MW01040226

# OUR RICHFIELD STORIES

## VOLUME ONE

*A Collective Time Travel of Memories and Tales From Richfield's Past...*

**Compiled by**
**Terry Ahlstrom**

Our Richfield Stories
Volume One
A Collective Time Travel of Memories and Tales From Richfield's Past


ISBN: 979-8-35092-106-9:

# ACKNOWLEDGEMENTS

I would like to say a huge thank you to all of you who submitted stories. Many of you submitted more than one. At the end of the day, we had a whole lot more than we had room for. There is a very good head start on volume two if that were to happen. We tried to limit it to one story per person, but in the case of a few used a second story if it had some historical significance such as a business, organization, building, special topic, activity, childhood or neighborhood memory or a place that may no longer be in existence.

Stories in this book were supplied by their Author. Many of the photos used in this book were also supplied from the stories Author. They are credited. Thanks also go out to the Richfield Historical Society for the use of photos from their archives including yearbook and Tax Assessors photos. Many thanks to the Richfield-Sun Current and their parent company for the permission to use images from the Richfield News and the Richfield Sun for this project and to the Star Tribune for licensing some very old images that help support some of the stories. Lastly a huge shout out to Mike Mason at Mason Graphics for his help in designing the cover and making my cover vision come to life.

This book is dedicated to all those Richfield people who came before us and played a big part in our lives growing up. Parents, Grandparents, Teachers, Coaches, Friends, Siblings, Neighbors, Mentors, Civic Leaders and so many others. You'll find in many of these stories they played very big roles and it's maybe taken us getting a little older to realize and talk about it.

The quote "Home is a place you grow up wanting to leave and grow old wanting to get back to" by John Ed Pearce has always had a special significance to me as I have found it to be true. I am hoping a little of that sentiment rubs off as you read the book.

Finally, profits generated from the sale of this book "Our Richfield Stories Volume One" will be split equally between The Richfield Historical Society and The Richfield Spartan Foundation, Inc.

THE RICHFIELD HISTORICAL SOCIETY mission statement is to acquire, document and preserve the unique story of Richfield, Minnesota. In addition, their mission is to inspire a sense of place and history through the details of our past.

THE RICHFIELD SPARTAN FOUNDATION, INC mission is to provide support for unfunded or underfunded programs that provide co-curricular activities in the Richfield Public Schools. It exists for the purpose of providing support, equipment, material, and funds designed to develop, assist, promote, and support the activities of Richfield students.

# CONTENTS

# PROLOGUE

I am not exactly sure how the idea of putting together a book of Richfield stories ever came about. If you had told me, I'd be doing a book someday I would have told you you're crazy. I know that in my life hearing people tell stories has always been of interest to me. When I get together with friends (some of those friendships going back to grade school) we always go right back to where we were as kids spending endless time swapping story after story. What a gift that is. To this day I can probably tell you the chain most of my friends were in when we played Little League together.

My Mom and Dad built their home in Richfield in 1956. My wife and I live there today. In my family one of my cousins was Miss Richfield in 1956. Another cousin was on the basketball team that was defeated by Edgerton in 1960. Both cousins were from different sides of the family. (There were lots of related families in Richfield) I grew up hearing stories about these Richfield events and things in our family lore, but I just wasn't old enough to understand or grasp what they were all about. I would have liked to have known more. So, if you asked me what the purpose of this book is I guess I'd say, It's the preservation of memories of times passed and educating through memories what it was like to grow up in or be a part of Richfield.

I assumed when I started this project and asked people for their stories that we'd get funny, cute ones about someone or something in their lives and there certainly are a lot of those, but it also became clear that many other Storytellers had so much more they wanted to say especially about not only what it was like for them to grow up in Richfield, but also the importance they placed on that. I know in my life I have seen many of Richfield's ups and downs and as I look back no matter what I have seen, done or been involved in, the connecting piece to all has always been Richfield...and I have always been proud of that!

Thank you to all The Storytellers. Many of you sent more than one. Maybe for a future volume? This book is for and about you. I want to thank my sister Sandy who was right there from the start willing to pitch in and help with any support I needed. I am forever grateful for all the Basketball and Football games I got to attend as a kid in the 60's to watch you cheer. I appreciate all the support from the numerous friends I mentioned doing a project like this to who said that it sounded like a fun idea and how could they be of help. (You all know who you are). And of course, to my wife Deb who when I told her I was thinking about doing a book she said absolutely you should do it… I am very Fortunate to have the support of so many!

I often say to people "Ask a lot of questions while folks are here, because the answers to those questions often go away when they are gone" that theme shows up more than once in this book. Always remember that everyone has a story to tell, and they want to tell it…you just need to ask and listen!

Terry Ahlstrom

# RICHFIELD - ALL AMERICA CITY

**ROGER BUCK**

*75TH AND STEVENS AVE.*

I recall as a youth riding with my 3 brothers in the back seat of my dad's Studebaker seeing that sign as we entered Richfield and always thought it was special. My parents bought a new house on 75th and Stevens after World War II and friends and relatives would talk about George and Marvel buying a house in a place called Richfield, all we know is it's even south of Holy Angels. Growing up on a quiet block in a neighborhood packed with families was any kids' dream, some like us went to school at Assumption, others to Richfield Public, it made no difference as after school was play time. Rubber baseball in the street or whatever, few cars to interrupt, we were never inside unless the weather called for it. One of the highlights every summer was the Assumption Fun Fest, fun for all with a carnival atmosphere. 76th and Lyndale was the first shopping area I recall with: Langers Grocery Store, Rexall Drug, Gamble's Hardware store, and a family favorite Latham's Drive In, where my mom occasionally worked part time nights at. When they built the new Red Owl on 66th and Nicollet it was instant success and for the Grand Opening they gave away a new Chevy. Not long after the Hub came to life, and the 66th and Nicollet intersection exploded. A huge favorite was the Richfield Theater on 65th, back then a quarter could get you a movie, popcorn and a box of milk duds. In 1958 the 7th Voyage of Sinbad big time action movie came to the Richfield screen; I recall our first attempt to see it was the disappointment of admission lines trailing all the way down the block to the Hub's JC Penny's store. Assumption was for 1 to 8 years, grade 9 was at East Junior High a huge culture shock where every class was in a different room and class options such as shop were available. Then came Richfield High School with an entire new wing and 3,000+ students. Walking to attend fall football games, the air heavy with the smell of burning leaves, is a lasting memory. As a high school sophomore, I recall my first pep fest which they held before big Friday football games and the chant "Were from Richfield couldn't be prouder, you can't hear us now we'll yell a little louder!" Richfield was a great place to grow up.

# THE PITS – RECOLLECTIONS OF THE SAND PITS

**P.K BARTELME**

*76TH AND WASHBURN AVE.SO.*

My Family moved to Richfield in 1956. We lived on 69th & Vincent. In 1965 we bought a new house on 76th & Washburn. We lived on both sides of Adams Hill Park. That Park known by neighborhood kids as "Devils Point" had a skating rink, warming house and great sledding hills. The park was also known as "Suicide", supposedly someone hanged themselves there. I recall walking the four blocks to the rink with my skates on once, so I did not need to change there, it was a painful walk home. Before the area south of Southdale Shopping Center was developed, I recall watching fireworks where the Hennepin County Library now sits. I remember my brothers & I were dressed in pajamas to see the show because it would be past our bedtime when we got home. At that time the area roughly from 70th street south to Hwy 494, and from France Ave. east to Xerxes Ave. was open land, owned by gravel companies; Glacier, Hedberg & Sons, and Mapco. There were large open pit mines with conveyor belts which moved sand & gravel to large structures where it was washed & separated. Much of the land was open fields dotted with stands of trees. This area known as "The Pits" was a great place for kids to explore, build forts, plink with BB guns or ride the trails on bicycles and later mini bikes & snowmobiles. Jumping off the tall cliffs of sand to see how far we could land insured our shoes would be filled when we got home. Carving out hand & footholds in the cliffs to get back up ensured our jeans pockets would be sand filled too. Deer lived there along with fox, raccoon, woodchuck & skunk. We used to trap gophers because we heard there was a bounty on them, but we never did find someone to turn them in to. There was a small stream of brownish water we named red river that ran from the Glacier Company buildings to a low spot we called the "lake". We learned there that if they had to, garter snakes can swim. As time went on development chipped away at the pits. By the early 1980's little was left, having given way to high-rise housing, stores, and restaurants. Today there is Centennial Lakes, a far more civilized area for kids to explore. They have a water feature, maybe almost as good as the red river.

# GROWING UP IN THE HOOD ON KNOX

**DEBBIE GOODSPEED DOUBEK**

*65TH AND KNOX AVE. SO.*

Closing my eyes brings me back to a time and place I call the "Camelot Years." My first Richfield home was 6520 Logan Ave So. A small two-bedroom rambler, one bathroom, one car garage with an attached porch. Often the neighborhood ladies met in the morning in the back yard for coffee. None of the yards had fences. My favorite babysitters lived on 65th and Morgan, the Rowe kids. Mom was eyeing a new home just one block over. A special place called home is 6514 Knox Ave So, phone number UN 9-4488 a soft yellow two-story house with three bedrooms, one bathroom and a one car garage where lived a mom and dad with two kids. Tree lined street with 12 other homes. Lots of kids come out from those homes. There was always someone to play with. One of my favorite memories was the summers of 5th and 6th grade. This was when us girls made the "She Shed" in the attic above the garage. I can still climb up the ladder, but the attic is long gone. The chalk written signage "No Boys Allowed" is still visible, even though its faded, it says it all. There was a lot of stuff up there: Christmas decorations, old stuff from the house, etc. We cleaned, rearranged the junky stuff and decorated it from items gathered from my girlfriends' homes. We had the record player up there and a radio and we listened to WDGY playing rock and roll. Summer days were really hot up there, but we didn't even care. Special smells: Mom's silver percolator making

Hills Brothers coffee, Dad cooking Saturday morning breakfast of link sausages and over easy eggs with toast; crawling into the freshly washed and ironed white sheets then taking a deep breath into the fresh cool feel of the sheets at night; Raking leaves into the street with neighbors and the smell of burning the leaves. The neighbors were all friends. Special sounds: riding bikes with playing cards in the spokes held with clothes pins. Kids playing hide and go seek till dark. Baseball in the street. Then Mom would ring the old Woodlake School bell and it would signal either dinner time or twilight time and to come in for the day. Saturdays were for watching cartoons, but my every day favorite was Axels Tree House after school. And afternoon movies with Mel Jass, don't forget Casey Jones and Roundhouse Rodney. Then in those teenage years it became American Bandstand with Dick Clark. Showing us the latest dance steps along with current pop music. Penny loafers with wool socks and saddle shoes. Grandpa's home on 719 Graham Ave. The gray, four-square, two-story stucco house, covered with ivy. Every room held an adventure. My Great Grandma Maggie Minnesota Goodspeed lived there with her son until her death in 1955. The time for Grandpa John Graham Goodspeed to move from the big family home into an apartment. Which meant that his dog Nutmeg a Boston Terrier would get to live with us. An auction of the contents of the house was scheduled but Mom got to go in and choose what items she wanted such as Great Grandma Maggie's Haviland China dishes, silver and other hand-picked antiques. My favorite was the Victorian love seat. Upholstered in black, stuffed with horsehair. I still have all that stuff and more. Chickens in Richfield. One Easter Grandpa bought us little chicks. All different colors. They were so cute. But the little chicks grew into chickens. They started to jump out of the box since they were growing so fast. And they started to stink in the house. Mom said they had to go. Grandpa had a plan. He built a chicken coop in his garage and fenced in part of his yard. We could still visit the chickens until we began to see there were less and less of them. Sunday chicken dinners never tasted so good. Growing up was happening way too fast. Before I knew it, Sheridan Elementary School was behind me, and West Junior High School held new adventures and new friends. Football games, teen club dances, coffee houses and movies at the old Richfield Theater. Southdale became the newest hangout. Meet me by the bird cage. Also, the Mann Southtown Theater with the fancy bathrooms. Then walking over to the Southtown Bowl to just hang out. The new pool on Portland was a great place to hang out too. The Beatles and the British invasion of music and don't forget Twiggy that set the standard for fashion in the '60's. Every kid that grew up in Richfield has their own story, some memories are good and some not so much. The Richfield History Center is a good place to begin to find some memories. It has some written materials, and some visual historical items. Your class reunion is another place to connect with old friendships and memories of the past. I'm helping to plan my 55th class reunion. Hard to believe. My long history really began around 1859 when my Great Grandparents, the Grahams and the Goodspeed's began their Richfield journey. They had a home (Woodlawn) on 66th and Lyndale, (overlooking Woodlake) and their farm stretched as far west and east as 68th street then up to Portland. As Minneapolis grew, Richfield shrank in all directions. The last piece of Goodspeed land was sold under the name of Fairwood Shores. A plot of land on what was Graham Avenue became the new and last home for the pioneering family. Urbanization took over making way for young families after WWII. Doing my genealogy search brought me up to Oak Hill Cemetery (across from Bachman's) where most of my family's journey ended. And one day my journey will end too. I will then rest with my ancestors and become part of the Richfield story. As I open my eyes driving through Richfield and so much has changed, I can hardly recognize it. But when I turn down 65th and Knox it still feels like I'm going home. Thankfully I can still go home, my brother and his wife bought my mom's home, raised their family and still live in the house. The neighbors have changed but the old feeling is still there. When I close my eyes, I can still hear children playing, neighbors talking, it's like going back in time.

# THE NIGHT THEY KILLED FRED

**EDWARD M. CHRISTIAN**

*69TH AND OLIVER AVE. SO.*

Fred Babcock was a member of the Richfield Police Department and is the only Peace Officer in the Village of Richfield to have been killed in the line of duty. Most Richfield residents have heard of the name, Fred Babcock, one way or another. In fact, the Richfield VFW Post 5555 is named after him. VFW Post 5555 is located on Lakeshore Drive and Lyndale Avenue South. I knew Fred because my father, Edward H. Christian, was also a member of the Richfield Police Department and was one of the first five officers that formed the force in 1939, the year I was born. My Dad figured that if he was going to continue having kids that he would not be able to support our mother and the kids' raising pigs on our small farm at 64th & 12th Avenue. He applied and was accepted, together with Cy Johnson, George Brening, Claude Robison and Alfred Peterson. My Dad was badge #3. Prior to becoming a Police Officer, Fred had served our country as a member of the U.S. Marine Corps. After World War II he settled in Richfield and owned and operated a small 3.2 tavern on 66th Street and 14th

Avenue, called "The Frenchman's". When he applied for the Richfield Police Department, Chief Cy Johnson told him that if he was to be on the Police Department, that he could not own a bar in the city. Fred then sold the bar and became a member of the Richfield Police Force. Often when my dad and Fred were patrolling, they would stop at our house for coffee, and sometimes for breakfast, which my mother was more than willing to serve. On the evening of June 4, 1949, Fred and Lee Poulter were patrolling together when they received a call about a possible burglary at the National Tea store on 76th and Lyndale. Fred was not supposed to be working that night, but he had switched shifts the week before so that he could attend a wedding. Fred dropped Lee off behind the store and drove around the front. As he exited the squad he confronted the lookout, Carl Bistrom, who was armed with a 30.30 deer rifle. The lookout shot Fred through the neck and he was dead within five minutes. My recollection of that night will never be forgotten. I was ten years old at the time, and three of my brothers were sleeping in the upper floor of our expansion home on 69th and Oliver Avenue when I heard the phone ring. My mother answered and then said to my dad, "It's Cy Johnson and he wants to talk to you." I then heard my dad's voice. "Hello. What?... I'll be right there." My mother then said, "What is it Hattie?" My Dad responded, "They just shot Fred, I have to go." He got dressed and then left for the scene and joined in the hunt for the perpetrators. Fred left a wife and two small children. R.I.P. He was only on the Police Force 16 months.

# THE WOODS

**DORI HIGGIN PERLEBERG**
*76TH AND EMERSON AVE. SO.*

Before my childhood block on 76th & Emerson Ave was shortened by half for The Shops at Lyndale development, our family lived in the middle of that block from 1959-1986. Across the street was a wooded area, a vast piece of mostly undeveloped property bordered by 76th Street on the north, 494 on the south, 35W on the west and Emerson Avenue on the east. Two blocks long and 2 blocks wide of heavily wooded land at the north end, a large meadow at the south end, plus the Cloverleaf Motel set in the NE corner of 35W & 494. We called the whole thing "the woods". Our family's front door was directly across the street from the natural entrance to the woods and we had a clear view of people entering. It was a dark and mysterious place that lured many of us in to explore. Since it was privately owned, people were always on the lookout to avoid getting caught trespassing, but the Lyons family who owned it, were tolerant. The Lyons house was set far back in the woods about where today's Bethel's Rock church stands - a church that was originally Emerson Ave Congregational church at the corner of 77th & Emerson before that church, too, was moved for the Shops at Lyndale project. It was commonly occupied by teenagers as a hangout, a playground for children, and a dumping ground where many thought they were invisibly leaving hazards of all sorts, from yard waste to refrigerators, it served as a private dump for those who dared. Wildlife was abundant and the pheasants were invited to my next-door neighbor's yard with corn feed. The meadow at the south end was full of native plants and wild strawberries where my sister and I spent many hours over many years, getting our fill. It felt safer in the meadow where we could easily be seen. I eventually had one of my first jobs at the Cloverleaf Motel as a maid, alongside Mrs. Lyons, who told me the story of her and her husband building the motel in the late 50s with plans to develop the woods into a shopping center, before Mr. Lyons' untimely death. Mrs. Lyons quietly continued to live with her children, work at the motel, and leave the property undeveloped. Those of us fortunate to live adjacent to her beautifully wooded property, with its plentiful meadow, were grateful it remained a wild place for us to explore, and to scare ourselves with what we might discover there. Today, as you drive east on 76th Street and turn south at Bethel's Rock Church heading to 77th Street, you are driving through the heart of my childhood woods.

# RICHFIELD MINNESOTA TWINS

**BOB AND BARRY BISHOP**

*64TH AND NEWTON AVE. SO*

We lived at 64th and Newton Ave. in west Richfield. The community was an excellent place for us, and our younger brother Jim, to grow up in the 50's and 60's. There were many well organized activities for 3 active boys. We found ourselves gravitating toward sports, especially baseball and basketball. At that time there were over 700 participants, ages 10-12, involved in the Richfield Little League program, as well as the Babe Ruth league, ages 13-15. There were also many church sponsored basketball teams throughout Richfield. We spent countless hours playing pick-up basketball games at the many parks in Richfield as well as in our back yard, where our dad nailed a backboard and basket to a big elm tree. These youth activities were the foundation of our involvement in athletics which would continue through our high school years. We remember the many excellent teachers and staff in the school system. For example, Mr. Jim Hamblin, a sixth-grade teacher at Sheridan Elementary school, was in charge of many activities before and after school, as well as Saturday morning basketball instruction. He encouraged us to play basketball (we were tall-5'10"-for our age) because he was sure we were going to be 7' tall. We did not quite make it to that height. In fact, we grew only a few more inches. However, because of his encouragement, we began our lifelong connection to the game of basketball. Barry remembers a situation with Mr. Jim Carlson, one of our favorite history teachers, as well as a favorite teacher of many students. As Mr. Carlson was handing back a daily quiz, which Barry did not do very well on, he mentioned to Barry that he hoped Barry would score more points in the basketball game that night than he did on the quiz. Barry complied with the request with one of his better games of the year. This was just one example of Mr. Carlson's interest in students' lives outside of the classroom. Another example occurred in Mr. Joseph Michel's biology class. He noticed that both of us were a bit squeamish about dissecting a frog, so he allowed us to work together. Mr. Michel had no problem when we pretended to be Dr. Casey and Dr. Kildare, two popular TV doctors in the 60's, to ease our discomfort with the activity. Teachers such as these, along with our basketball (Vance Crosby) and baseball (Gene Olive) coaches, enhanced our enjoyment of school and sports. We were privileged to be part of two very successful teams our senior year. We were honored to be co-captains of the basketball team, winning the Lake Conference title with an overall record of 18-3. Barry was named to the Minnesota All-State Basketball Team. The baseball team won the State Championship with a record of 25-0. Bob was named to the Minnesota All-State Baseball Tournament Team. A combined record of 43-3 (93.5%) our senior year was the culmination of the many positive experiences Richfield provided as we grew up. We remember the tremendous support from the students and community. Most of our basketball games were played in front of capacity crowds. In one away game against Edina, the gym was full at 5:30 for a 7:30 game. There were 18 bus loads of fans attending our district final basketball game at Williams Arena on the campus of the University of Minnesota, against the eventual state champions, Minnetonka. In spite of a very wet spring and historical flooding throughout Minnesota in 1965, our baseball games drew hundreds of fans to both home and away games. Now, 50+ years later, Barry is fortunate to be able to watch his grandkids play on many of the baseball fields and basketball courts as we did. Bob is the proud grandfather of five-year-old twins, looking forward to watching them grow and experience many of the positive aspects of being a twin.

# ONE MORE PIZZA PLEASE!

**DENNIS CRASWELL**

*66TH AND LYNDALE AVE. SO.*

In the 60s I lived at Craswell Studios. Around 66th and Lyndale. I was about 14, and played drums, Larry Wiegand played bass, Dick Wiegand played guitar and Lonnie Knight played guitar. On Friday nights all the junior high school kids would meet at Miller's fireside pizza on around 68th and Penn. Miller's Fireside Pizza would turn out to be the birthplace of two million seller bands from Richfield, MN:

The Crow and The Castaways…I guess the definition of a professional is when you are first compensated for your services. So, the idea was to ask Mrs. Miller if we could play music on Friday night. And in return we would be compensated in pizza **One large pizza** for our services. That night was just the greatest. All the kids from school eating pizza, dancing, and having a blast. So, after our first professional gig I went to pick up our pay, One large, One topping Pizza. It was like monkeys grabbing at a pile of bananas. It took exactly 35 sec. for us monkeys to make the pizza disappear from the face of the earth. Heck after playing all night we all could have eaten the whole thing. Lonnie said, "we did really great, didn't we?" and we all agreed. Yes, we really did great… Lonnie said, "Denny why don't you go and ask Mrs. Miller if we might be able to get just one more pizza?" So, I was elected. I went to Mrs. Miller and asked her how we did she said, "you boys really did a good job". I said" thank you". The boys were wondering if by chance if it's not asking too much if we could get one more pizza… Well, she was quick to answer "NO, the deal was for one pizza that was the deal" First pro gig lesson learned… ask for the world maybe they will give you Minnesota!

# THE LEROY HOWE IMMACULATE DECEPTION

**MIKE EDBERG**

*64TH AND 2ND AVE. SO.*

One day back in 1972 my buddies and I decided to go to the Richfield Legion for amateur boxing night, we were all seated on the stage for prime viewing of the ring, there was an intermission and the ring announcer got on the mic, in the middle of the ring and said,"alright we are going to draw for the $ Cash door prize". He bellows out the name "Leroy Howe come up and claim your prize. Nobody......he says Leroy Howe 3 more times and then...., last chance Leroy Howe in the house or we draw again"? I say to my friends I'm going up there. One friend says no don't! The rest are like do it! I dare you. well, it doesn't take much for me to pursue attention and follow the majority. Plus, I thought it would make my mark as a fearless sophomore in high school with all the cool dudes, As I go up into the ring and claim my big winnings, and they ask so "you are Leroy Howe"? I said yes, he goes "what took you so long"? I said, "I don't know I guess I'm a little shy." Well congratulations, he hands me an envelope with a $10 bill in it. No questions. I go back to my friends and lo and behold there is a reporter from the Sun newspaper there, and he asks for more info from me, and to take a picture. Well of course yes, me trying to save any stupid integrity that I still may have had, I give the reporter my real address. Wait, there's more, it gets better or worse. After the paper came out the picture and info, they took revealed me and friends celebrating. Well, a week or so went by and I got a call from the athletic office to see Mr. Collison, the athletic director, in his office now. At this time, I seriously had no idea why. I walk in he says well Leroy Howe I thought we would never meet! I was shocked. I started to laugh a little out of fear. He says where did you get that stolen hockey jersey.? Now, you can ask my parents, I wasn't a very good liar, so I said it's my brothers, he says you and your brother are wrestlers why would he or you have that jersey? Well, he says "since it's an old jersey that we don't use anymore. I'll let it go, this time but if I find out you ever take anything else, I won't be so forgiving, and you may not be able to participate in any after school activities again. Now I know you are better than this and are a good valuable student and athlete to have here. Please don't disappoint me?

Just be careful next time you wear stolen property, especially from here. I believe since I was a loyal Spartan athlete, he thought the story was entertaining. I also think I was one of his favorites I was very adept at brown-nosing by that time. I even eventually became the intramural athletic director in the early 80's with him.

# THE NIGHT I MET THE BEATLES

**DONNA JOHNSON NEU**

*75TH AND CLINTON AVE. SO.*

I was in love with the Beatles from the first time I heard them on the radio. I knew every word of every song. I watched them on the Ed Sullivan Show and screamed at the television set in the basement when they sang "All My Loving" and "Till There Was You." But when I heard that the Beatles would be performing at Metropolitan Stadium near Richfield in August of 1965, I never in the world imagined that I would be able to see them. Spending money on a concert was something our family didn't do, and besides, I was just 12 going on 13 years old, so who at that age attended concerts like they do now? Not at our house. On the night of the event, as I moped around the house, my parents suddenly said, "Why don't we drive to the stadium and listen outside?" So, my neighborhood friend and I jumped in the back seat of our car, and we were off. My parents parked the car on the bleacher side of the stadium, and we all rolled down our windows to listen. We could hear the Beatles! But.... barely. Then I noticed other kids standing at the outside of the bleachers, looking through the knotholes, so my friend and I climbed out of the car and did the same as them to get a peek and hear the music better. After a while, there was some type of intermission, and suddenly the big wooden gates to the bleachers were opened by a very sympathetic usher. We few excited kids rushed in, climbing the bleachers to get a view of the concert (looking all the way across the field to the second base where the Beatles were set up.) Soon the Beatles started their next set, and we screamed and jumped excitedly. We were seeing the Beatles (from the rear of course, as they were playing to the main seats & upper decks on the opposite side of us). But it didn't matter. We were there, seeing a bit of the Beatles and screaming along with the rest of the crowd who were on the other side of the stadium. Without a large screaming crowd around us, our screams sounded like weak little "yeas…." that dissipated quickly into the air. But we didn't care. Recently, I visited the Beatles Story Museum in Liverpool, England. And amongst the enormous amount of exhibits was one that listed all of the American concert tours, including those performed in 1965. And there was listed the Minneapolis tour – August 21, 1965. I had really been there!

Thinking back, I remember fondly that we didn't have regular tickets, we didn't have fancy seats, we saw the Beatles only from the rear from a very long distance away, and we couldn't hear the music that well at all. But that was okay because it became an experience I'll never forget. I can always say I saw the Beatles in concert! And I still love Beatles music.

# THE PASSING TIME

**DAVID MALMBERG**
*66TH AND KNOX AVE. SO.*

In 1967, Richfield High School staged its first musical production ever in the history of the school. Directed by James Marcell, it was the beginning of a long illustrious history of RHS musicals. But 1967 was the inaugural year. And the musical was Finian's Rainbow. I had at one time asked Jim Marcell why he chose Finian's as the first RHS musical. His response was that it was the most accessible for high schoolers as a first musical outing. Interestingly, Marcell reprised Finian's again in 1980.The play was a huge undertaking. The cast was enormous, as was the stage crew, costume and set designers along with the school band and orchestra. It seemed like a large percentage of the student body was involved in some capacity! Math teacher Stan DeFreese also came on as a vocal coach, which began a long and fruitful partnership until both men retired. We rehearsed like crazy. After school every day for at least 2 months, possibly more. I had the lead role of 'Woody,' while the leading lady was Elena Dress Biessener. She was really the star of the production. All of this rehearsal for six performances in April 1967. 56 years later people still talk to me about what a magical experience it was for them. The shows were sold out every night. Many students attended multiple performances. Some took jobs as ushers just so they could see the play again and again! It was really quite the event. For me? I am forever reminded of the kind of magic produced by the Finian's team. Of the thousands of solo performances, I have done in my career, the cast of Finian's Rainbow looms singular in my consciousness in terms of richness of experience. I stayed in touch with Jim Marcell through the years until his passing. For each play he did, along with minutely constructed model sets, he would make up a small stained-glass window with symbolism in each pane representing the musical he had done that particular year. One day I was visiting at his home in Golden Valley, and he picked up the stained glass pane he had done for Finian's and said, "I want you to have this." It has a place of honor in my home today. It is my understanding that he gave many students involved in his production's mementos of those shows. So, that was the beginning. 1967. The first musical in RHS history. Truly an honor for me. Six performances creating almost 60 years of memories in my life.

# ERIK THE BIKE MAN

**ERIK SALTVOLD**

*66TH STREET*

I grew up in one of the original farmhouses in Richfield on 66th St. between Girard and Humboldt. It truly was farmland before becoming "Rich Field." When my parents bought the place in 1964, the barn was ready to fall over. My folks decided they would fix up the house and the barn. My parents were resourceful and Norwegian frugal, when we needed to put a new driveway in, they drove down to Minneapolis and got free bricks as the city replaced brick streets with asphalt and concrete. That driveway is still in pretty good shape 60 years later. My early years were spent sitting in the yard amongst construction as I literally played with nails from the site. My parents spent over 45 years loving and caring for that house and barn. Little did they know that that barn would become such an important part of my life. In 1977, at the age of 13, I started ERIK'S Bike Shop in that same barn. They let me take it over with a showroom and a shop. They were great and supportive parents; they would have supported anything I wanted to do. It was a great place to incubate ERIK'S. My parents supported me, Richfield Schools supported me (my Business teacher, Ken Hess, became an early mentor), and my accountant and attorney all had Spartan connections. BMX racing was big for my business and Mothers Lake Park (62/Cedar) built out a track and was a big time BMX racing track. One of the biggest promotions we ever had in the early days was driving a truck in the Richfield 4th of July parade while we had a BMX stunt team (Haro) doing tricks right on the route. In 1982 as a senior in high school, I moved from the barn into a real store at 72nd and Chicago and cultivated my growth from there. I went to one quarter at the U of M, but Richfield High School and real life was where I got my education! The Richfield connections go even further as I met my future wife when she lived on Diagonal Boulevard and became a customer. Fast forward to 2023 and we operate stores in 9 states and recently re-located a store in Richfield at 66th and Cedar. Richfield has become a metro leader in bike trails and transportation with the recent 66th street parkway and bike/walking trails. I can't imagine a better place to grow up. I have lifelong friends and memories of my childhood in Richfield.

# SENIOR ENGLISH RHS 1966-1967

**CAROL SCHIEBOLD**

*74TH AND 4TH AVE. SO.*

Senior English was a struggle for me. My teacher was Mrs. Hendrickson. At the time I was often in tears because I only received "C's and "B's". I felt Mrs. Hendrickson was too hard on me but I kept trying and spent long hours writing papers most weekends. Little did I know how well that time was spent and that it would positively affect the rest of my life. First, I attended Bemidji State my first two Years of college. I aced Freshman English and received many compliments from my instructors on my excellent writing skills. One afternoon in 1967 at the end of the school day I went back to RHS and found Mrs. Hendrickson in the hallway. I thanked her for how hard she was on me because I realized she made a difference early in my life. I already recognized that what she taught me would help me for the rest of my life. Mrs. Hendrickson eyes welled up with tears as she profusely thanked me for taking the time and making the effort to come back and thank her. She felt that students never recognized what she was doing for them. Later in life I wrote newsletters for various jobs and groups. As an RN I wrote lengthy instruction manuals for caregivers and for parents of disabled children. A supervisor in one of my jobs had me review her business-related letters. She was brilliant with numbers but could not write a sentence. Rest in peace Mrs. Hendrickson for a job well done.

# A FLOAT PLANE ON WOODLAKE

LAURIE KOLLAR SMYRL

*75TH AND COLFAX AVE. SO.*

My dad, Paul "Bert" Kollar, was born in April 1923 and served in the Army Air Force on a B17 as a top turret gunner and engineer in the European arena during WWII. Dad loved flying and challenging projects and, in the Winter of 1954, he brought home the "Wowzer" of all backyard projects. I have vague memories of this project but my cousin, Dennis Hoyne, who is a few years older remembers it well. Dad's flight logbook entry for December 20, 1954 documents that he purchased a Taylorcraft single engine float plan in Hibbing, Mn and, on April 10, 1955 (three days before his 32nd birthday), he flew it to Wold-Chamberlain (Minneapolis St. Paul Airport) where it was dismantled. From Wold the parts were transported to our small garage on the corner of 75th and Colfax which was converted to a quasi-hanger. I wish I could remember my mom's reaction when she saw that dismantled plane coming down the street heading for our garage. What a coincidence that as I finish this story today is April 10th, 2023, and dad would be turning 100 years old in three days. In that small garage all the exterior fabric was removed from the plane, and it was stripped down to the bare bones of the frame. The floats were stored across the street in Cousin Denny's backyard. Dad entirely rebuilt his favorite plane in that small garage on Colfax Avenue. Once the rebuilding was complete the floats and wings were returned to the fuselage and the plane was loaded onto a homemade trailer. The flight record documents that by July 24, 1955, the plane was ready to fly. And fly it did … right off Woodlake. My Cousin remembers the journey down 75th Street to Humbolt then down the dirt road that would become 35W, and on to the SW side of Woodlake where it was launched. Dad flew his Tcraft to Sky Harbor Seaplane base on Ely Lake in Eveleth, Mn where it was inspected and certified as flight worthy. I remember as a young child the trips riding behind the seats of that plane in a small baggage compartment as dad flew mom and me to my grandparent's cabin on Bay Lake near Garrison, MN. Thank you, Dennis Hoyne, for sharing your memories of Dad and his project, for searching through his log book and for finding out the final resting place of Taylorcraft BC-12D, N96420. After spending its final days in Kotzebue, Alaska (26 miles from the Artic Circle) it was destroyed in a windstorm and deregistered in 2018. How I would love to know the stories that old plane could tell.

# GOING TO BAT FOR THE MINNESOTA HEART ASSOCIATION

**DAVE JACKELEN**

*72ND AND BLAISDELL AVE.SO.*

While hanging around in the early 70s at the Teen Center located in the Augsburg Park warming house, the idea arose, how about a softball game to raise money for charity. After some planning with our teen center leaders Bob Kaitz, Dick Thomas, and Judy Reasoner (Richfield Parks and Recreation Department supervisor) we were ready to host a really long softball game. The following information came from a story published in The Richfield Sun… The Richfield Teen Center staged a 24-hour marathon softball game that raised more than $1,400. Ronald McDonald was among celebrities who played for the challenger teams. The final score was 248 for the Teen Center to 245 for the visitors. Celebrity umpires included former Gopher hockey coach Glen Sonmor, now coach of the new Minnesota Fighting Saints; North Star John Mariucci; and Prince Jim Bradshaw along with Princess Kathy Pederson of the St. Paul Winter Carnival. Mayor Loren Law led off the 130-inning game by tossing in the first ball at 4 p.m. on a Friday afternoon at the long-gone Augsburg Park softball field. The" new library's" parking lot now occupies that space. The team looked ready sporting their PARK PEOPLE T-shirts and settled in for some serious softball. Visiting teams included: the Richfield All-Star Girls; McDonald's; Schooner Bar; the Jockettes; Chopper's Whoppers; Korner Plaza; Richfield Park Leaders; St. Peter's Girls; Bob's Park; John Holter's Heroes; the Frenchman's; WWIC and Friends; and the Gang from Highland Park. Teen Center member Rick St. Martin pitched several hours and then moved to some of the less demanding roles of other positions. He missed barely more than two hours of the game. Other players included Mitch Stevenson, Dave Jackelen, Mike Volz, Mike Gleason, Billy Baribeau, along with Paul "Byrd" Barrett and his brother Bob played almost all of the marathon skirmish. The marathoners yielded only infrequently to catch short naps in the teen center clubhouse. Two from the Teen Center female contingent, Debbie Friendshuh and "Sunny" Pemble, missed only a few innings. Karen Vrchota, who is known as "Taco" to her friends, spent the full 24 hours at the concession stand, which she ran efficiently. Lee Ann Johnson likewise donated a full day to working behind the makeshift counter. The Teen Center, which includes members from 13 through 18 years old, does not have a regular softball team. The organization has sponsored canoe trips and bike hikes this summer as well as just "hanging out".

# A RICHFIELD STATE OF MIND

**DON HOULDING**

*71ST AND 13TH AVE. SO.*

Richfield in the 50's and 60's wasn't a place. It was a state of mind. It wasn't a city; it was a way of life. For all of us lucky enough to have experienced it back then, we were truly blessed. It was a place where road graders plowed up the streets and oil trucks sprayed oil while kids played in the sticky black goo. We had Kool-Aid stands and baseball games. Cowboys and Indians ran rampant through the neighborhoods and bicycles raced up and down the streets. In the heat of the summer, there were sprinklers to run through and penny candy to be bought at Roith's Drug. The parks had games like four square, space chase, box hockey, and something called "beans". I learned 30 years later that what they called beans was really a game called mancala. Arts and crafts kept our creative juices flowing as we made potholders and whistle straps by the dozen. Many of us mowed lawns, washed cars, baby sat, or delivered papers, to supplement the allowance, if any, that we were sometimes paid. We had to take out our garbage, and in those days, every driveway had a "trash burner" where we burned our waste papers. In the fall, there was always the wonderful smell of burning leaves as we raked up what a literal forest of huge elm trees were dropping upon us as the daily temperatures dropped and the days got shorter. Every kid from those days knew the phrase: "You be sure you get back home tonight before the streetlights come on!" Good advice from our parents. Words to live by if we knew what was good for us. Invariably, cold winter weather meant skating and sledding at places like Wilson's Pond and Christian Park. The warming houses, manned by older kids, often had wood burning stoves. If we were lucky, when we got home, there would be hot chocolate. As we left our youth to enter young adulthood, those feelings and smells and memories would live on in our hearts, always reminding us of a world we could not go back to but were so lucky to have been a part of. My parents are gone now, and I no longer own the house I grew up in. Most of the toys I had growing up have been sold, given away, or just plain tossed out. Luckily, I still have a treasure trove of memories from those days that I will always cherish. I grew up in those times and consider myself lucky. I may not have understood that back while it was happening, but I sure do realize it now...I still have that Richfield State of Mind.

# THEATRE KID

**BRIAN SULLIVAN**

*77TH AND NICOLLET AVE. SO.*

We lived on Nicollet Avenue, near 77th Street. When the house was built for my family in the late forties, it was in the middle of farmland. Not anymore. I was a theatre kid. In the spring of 1973, I was rehearsing in the afternoons for *Kiss Me, Kate*, the musical at Richfield High. Fortunately, I was not one of the major characters, for I was also rehearsing in the evenings and weekends at Holy Angels High for their musical, *Oliver!* (Yes, the exclamation point is part of the title.) I played one of the leads, the Artful Dodger, so it was a lot on my plate. (At the time, Holy Angels was just starting the change from an all-girl school to a co-ed one, so they needed to "import" their male actors. To this day, when I hear about a football team at Holy Angels, it sounds odd to me.) At the same time, I was also designing and applying makeup for a one-act play at RHS called *The Good Woman of Setzuan*. Since each actor played more than one Asian character, that was a bit of a task. Eyes and eyebrows needed to be transformed, beards needed to be constructed and then pasted on and off. That spring I also served as one of the editors of the Spartan Spotlite, the RHS newspaper, so I had substantial writing and editing duties. Coupled with attending classes and doing homework, you could say my calendar was full. As a matter of fact, each activity on my physical calendar for that period was color-coded so I didn't miss or overlap any rehearsals or meetings. I loved doing plays and musicals in the area. Being someone else for a while and entertaining people made this short little kid feel special. (As a weird side benefit, I was – and am - very fair skinned. In the 70s, having a dark tan was a social necessity, so I could apply stage makeup and have some color on my face, if only for a couple of hours at a time!) My older sister, Mary Jane, had taken lessons at the Dolan Dance Studio near the Hub as a child. As a teenager, people encouraged her to perform in shows at the Bloomington Civic Theatre - now called Artistry - and I joined her there for a couple of musicals in the 60s, getting hooked on showbiz in the process. There was also a group called the Richfield Village Players at the time. I did a silly little children's play there called *The Hideous Ogre of Condor Cave.* We performed at Wood Lake Elementary School. My sister went on to become a professional actress, performing in some of the early musicals at the Chanhassen Dinner Theatre, which at the time seemed a very long drive from Nicollet Avenue. When it opened in 1968, I think the complex was also surrounded by farmland. The south metro has certainly filled in over the last few decades.

# JUST CHARGE IT!

**SUSAN LINDBLOM CULVER**
*72ND AND OLIVER AVE. SO.*

One of my favorite Richfield stories happened when I was about 4 years old. It was summer and I had a friend who lived across the street from me on Oliver Avenue. His name was Tommy Niedenfieur (spelling on that last name may not be correct) and he was just a few months younger than me. He and I were best buds. One summer day, he and I decided to take my little red wagon and hike from our homes on 72nd and Oliver to Hjalmer's Drug Store on the corner of 66th and Penn. We walked up there, went into the store, and put all sorts of candy and stuff in the wagon. Didn't fill it but we didn't leave it empty either. On the way out the door, I called out to the druggist "Charge It" like my mom always did when we shopped there. We went home only to have two mothers waiting for us. It seems that after he stopped laughing, the druggist called my mom and told her of our visit and that he had charged their account accordingly. WHY two 4 years olds were running about, I have no idea. I always tell folks that we were feral children and did as we pleased, when in reality, our parents were very aware of where we were and what we were doing (most times) when we were that young. This may have been a case of my mom thinking I was at Tommy's house and his mom thinking that we were at my house. Anyhow, a couple of weeks after that, Tommy and I wandered away again, only to be brought home by the police and handed over to our moms. I was able to give him our address (Tommy had no clue what his was) and we were pretty much on yard arrest for the rest of the summer.

# MY GRANDPARENTS' DRIVING RANGES

**PAUL HARDT**

*62ND AND SHERIDAN AVE. SO.*

My grandfather, Otto Hardt, was a teaching professional golfer and member of the PGA. He was president of the Senior PGA in 1953-54. He never played on the tour, but what qualified him as a professional were two facts...he was a very active golf instructor in south Minneapolis in the 1930s to the 1950s, and he owned two driving ranges. The first range was located about 54th and Lyndale, starting in the early 1930s and was sold in about 1947. The range was situated in the "Y" that is made today by Lyndale Avenue dividing between old and new Lyndale at 54th. Grandpa Otto bought a new range at 76th and Lyndale with the money he made from the 1947 sale, and built the newer range, once known as the "Airport Driving Range." Planes would buzz the range, as they took off and landed from the old Wold-Chamberlain Field. My Grandfather invented an automatic tee, which allowed you to tee up a ball on a practice platform, by pressing a foot pedal. When you lifted your foot up from the pedal, a ball emerged from below the platform. He owned that driving range until the late 1950s or early 1960s, when he and my grandmother retired full-time to Florida. Mr. Friedan bought the range, and continued to operate it, and a little putt-putt golf course for several years, and then he sold it to be developed as an apartment complex, which it is today. The Airport Range was just south of a trailer/tourist cabin park, which is still there on 76th and Lyndale. We have pictures of the park in the distance, when photos were taken of the Airport Driving Range.

# IS OLD MAN WALLER YOUR DAD?

**DAVID WALLER**

*72ND AND GARFIELD AVE. SO.*

This was the greeting I got when I started my three years at Richfield High School. You see, my dad was a 9th grade Social Studies (Civics) teacher at East Junior High, the other Junior High School in Richfield. Given that the person asking the question was considered to be one of the "tougher" guys from East Junior, I had but a moment to consider the possible ramifications of my answer. I had no idea what experiences he may have had with my dad or how he may react, learning Mr. Waller was indeed my father. I was always proud of my dad, and he appeared to be a popular guy, as I noted on numerous occasions when as a young kid, my Dad would accompany me to the Richfield High Friday night football games. Dad would be greeted with shouts of, "Mr. Waller" by many of the students. He was amazing with the way he remembered the names of current as well as former students. However, the question above still loomed large and needed an answer. I responded that, "Yes, he is my dad." I waited for the reaction or response, which seemed like a long time coming. Imagine the relief when this individual spoke words I heard a lot in school and have continued to hear throughout many years of running into former RHS students… "He was the best teacher I ever had!" This interaction began an unexpected friendship that has continued to this very day. RHS was always the merging of two different schools with mostly friendly rivalries. This experience proved to me that RHS was a great place to meet new friends and develop friendships that have lasted almost 50 years.

# A FORT SNELLING KID EXPLAINED

**JANE WATSON O'REILLY**
*TAYLOR AVENUE (OFFICERS ROW)*
*FORT SNELLING*

The whole time I was a student in the Richfield Public Schools, I was a "Fort Snelling kid." Most people thought we were military families but living at the "The Fort" simply meant one of our parents worked for the Veterans Administration and was lucky enough to rent a house at Tower Town. My dad was the eye doctor at the VA from 1946 until he retired in 1984. In its heyday, there were about 80 families in the various Fort neighborhoods. Many of the families had several kids with a child in every age group, so we were never at a loss for a playmate. To top it off, we all rode the same school bus—typically a rundown city bus that filled up back to front with highschoolers down to kindergartners. I can still hear Doug Gibson calling from the back of the bus, "Hey Janie Watson, whadja have for breakfast?" When the Minneapolis schools became overcrowded, we were bused to Richfield, a school district still in its infancy. Our bus made one round through the Fort and dropped us at East Junior High, Central Elementary and Richfield High School, and later Lincoln Hills and West Junior High—

unless it broke down and we all went to the Fort's canteen for Hostess cupcakes instead. Of course, if it snowed heavily, we had to leave early and the dreaded words, "Would the Fort Snelling kids please come to the office," resounded over the loudspeaker. Sometimes, being a Fort Snelling Kid was embarrassing. With a pool, park, tennis court, polo grounds and a golf course, Fort Snelling was considered the country club of military posts. When it was decommissioned in 1946, the amenities remained, yet we didn't take our unusual childhoods for granted. I grew up on Taylor Avenue, AKA Officer's Row, in a yellow brick house built in 1905. The year we moved in, it was 53 years old, far younger than the housing stock in Richfield today. Rent was approximately $91/month. Everybody knew everybody and no one locked their doors. My mom played bridge in the Commandant's house. My best friend, Cherie Church, and I played with our Barbie Dolls in the Round Tower. I kissed Joey Tonozzi before kindergarten and married Eddie Sako in second grade. We made forts in the giant lilac bushes. Our front lawns were as big as ball fields. We sneaked out at night and ran amok on acres of land that spanned the river bluff. We rode our bikes no handed down the steep hill behind the Hexagonal Tower all the way to the Mississippi. We trick-or-treated from the Round Tower to the airport. We were nicely contained, and somewhat isolated, on the Fort when we were young, and I remember thinking I had school friends and Fort friends. As we got older, hide and seek spots became make-out spots and the golf course became the best spot for parties. Once we got our licenses, we were no longer confined to the Fort on weekends. Fort friends mingled with the school friends and being from Fort Snelling was suddenly cool. (Think about it. It was the Seventies.) But if you didn't have your license, you needed a good friend to pick you up 15 miles away and make the trip all over again at the end of the night. I owe my best Richfield memories to Anne Budroe, Don Gillette,

Pattie Rosch, Kathy Leighton and Jon Nichols—dear friends who were willing to make the drive. Twice. But I can still feel the wave of sadness when I recall the car—whosever it was— turning onto Highway 62 and heading east. The night was over. No more Mr. Donut Swiss vanilla creams (10 cents apiece plus a penny tax) or Hot Fudge Vicky Kay brownies a la mode, or wandering Southdale, or Southdale Bowl, or the Quarry, or hanging out at a party—until someone came back for me. In 1968, Fort Snelling was turned over to the state, and in 1973, the year before I graduated from RHS, Fort Snelling residents were evicted from their homes. We moved to Minneapolis and the Fort's buildings were boarded up and abandoned for the next 49 years. Today, the Fort is a development of affordable housing for veterans; my old home is likely to house three families. Ironically, my dad's office, Building 18, is the new visitor's center for Historic Fort Snelling. And I can finally drive myself there and back.

Proving one thing: You can go home again.

# RICHFIELD SPARTANS STATE FOOTBALL CHAMPIONS 1963

**MIKE PALMQUIST**

*70TH AND 15TH AVE. SO.*

It started in the spring of 1963 when Richfield High School Football Coach, Bob Collison, suggested that all of the players set up workout groups to do weightlifting and workout sessions in groups of 3 or 4 players. Three times a week I would go to Rick Rosen's where he and I and two others would lift weights and do a simple workout program.

By the time the fall practices started we all, the entire team, were a lean mean fighting machine. When the fall two a day practices started, we were all of one mind. We wanted to put the best football team we could on the field. Coach Collison and Assistant Head Coach Archie Ward told us they were going to try something that had never been done in Minnesota High. School football. We were going to play two platoon football. We were going to have a starting offense and a starting defense, and no one was going to play both ways. Chuck Birch and I had both been fullbacks, but Chuck was also a great defensive linebacker, so he became the starting linebacker and I became the starting fullback. Dick Metz was a good running back, but he was also a great defensive back, so he became a starting defense halfback and Kip Myre became the starting halfback. Mike Sadek and Rick Rosen were both excellent quarterbacks, but Rick was also a great defensive safety. There were as many stories as there were players. Once the teams, offense and defense, were set up it was our job to make them work. We had two full teams, a first and second team offense and a first and second team defense. After our first few games it was obvious that the coaches had come up with something that was going to work. Practices were a contest between first team offense and first team defense, second team offense and second team defense. During the week we were playing against the best team in the Lake Conference, Richfield. Our first real test was the third week of the season against Robbinsdale. Robbinsdale was considered to be one of the best teams in the state. Although the score was only 20-13, we were in control from the start. We had a couple easier games but then for Homecoming we were playing Sioux Falls Washington High School from Sioux Falls, SD. Throughout their history, SF Washington had never lost to a Minnesota team. We scored the first touchdown and never looked back. We won the game 46-7. After the Sioux Falls Washington game, we faced Edina, our #1 rival and our final true challenge. On Monday after the Sioux Falls Washington game the Minneapolis Star & Tribune and KSTP moved us up to the #1 ranked team in Minnesota and ranked Edina #2. Our record at that point was 7-0 and Edina was 6-0-1, having tied Robbinsdale. We had to play them on Wednesday because of a short week for teacher's workshops on Thursday and Friday. We also had to go to Edina to play the game. A win would guarantee us a Lake Conference Championship, but a loss would have put us in 2nd place behind Edina. At game time it was estimated that there were 12,000 people in attendance in a stadium that sat 6,500 people. There were snow fences behind each end zone and people were standing 8-10 deep. They were also standing on the track around the field. There was a picture of Viking great Fran Tarkenton standing behind the snow fence in one of the end zones. It was a hard-fought game, but we prevailed 14-12. We were in control throughout the game and even though the score was close there was no doubt we would win. It was, in my opinion, probably one of the best games ever played in Minnesota High School Football. On a personal note, on the 3rd play of the second quarter, I injured my knee. I managed to play the rest of the game but the next day after a sleepless night I found out that I had torn the ligaments in my left knee. I ended up in a cast for the next 3 weeks and was unable to play in the last game of the season against St. Louis Park. We won the game 12-0 and secured the Lake Conference Championship. After the Edina game we stayed at #1 in the state and Edina dropped to 3rd or 4th, I can't remember for sure, but Rochester was moved into the #2 spot. As luck would have it, Edina's last game of the season was against Rochester and Edina won 33-0 which solidified our #1 ranking. We ended up being crowned the State Champions and our coaches, Bob Collison, and Archie Ward, along with our team captains, Tom Langseth and Dave Miller, went on KSTP, a couple of weeks later, and received the State Championship Trophy which has been in the school trophy case for decades. Several weeks later we had our Football Banquet and Fran Tarkenton was our speaker. We all learned a lot about teamwork and comradeship that season. Our coaches, especially Collison and Ward, were like fathers to all of us and they taught us a lot about how to be a man. Coach Collison's philosophy pretty much summed it up, "Winning isn't everything, it's the only thing". That didn't mean that you played dirty or cheated, it just meant that you could learn everything you wanted to about losing by losing once. In other words, don't make a habit out of it. Coach Collison and Coach Ward are both gone but their memory, as well as all the assistant coaches, lives on in every one of the players who was on that team. We couldn't have done it without you.

# TODAY'S TEENAGERS' HAVE NO IDEA...

**ROBERT "BOBO" PATRICK**

*68TH AND 18TH AVE. SO.*

Today's teenagers have no idea how difficult it was with one phone on the kitchen wall and a family with 3 teenagers. We lived on the corner of 68th and 18th Avenue South in Richfield. Our Dad was a strict disciplinarian. The rules were simple. His way or the highway. There were 3 teenagers, Mike Patrick RHS 64, me Bob or Bobo Patrick RHS 65, and Kathy Patrick RHS 67. One day Dad announced that all phone calls were limited to 2 minutes, or we must walk to the pay phone in the parking lot at the newly constructed Richfield Liquor Store, a block north on 67th and Cedar Avenue. What Dad said was our rule. One cold winter evening I had to have a talk with my girlfriend, Joanie Peterson RHS 66. Of course, Dad said, Bo get off the phone and walk to the liquor store booth. It was a cold and snowy evening and I put on my warmest clothes and added a bright orange ski mask. I hadn't thought that it was a knitted face on the back of my head, but I knew it would keep me warm. I took off to call my girlfriend. I got to the aluminum and glass structure in the lot on front of the liquor store. I stepped in and the ceiling light came on. I stood inside with my back to the liquor store and put my dime in and called Joanie. We were talking for about 10 minutes when someone behind me pounded on the glass door. I didn't turn around and just yelled, " I am on the phone". The rude person pounded again and pushed the door open and held up a police badge and said, "Get off the phone". I told Joanie I had to go. The Richfield Detective told me the liquor store cashier called the police because she thought I was going to rob the business. I guess she kept seeing the knit face on the back of my head. The Detective drove me home and explained the situation to my folks. He also suggested that Dad relax the rules a bit. Kids these days have no idea what we went through. After 4 years in the US Navy, I got a job as a Deputy Sheriff in a rural county. About 1979 I responded to a bank robbery, and I apprehended one of the robbers at a phone booth by a gas station. How ironic was that?

# AN EVENING UNLIKE ANY OTHER

**GORDON HANSON**

*63RD AND SHERIDAN AVE. SO.*

The day started like any other and ended in a way I'll never forget. I was a teenager living on 60th and Oliver. I grew up as a Minneapolis kid but knew Richfield well because it's where my parents shopped. One of those shopping trips is a night to remember. On a chilly December day in 1974, I boarded the bus to go to my carryout job at the Walsh's grocery store at the Southtown shopping center in Bloomington. It was an ordinary day at work, ending with a return ride on the bus to go home. As the bus headed north on Penn Avenue, it was forced to detour onto Oliver Avenue because of a robbery with hostages at the Country Club market at Penn and 66th. Wow! I couldn't wait to break the news to my parents. When the bus stopped at Penn and 60th, I hopped off and ran to tell my parents. I burst into the house to find it empty with no one home. I waited, and waited, and waited. With each passing moment, the thought crept into my mind: "Could my parents be there? After a while, I left home and walked to the Country Club. A crowd of spectators had gathered around a perimeter that police had set up. I could get as close as the north side of the Embers restaurant building at 65th and Penn, which today is America's Best Eyewear. I stood in the cold of the night looking at the store, knowing my parents were in there. Earlier in the evening, four men had entered the store with guns. They waved their firearms and demanded money, emptying cash register drawers. It was a chaotic scene with shouting, pushing and threats being made. Before they could leave, police arrived on the scene, cutting off their escape. My parents had just finished checking out. My dad was near the door and could probably have slipped out in the confusion. My mother was still near the check stand and had no way to escape. My dad returned to her. Being trapped inside the store, the robbers gathered up all the employees and customers they could find and forced them to lay down on the floor in the front of the store. According to my parents, the robbers took butchering knives from the meat department and brought them up front, occasionally stroking the blades. It was a night of high tension. A helicopter flew overhead. Sharpshooters were stationed on the rooftops of buildings across the street. Then-Governor Wendell Anderson was being apprised of the situation. Two robbers surrendered earlier, and the final two gave up shortly after 1 am. The siege lasted about 5 hours. I walked home and waited for my parents, who came home in the wee hours of the morning. I was so grateful to see them. The night ended without any hostages being seriously injured, but it did steal a certain innocence that the community had known before.

# THE BEST PLACE TO GROW UP

**PAMELA BEESON PREISS**

*64TH AND 19TH AVE. SO.*

My family moved to New Ford Town in 1956. At that time our family consisted of my mom and dad, my three brothers Gene ('70), Ray ('73) Dan ('74) and myself. Two years later our family grew with the birth of my sister, Terry ('76). Our address was 6405-19th Ave. S. New Ford Town was at the very East end of Richfield with the boundaries being 63rd Street to 66th street and Cedar Ave. to the airport property… My mom called 19th Avenue Incubator Alley because there were so many young kids on those three blocks. I believe at one time there were between 60-75 grade school kids living on 19th Ave. from 63rd Street to 65th Street. There was ALWAYS someone to play with and ALWAYS something to do. We would go play in the swamp (Mothers Lake), play at the vacant lot (The Tree Fort), sneak into the airport property, and build forts or go watch/play baseball or softball at East Richfield Babe Ruth and Little League fields. There were a couple of things that stand out in my memories of living in New Ford Town. One was in the early 60's. We were playing ball in the street, and we heard an airplane that sounded like it was in trouble. Sure enough, we looked up and saw a small plane flying low and smoke coming out. It was headed toward the airport property. We ran in the direction that it was flying, and it crashed just past the swamp and almost on airport property. I cannot remember if the pilot was killed or not. Another fond memory was when the Circus came to town. After it unloaded somewhere in Minneapolis, part of their path to the place where they held the circus was right in front of East Elementary. We watched the elephants, performers and other animals walk right by the school. East Elementary was a small school. When I attended there, it was Kindergarten through 6th grade. There were two classes per grade. When we first started going to school, we walked the two blocks and then had to cross 66th street to get to the school. There were only school patrols with flags to stop the cars. On Memorial Day in 1961 we convinced our parents to let our jr. high school neighbor take us to play on the playground at East School. We played for a few hours and then headed home. As we were crossing the street my little brother got hit by a car.

He was taken to the hospital but was ok. Thanks to him getting hit by the car, East School got crossing lights. In the 60's we had bomb drills at school. We would have to hide under our desks when we had those drills. They didn't seem silly then but now all I can say is WHAT GOOD WOULD THAT HAVE DONE? The Metropolitan Airports Commission decided the airport had to expand in size, so they bought out New Ford Town in the mid 1990's. By then my parents had moved to Lakeville in 1977. Many of the houses were sold and moved but some were demolished. Our house sat on a hill and couldn't be moved. I found out the date when they were going to demolish our house so my oldest brother, mom and I went to watch. As the bulldozer started to crush and flatten our house, I shed a few tears and thought that a part of my history, my past, was being destroyed. I was able to get the street sign for our block—64th St. and 19th Ave. S. That street sign is in my yard now. I still have the key to our house. I now realize that yes, the bulldozer did demolish some of the physical aspects of my childhood but not all the wonderful memories of my life in New Ford Town. It was the best place to raise a family, even with the airplane noise. There never will be anything like New Ford Town again.

# THE PETERSON FAMILY

**PATTY PETERSON**

*63RD AND MORGAN AVE. SO.*

In 1951, a very musical couple moved their daughter, Linda, and baby son, Billy, from Minneapolis to Richfield Minnesota. That musical couple was Willie and Jeanne (Arland) Peterson of WCCO Radio and Television fame. They built their home on Humboldt Ave and quickly added 2 more children to their family, Patty, and Ricky, all while working nightclubs, parties, and 'CCO Radio and TV. In 1958, they moved a few blocks away to Morgan Avenue, and 2 more children joined their family, Jeffrey (who passed from Leukemia at age 2) and Paul. In 1961, Willie became the first organist for the Minnesota Twins at the Met stadium. He continued for the next 8 years until his early passing in 1969, on opening day of Twins Baseball. After he passed, Jeanne took over for him for three years. We loved going to the baseball games. Bob Casey, the Twins live announcer for the games, was in the same booth as the organ. Wow, did we ever have great seats! In both Richfield homes, as the kids prepared for school and music lessons, Jeanne and Willie had rehearsals and writing sessions for commercials and big bands in the homes. This life in music became a language between everyone in the family. Little did we know that we would all end up in the music business for our own careers. This is how Linda, Billy, Patty, Ricky, and Paul, got their start. We absorbed music on a daily basis and then we had lessons on top of that. Piano lessons started early, but not with our folks. They sent us to Holy Angels to study music with the nuns, or, as in Billy's case, he learned how to play the organ from Larry Malmberg, another Richfield Resident. As a family, we often performed for musical events at St Peter's Church, where we attended, and even did a corporate party on occasion. Since rehearsals happened in our Morgan Avenue lower level, neighbors and music lovers would stop by the windows to hear the different bands practicing. Dan Chouinard, whose family were Richfield residents, tells a very fun story of how he and his brother, also musicians, delivered the newspaper to the Petersons. He said that they would stop and listen to what the music was being played as they delivered those papers. Fun memories. Willie, our dad, also became a coach for a speedskating team and led many kids into this new kind of sport. Billy became quite successful as a speed skater and was recognized for this throughout his life. Everyone but brother Paul graduated from Richfield High School. He graduated from Holy Angels along with his wife, Julie. Paul still helps with some of Holy Angels events, taking on a role that our dad had for so many years in the Twin Cities: booking music for special events. One of my personal favorite memories was moving from Holy Angels to Richfield High School as a sophomore. I remember trying out for the spring musical in 1971. It was going to be "Guys and Dolls". I had been singing with my family for years, and even on some commercials as a kid, but this was different. I prepared a song from Mame called "If He Walked into My Life" for my audition, and my mom, Jeanne, came waltzing into Richfield's Auditorium to play it for me. It was January, so it was cold. Mom breezed in, removed her fur coat, and threw it on the auditorium chairs. Jeanne sat down at the piano, went into an arpeggio, and then I began to sing. Jim Marcell was the director and he told me years after the fact that he said to himself, "Oh my goodness, who is this?" I think mom's talent knocked him out and luckily, my voice got his attention too. I got the lead in "Guys and Dolls", and in those days it usually went to a senior. That musical was the gift that made me realize that the audience liked me for ME. It wasn't because I was singing with and for my family. . .I got this role by myself, and that applause was for *ME* during the show. This is what propelled me into realizing singing was so much a part of me, I had to do it forever. Many years later, Jim Marcell passed away and being that he was an artist himself, he had a sketch pad that had the names of those he wanted to perform at his funeral. My name was on that pad. To me, that was one of the greatest honors to receive. We touched each other's lives in such a wonderful way on that cold January day. I am so grateful that happened. Today, our brother, Paul, and his family live in the Richfield home. It has continued to hold many family parties, rehearsals, and jam sessions, just like in our Parents' Day. There have even been some celebrity sightings at the home, coming over to spend time with the Petersons and taking part in a song or two. Afterall, our family loves being together, and that precious Richfield home is as big of a part of us as we siblings are to each other.

Thank you, Richfield!

# MY CHILDHOOD FRIEND FROM RICHFIELD MADE THE BIG LEAGUES (AND WHEN I FIRST SAW HIM IN ACTION!)

**RON BERGLUND**

*68TH AND STEVENS AVE. SO*

One of my favorite things about growing up in "Minnesota's Oldest Suburb" was East Richfield Little League. My first memories of "Little League" (as we called it then) go back to 1957, when I was only seven years old. My best childhood friend (Dayton Wightman) and I started in what they called "the clinic" when we were seven, and then each following year we moved up the ranks from "juniors" to "minors" to "international" and – finally- to the "majors"! The big time! The larger field for the major league had a larger grandstand for fans and a large elevated "press box" which usually had someone announcing the games on a loudspeaker. I cannot remember how many diamonds there were in 1957 and 1958, but by 1962 I believe there were about a dozen. Most were for the different levels of Little League, and there were the larger diamonds for Pony League and Babe Ruth. The fields were meticulously maintained by a hardworking crew of Little League dads, and when you set foot on one of the diamonds you felt like a big leaguer! To me- as a youngster-- it was all heaven on earth. I can still fondly remember the little snack shacks selling the delicious ice-cold pop such as black cherry and crème soda on a steamy hot summer day. My buddy Dayton and I would often ride our bikes a couple miles due east from Nicollet Avenue all the way up past Cedar Avenue along 66th Street (originally called Fort Snelling Road way back when) to the Little League fields just to watch other games even when our teams weren't playing that day. One fine day when we were both 11 years old and playing in the International League, as we walked from diamond to diamond observing the play, we heard the announcer at the major league diamond proclaim: "Home run....Kingsriter". This certainly caught our attention, as neither one of us had heard that unusual name before. Literally ten minutes we heard it again ("Home run.... Kingsriter"). And... maybe 15 minutes later we heard it AGAIN! Holy crap! Who is this kid?! Of course, by now Dayton and I were sprinting over to the major league field. When we arrived at the diamond we observed an adult-sized 12-year-old playing amongst the other 17 children on the field. So, this was the famous Doug Kingsriter! And the legend has continued for the past 60 years...Doug was the East Richfield Little League-leading home run hitter the next year (1962) when Dayton and I were also playing in the majors. Doug played for the Bridgeman's team which also featured the feared "David A" Johnson. As I recall (and it WAS 60 years ago for goodness' sake), Doug hit 12 home runs in his last year in Little League (before he graduated to Babe Ruth) but he was also a feared pitcher. He was adult-sized by age 12, so if you can imagine a grown man pitching from a rubber that was only 44 feet away from home plate you can get an idea. I never had to bat against Doug, but my friend Dayton did. Doug not only had a fastball that could break your flimsy plastic helmet in half if he hit you in the head, but Doug could even throw big curve balls! Once, Dayton hit the dirt when Doug threw a big curve only to have the umpire scream "strike" as the ball crossed the middle of the plate! Dayton was scared to death! Not too many kids could throw a curve ball at age 12. Doug eventually became a very good friend of Dayton and me and several of our other pals, and we have a number of stories about what it was like growing up with someone who became a fantastic high school baseball, football and basketball star. When Doug played ball with us back then it was like a bunch of kids were playing with a grown man! Doug went on to play for Murray Warmath's University of Minnesota football team and was an All-American tight end. Then, he went on to play for the Minnesota Vikings. Today, he proudly sports TWO Super Bowl rings! Even though the Vikes have still not won a Super Bowl in over 60 years, we can all be proud that one of our fellow Spartans played in two of them! And he is a great guy- and a great friend- in addition to being an amazing athlete.

# CONCERTS AT THE POOL

**BRAD KORKOWSKI**

*76TH AND NICOLLET AVE. SO.*

In the very early '70s, the city sponsored several evening "Pool Stomp" rock concerts, featuring local bands. The concerts were held at the swimming pool parking lot and were quite well attended. As I recall, they were very enjoyable and without incident. Richfield police patrolled the area, mostly enforcing no smoking by minors!

# POOL STOMP SLUMBER PARTY

**MARIA MEADE**

*66TH AND 2ND AVE. SO.*

In that magical year 1969, I was a Richfield Tween, famous in my St Peters School friend group, for hosting the best tent parties. August 2nd, 1969, was my best party yet. I was going to be 12 years old, and the Richfield Pool, where we "lived" from Memorial Day to Labor Day, was hosting a Pool Stomp that evening. The Pool Stomps were a City of Richfield sponsored dance, complete with a live band playing on a flatbed, that was set up in the Richfield Pool parking lot. The band Fairchild was the featured band that night. My friends all came over during the day, and we built our giant tent using my mom's clothesline in the back yard. My friends all brought blankets and sheets, clothespins and sleeping bags that we draped over the clothesline to create a shelter. WDGY, and KDWB played on our transistor radios as we drank Kool Aid and ate platefuls of Oreo cookies and watermelon while we discussed what fabulous fashions we would be wearing. We dreamed of dancing and falling in love with the rock stars on stage, or with the neighborhood boys who might dare to dance and take a chance. We were Catholic Girls, and the pool was a place where all the parochial and elementary school kids mixed and mingled. It was all so exotic and intoxicating. Everyone met back up at my house later, clad in our finest polka dot bell bottoms, and hair up in pigtails with big yarn bow ribbons. Presents were opened, hotdogs and chips, and birthday cake consumed, and then off we walked the 6 blocks to the pool. Fairchild played our favorite songs in all their paisley shirted, bell-bottomed jean splendor. Stealing our tween hearts away. We danced with each other and admired the public-school boys who fearlessly danced with their blonde public-school girlfriends. We dreamed of being cool. We wished the night would never end. Walking home to my house, we camped in our makeshift tent anticipating the arrival of the boys we knew from school, who vowed to sneak out and come visit us in the wee hours of the morning before their paper routes. We had to stifle our laughter to not wake up the neighbors as we talked and joked through that summer night... telling ghost stories, discussing movies, hippies, makeup, and fashion, and making plans for bike trips to Minnehaha falls. We were tweens that magic year of 1969....It was Endless Summer in Richfield.

# AUGSBURG PARK

**PAUL KUEHN**

*69TH AND BLAISDELL AVE. SO.*

For those of us with the distinction of being known as "Boomers", growing up in Richfield during the 60's was an idyllic time. Many of our freedoms and adventures were certainly taken for granted at the time but now, looked back on with nostalgic tears in our eyes. Summer months could find us riding our bikes, one hand on a handlebar, the other carrying an inner tube, on our way to Lake Nokomis or Minnehaha Creek to languish in their cool refreshing waters. The only concern was to be home by dinnertime. The Richfield pool was about a mile away so walking there, barefooted (of course), was another way to beat the unforgiving humidity of Summer. For the kids in our neighborhood, that meant crossing the endlessly wide and hot as Hades' cement of Portland Avenue. For those of us with the good fortune to live on the fringes of Augsburg Park, much closer to home, fun awaited; dangerously high (and hot) metal slides, merry go rounds, teeter totters, a pond and seemingly ancient Oaks. Although the lakes, creeks, pool, and playground equipment were only available during the warmer months, Augsburg Park was a four-season wonderland. Spring offered community sponsored Easter egg hunts and May Pole dances. The Fall, mounds of Oak leaves and Richfield High School football games. But Winter was especially enticing as the park hosted steep hills for sledding, rinks for ice skating and hockey, and even a warming house. But, of course, one needed to know how to skate. In my case, it was grandma to the rescue. (She lived with our family those years.) I'm not sure of my age but I'm guessing early elementary school, when she took it upon herself to teach me to skate. We trudged the five-house distance from our house to the pond in the West side of the park carrying with us a shovel and her ice skates. Together we'd shovel off a good-sized patch. Then, with old socks balled up in the toes of her skates so they would fit me, she'd lace up "my" skates, stand me up on the ice, face to face. Then she'd grab hold of my hands, her sliding her feet backwards one foot at a time, and me sliding mine forward in sync with her movement, one foot at a time. It didn't take too long before I could officially skate and, with the other neighborhood kids, trudge through the snow on our own to the skating rink and that blessed warming house. So many memories exist from those days, but grandma's loving, maybe unique, patient lessons afforded me many years, decades, of Winter ice skating fun. Even after relocating to California, we'd be sure to find ice skating rinks during the Winter to experience it with our own children.

# IN REMEMBRANCE OF AL PAYNE

**ROGER MAHN**

*74TH AND PLEASANT AVE. SO.*

People frequently called Al Payne, Mr. Richfield. If you went to Richfield High School between 1962 - 1965, you most probably saw Al play for Richfield. If you went to a football game, you saw him catch passes. If you attended a hockey game, you saw him skate fast and check hard. And if you watched a game of baseball, there was Al on the mound throwing heat. Richfield won the State Baseball Title in 1965, they were undefeated, and Al was a big part of that championship season. If you went to the pool or the rink in later years, you probably saw Al Payne. Earlier in life, Al was placed in a Richfield foster home. Al's foster mother was kind, understanding and tough. Al said he loved her, that he was afraid of her, but mostly afraid he might disappoint her. She told me once that Al really liked being a part of Richfield. He was to become a really large part of that city where he became beloved and where he rarely disappointed anyone. After high school, Al attended the University of Minnesota where he threw baseballs for them until something terrible happened to his arm. He finished his college education at Saint Cloud State College where he earned a degree in elementary education. Teachers with whom he worked thought he was a wonderful teacher. However, the city of Richfield wanted him back. He became the manager of the Richfield swimming pool and the hockey rink. His co-workers loved him. Folks who used the facilities praised him, especially the parents. He told a few girl skaters that he thought girls' hockey would be a future thing. He was about ten years ahead of his time. Al invited many of us to come back to support the high school and the Richfield Foundation. At Al's insistence, we paid our dues and formed the worst team of golfers on the course. Al was a wonderful athlete and an even better human being, but no one watched his golf swing twice. Laughing was not encouraged. The last year we got to play he told me that he had gotten much better. As far as I know, that was the only untruth he ever uttered. The next year he called to encourage my participation. He was coughing and said he couldn't play but he wanted the hat from the Foundation's golf tournament. Al was diagnosed with stomach cancer and died before I could bring him the hat.

# SHULE'S RIDING STABLE

**THOMAS ABALAN**

*73RD AND NEWTON AVE. SO.*

I remember when I was 6 or 7, Tim Patrick and I were riding up to Shule's Riding Stable on our bikes. It was near the gravel pit. I remember that there was no one around, as for workers, being there. Tim and I walked around inside the barn, where all the hay and feed were. Suddenly, I felt something climbing on my neck, it was a big barn spider! I slapped it off me, it was huge, at least, I thought it was. So, we went outside where the horses were. Tim decided to climb on one of the horses, while he said for me to tie a rope around the other horses' neck. Because of my inexperience around horses, I had no idea what I was doing. Tim jumps from one horse to the one I was holding on to, and that was when the horse reared back and ripped the twine out of my hands. At that time, I started to high tail out of there. The horse ran at me, and stepped on my foot, while I was running. I dropped to my knees and the horse came down and bit me on the top of my head. I then ran to the fence, jumped through, and got on my bike and road home, bleeding all the way. When I got home, and walked inside, my mom saw me bleeding, and asked what happened? I said I got bitten on my head by a horse! Mom said a horse! Where are there horses?... This is just one of the stories. I have more!

# A SNOWPLOW DRIVER SAVES THE DAY!

**LESLIE GERSEY BENTLEY**

*68TH AND VINCENT AVE. SO.*

I was so fortunate to grow up in Richfield, MN. My family moved to 68th and Vincent in 1954, when I was four. I enjoyed a classic 1950s childhood, complete with door-to-door selling Girl Scout Cookies, neighborhood picnics, annual trips to the State Fair, and Saturday afternoons at the Woolworths lunch counter. I was one of the overly curious 1st-graders who licked the frosty stop sign, temporarily welding my tongue to it. We played marbles in the street, rolling "purees" and "cat's eyes" into divots in the asphalt. The neighborhood kids constructed a baseball diamond in the vacant lot across the street, and my mom was our occasional umpire. We ventured far and wide on our bikes, visiting Shule's farm for an occasional horse ride or camping out in the fields at 68th and Xerxes to watch the construction of Southdale. We played "annie annie over" and "olly olly oxen free" with our friends on those long summer nights until the streetlights came on, everyone's signal to head home. In the winter, I huddled around the warming shack stove with my friends before heading back out for some laps around the skating rink. There were grade school pageants, junior high school talent shows, high school theater productions and debate tournaments, band concerts, Friday night football games, and sock hops to keep us involved. I moved away from Richfield in 1969 to join my husband at Ft. Carson in Colorado, but I maintained my connection by reading the Richfield News that my mom faithfully mailed to us weekly. It kept our bond to Richfield strong, and after his service, we bought a little house on the corner of 75th and Washburn in 1972. I eventually landed in Southern California, where I lived, when I had my most memorable Richfield moment. My Dad was diagnosed with three coronary artery blockages and was in the hospital awaiting bypass surgery. My brother and I both flew in from California to be there for his surgery. We stayed at our parents' home, sleeping in the bedrooms we'd grown up in. A winter storm blew in on the eve of my dad's 8 a.m. surgery. I awoke to lights on at 4 a.m. and found my mom staring out the window at the snow-drifted street. With tears in her eyes, she said, "How are we ever going to get to the hospital to see Dad before his surgery?" Not willing to give up, she took action. At 5:00 a.m., she started calling numbers for the City of Richfield and didn't give up until she found someone to speak to about the plow crew who had started clearing the streets. I remember her words clearly as she pleaded with the plow crew supervisor on the phone: "I have been a loyal and active resident of Richfield for almost three decades. I have never asked for anything from my city, but today I have an emergency." She explained that the drifted street would make it impossible to get to the hospital in time to hug her husband before his major surgery. I'm not sure what the man on the phone said, but she told us to get dressed and returned to the window. Within 15 minutes, a snowplow showed up at our house and plowed a path down Vincent Avenue to 69th

Street, and then down to Penn, where the plow had already cleared the snow. We followed the plow in our car and made it to the hospital with moments to spare before they took my dad for his surgery. The relieved look on his face made me realize how much he needed those parting hugs. He made it through his surgery. That was like a Richfield miracle to me, showing how much the city cared for its citizens. Though it may have created some havoc in the plowing schedule that morning, someone had responded to our emergency. I wonder how many other cities have such stories of compassion in their histories. Richfield will always hold a very special place in my heart.

# COMING OF AGE WITH WDGY

**MARK FOSTER**

*72ND AND PILLSBURY AVE. SO.*

Jimmy Reed - the disc jockey from 7-midnight at WDGY got to know me and Skip Vandinburg from calling in every night to do "dedications" to our girlfriends…that turned into long/off-air conversations, which eventually turned into putting us on the air to do the dedications and, eventually, visits out to WDGY studios out on 35W to watch him do his show live…Jimmy would also come to watch us play Babe Ruth baseball games at the old Donaldson's Park/fields (we were on Tait's and my Dad was the head coach)…I especially liked the fact that he would give me stacks of 45's, most of which were "promotional/DJ" copies only, and I would have "HIT" songs before any of my friends even heard them…even have a picture of Skip and I posing with Jimmy Reed and Santa Claus out at Southdale which was used for a picture in the WDGY "Top 40" playlist that they published and circulated at ALL the record shops in the Twin Cities…After graduating from Brown Institute on Lake Street, I eventually, ended up in radio broadcasting myself in Texas as an on-air personality and a Program Director and eventually a consultant for other stations…all because of those late night dedications to my Junior High School sweetheart…and Jimmy Reed…

# SHAWN PHILLIPS - OCTOBER 5TH, 1972

**JAN HATFIELD**

*RHS CLASS OF 1973*

It was a Thursday and something awesome was happening at Richfield High School. A & M Recording artist Shawn Phillips was doing a show at our school. How the people in charge were able to set this up I will never know, but it was a fantastic event to me. To be honest the show was not my favorite memory of it because……Not only did Shawn Phillips do a show at our school but he also came and spoke at my "Poetry in Todays Music" class. I was in my senior year of high school at the time and this class was an elective you could take for a quarter instead of traditional English. It was so interesting to hear him speak about how he wrote lyrics to his songs. He said he read the dictionary page by page. I found that weird but cool at the same time. He looked like your everyday "hippie" but spoke more like a professor. All in all it is one of my favorite memories of High School. I still listen to his albums to this day.

# MR. DUANE WOLD

LEE WOLD AND SCOTT WOLD

Being the son of Duane Wold while growing up in Richfield was oftentimes like being raised in a small town. My dad was an employee of Richfield Public Schools in several capacities: as the Media Generalist, teacher, baseball, basketball, cross-country coach at the Junior High level at East and West, and as a driving instructor at RHS. Going anywhere in Richfield was to experience people greeting him as "Coach," "Mr. Wold," "Tuffy," or "Dewey." When we went out to run errands, there seemed to be someone who knew Dad. He would get a wave or would be stopped for a conversation reminiscing about a past school year or a sporting activity. When the person would leave, we would ask the question "Who was that Dad?" He would tell us a fun story of that person like they were famous. We lived near school and the students would know his car and they would wave or shout his name, trying to get his attention, and he would return the gesture with a horn honk acknowledging them. Today, when we introduce ourselves, we're asked if we're related to Mr. Wold. We need to clarify because his twin brother was also a teacher and coach from St. Louis Park. One of the most telling experiences on how far-reaching his network of students was occurred the day he passed away. When we called the funeral home, the person who answered the phone was leaving for the night. He recognized the name and stayed late to help. When Steve from the funeral home arrived, he asked if it was Duane Wold from Richfield High School who had taught behind-the-wheel driving. We confirmed it was Dad. Steve told us that dad was his driving instructor and told us the various sayings he remembered during his lessons. It turned out that the person who was going to be one of the last people to be with our father was yet another person who was touched by him during their own life. He said what many people said about our dad, "Your dad was a good man." We certainly agree. Our dad touched the lives of hundreds of students during his 30 plus years with Richfield Public Schools.

# MY CAREER AT BRIDGEMAN'S

**BOB KALWAT**

*68TH AND 18TH AVE. SO.*

I started working at Bridgeman's on 66th the spring of my junior year in '71. Previous jobs at Tastee Freeze on 66th, and Mr. Steak on 78th didn't pan out, so I walked into Bridgeman's on a whim. The manager on duty was the head guy by the name of Bob Burris. Vietnam veteran, and he wanted everybody to know it. Had me fill out an application, hired me on the spot and put me to work as a busboy the same night. Was a good starting job to learn the "lay of the land" and get to know the cooks, waitresses, managers, etc. There was a Drive-in section out back in those days. Open all winter. I did my stint as a dishwasher as well, and the opening to the drive-in was right across from the dishwasher portion of the kitchen. Waitresses would open the door when it was -30, cold air would come over and hit that hot, wet air and immediately turn to steam. Couldn't see across the room. SuperAmerica gas station was right in the back of the store. Burris was always sending me off on an errand to buy him two packs of "True Green" smokes at SuperAmerica. Imagine trying to get away with that today. The other managers were Kim (last name?) and Wendy (last name?). The manager on duty would have to inspect the kitchen after closing before you could leave. Bob Burris was a stickler, Kim was easy, and Wendy was somewhere in the middle. Wasn't too long (2-3 months) there came up an opportunity to take over as the "kitchen boy", when the current guy, Barney (last name?) moved to the grill as a cook. The Kitchen Boy stocked ice cream in the bins out front, kept the toppings prepped and filled and made whipped cream. The kitchen Boy also came in on delivery day to take the shipment and load the main freezer. Making whipped cream canisters was an experience. Stainless steel canisters, 1 ½ cups heavy cream, seal the lid and charge with CO2. Shake 150 times, repeat for as many empty cans you had. Was stocking the Hot Fudge one Friday night when I slipped on a wet spot and dropped the metal cannister. Hot fudge shot out the top like a shotgun, all the way to the ceiling. What didn't stick fell on the customers in the booth underneath. Needless to say Bridgeman's paid for their dinner (me in particular). I went back in later years to eat there, and the stain was still on the ceiling until they gutted the store to make it Pizza Luce. My favorite waitress was Daisy. When she had a lull, she'd come back to the kitchen and listen to WDGY. Her favorite song was "Rings" by Cymmaron. I had a standing order to come and get her when they played it. My goal on Saturday night was to get the kitchen cleaned up, inspected, be out and in the car before midnight. REASON – WDGY played the full-length version of IN-A-GADDA-DA-VIDA at midnight, and I wasn't missing a second of it. I worked there until the Marines called and I left in June of '72 - 13 days after we graduated at the Met Center. Good times ……

# RICHFIELD'S RAVE-ONS OUTDRAW THE ROLLING STONES!

**LARRY WIEGAND**

*74TH AND GIRARD AVE. SO.*

I know this headline looks like a misprint, but it really did happen...The year was 1964 and The Rolling Stones were playing that famous gig at DANCELAND Ballroom in Excelsior. On the same night, I was playing with the Rave-Ons (with Lonnie Knight ('66), Harry Nehls ('64) and my brother, Dick Wiegand ('64) at the Marian Ballroom in Bloomington. It was the peak time for all of the mid 60's crowd, and those Ballrooms, and we drew about 500 people that night. You could've had Daffy Duck playing there and he would've done the same...About halfway through the night, some friends of mine showed up. They had just come from the Stones gig in Excelsior. They said there were only 50 people there, so they left early. Sooooooooo.... The Rave-Ons outdrew The Rolling Stones that night! It didn't take long to figure out that there were probably 20 or 30 other local bands playing that night that could say the same thing. It's been a nice memory although quite a fantasy.

# THE LASTING IMPACT OF OUR WORDS

**JIM RAYMOND**
*64TH AND HUMBOLDT AVE. SO.*

In 1953, I was 12 years old and was just entering junior high, when my parents, like many other couples who had begun to raise a family in the early and mid-40's, moved from Minneapolis to the rapidly growing suburb of Richfield. I was beginning to attend a new school in a new neighborhood, and my parents later told me that they were very concerned as every day when school was out, I would come home, go into my bedroom, shut the door and listen to my music on my 45-rpm record changer. I was very non-communicative and apathetic according to my mother. My grades in school were noticeably lower than I had in grade school, and I seemed to be having a very hard time adjusting to a new school and making new friends. My dad encouraged me to join a neighborhood church basketball program to meet some kids my age and I met a few new friends. Then Spring came, basketball ended, and it was back to my room after school. In the summer between 7th and 8th grade I began to hang out with a cousin, who was 2 years older - old enough to have a driver's license - and with whom I was quite close and who had a buddy who had a 1950 Ford Convertible. My cousin, who attended Central High school in the inner city of Minneapolis, and now had transportation, spent more and more time in Richfield. But my parents were very concerned with the inner city influence this relationship had on me. When winter of my 8th grade came, the one friend that I had met in my church basketball program encouraged me to try out for an 8th grade basketball team that was coached by a man named Ev Schlaeder and somehow, I was selected. While I was still spending time with my cousin and his friends, my grades were still causing my parents to be very concerned with the direction things were going. One day, after practice, in the lockers next to the gym at the old Woodlake School on 66th and Dupont, a man whom I was told was the High School football coach came up to me and said," What's your name?" "Jim Raymond," I replied. "Raymond, do you play football?" "No, I haven't." Then he proceeded to say the words that changed my life … for him just a throwaway line that he probably had used many times …. He said, "Raymond, with legs like those, you should play football." That's it, just … "Raymond, with legs like those, you should play football." To say that I had no idea of the impact that comment would have would be the biggest understatement of my life. That night, I went home, and at dinner said to my dad, "Dad … the high school football coach said that with my legs I should go out for football." I had never played football, but he *was* the coach, and he noticed me. He didn't tell anybody else that they should go out for football. Maybe I should give it a try …. I didn't have anything to lose. And so, it was settled … I would go out for the 9th grade football team …. And that was the beginning of a journey, a new direction that would change my life forever and give my life a meaningful direction. The next Fall football practice began, coached by at least 2 men whose names I remember … Carl Martin and Jerry Stahlwick. I finally began to meet new friends, eventually meeting my closest friend, and who passed away in 2014, Wes Hatlestad, and … as I started to hang out with a new group of guys, I found out that many of them were not only athletes, but excellent students and I began to hang out more with them and less with my inner-city cousin and his friends. My grades improved and my involvement with school activities increased tremendously and besides that, I was enjoying and doing well at this sport that I had never tried before. It didn't hurt that I had well developed calf muscles!!The next year, my sophomore year, I was fortunate to not only play on the 10th grade team, but also suited up for the varsity games and played barely enough to receive my first athletic letter in a sport. By now my grades had come up and I was taking on a leadership role in both school and athletics that was instrumental in my development and maturing. Involvement in the youth group of my church along with high school student council and being elected Sophomore Class President reinforced my growing self-confidence and self-image. Somewhere in this rambling I want to acknowledge the part that some athletes who preceded me at Richfield played as role models for a me as young guy looking to older student leaders and athletes … guys like Al Andreotti in the class of 1956, Larry Molsather in the class of 1957, Dick Enga in the class of 1958 and others too numerous to mention. Also, I want to mention the positive influence of many teachers and coaches – Arch Ward, Vance Crosby, Gene Olive, Floyd Nordland, Doris Frankenstein, Lloyd Fezler, and Gene Farrell, among others. I ended up my high school career as Co-Captain of the football team in my senior year, and President of my class in both my Junior and Senior years, attended Boys State and was a 2-year member of the National Honor Society. I began to have visions of going to college after high school, something nobody in my family had ever done. With the encouragement of coaches and teachers and family friends, I was even bold enough to dream of one day attending dental school and becoming a dentist. Fast forward 6 years to 1965 … as I became the first Richfield High School grad to attend and graduate from the University of Minnesota School of Dentistry. Fast forward to 2015 … I was blessed to practice dentistry for 50 years in a profession that I absolutely loved going to every single day! I, along with my wonderful wife, Sue, lived in Richfield for 30 years and have raised 3 sons who attended Richfield High School, all of whom were fortunate enough to be able to participate in the athletic programs there, and 2 of whom played football for Mr. Dick Walker, and who was the successor to my football coach. To me, it is very obvious that the watershed experience - I could have gone in one of 2 very opposite directions - that watershed experience that led to the life I have had was the remark, those many years ago, by that football coach, "Raymond, with legs like those, you should play football." And to say that I am so very, very grateful seems to be so inadequate. But I sincerely and humbly say, "Thank you Bob Collison."

# SEEING THE BEATLES IN CONCERT... AUGUST 21, 1965

**SANDIE TANTTU**

*67TH AND MORGAN AVE. SO.*

Sue Taragos and I, Sandie Tanttu, class of 1968, were avid Beatles fans from the day we saw them on the Ed Sullivan Show February 9th, 1964. I already had Beatle pictures on all 4 of my bedroom walls. From then on, everything we did together seemed to revolve around The Beatles. Playing Beatles records, going to see them on the huge screen at the Minneapolis Armory, watching "A Hard Days Night "numerous times and later seeing "Help" numerous times. Buying all the teen magazines that we could find on the Beatles, buying Beatles bubble gum cards with Beatles cards inside. It was such a disappointment that they didn't come to Minneapolis the first year, but they did come on August 21st, 1965, to Metropolitan Stadium in Bloomington, Minnesota. We started shopping for our new dresses about 2 or 3 months earlier. Who knows, we might get to meet them! Sue came to my house and my dad drove us there. It was so exciting. Almost everyone was screaming but not Sue and I. We were just dreaming about being with them. We actually ran along their limousine and Paul was on our side. Beatlemania at its finest. My Dad came to pick us up, but Sue was getting a ride home with someone else, but first they went to find The Beatles. Sue wanted me to come too but I didn't even bother to ask my parents. I knew they wouldn't let me. We were 14 going on 15. The next day I heard they were at the Leamington Hotel and Paul had a girl in his room. But she was 21. All was good. When The Beatles did not come back in 1966, WDGY had a contest to fly the winners to St. Louis, Missouri. I must have entered 100 times and one day I got a phone call from Scott Burton that I had won! So there was 16 of us and 4 DJ's, Scott Burton, Jim Dandy, Johnny Canton and Bill Diehl flying to St. Louis August 21, 1966. That led me to getting a job at the WDGY booth at the Minnesota State Fair, passing out 45's and wearing Mary Quant outfits. I had a blast during those years!

# GIRLS IN "BOYS" CLASSES

**PAMELA SYVERSON**

*77TH AND 13TH AVE. SO.*

Back in 1972, girls were only allowed to attend "Home Economics" classes, cooking, sewing, etc. as an elective. My Mom/Grandma taught me those things, so I enrolled in the Wood Shop class. Immediately was called down to the principal's office and told I could not take a "boys" class... I then staged a "sit in", that is how we protested back then... was immediately called into the principal's office again! They agreed if I could get enough girls to populate a full class, they would let us take it, the catch was I also had to get enough boys to take a "Home Ec" class. We ended up with 22 girls signed up for Wood shop and enough boys in cooking class. It made the front page of the paper, using me as the example :) Mr. DeVries was the best! Built a chess table oak and Black walnut, with a pedestal that was lathed with a drawer to hold the pieces. Hence all classes were open enrollment for all genders in Richfield after that. New classes were added as well, like "powder puff auto mechanics" where we learned how to change a tire, check the oil, etc. Anybody remember this?

# SKATING ON WILSON POND

**CAMILLE LEMERE STRATTON**

*73RD AND BLOOMINGTON AVE. SO*

I think the fondest memory I have of living in Richfield was ice skating on Wilson Pond just around the corner from our house. In winter every day after school and every night after dinner you could find me on the pond ice skating. The road was usually frozen so I could skate to Wilson Pond. I learned how to skate from my dad. He'd effortlessly skate backwards while I moved my little legs as fast as I could, the sound of my snowpants... (you know that nylon sound I'm talking about) and falling down! Then on one foot my dad would make flawless figure 8's. Boy I miss him! When I was ready to get warmed up and wipe my runny nose, I'd skate up to the wooden steps that led up to the warming house. Ahhhhh the warming house, felt soooo cozy. There was always a fire in the stove and kids coming in and out of the door. I'd get warm and then head back down the wooden steps to the ice rink. As I grew up and became a better skater (now wearing jeans which froze), I'd play Red Rover Red Rover send……right over and Pom-Pom pull away with all the neighborhood kids. (I was always the last one caught). I also did flips into the giant snowbanks push up along the banks of the pond by the snow grader. As I got older boy crushes happened and I couldn't wait to see certain boys on the rink (which my dad wasn't too crazy about). As an adult, visiting family, I brought my husband Mark to Wilson Pond rattling off my many memories. The warming house is gone now, and the grasses and flowers surround the pond. Ahhhh the memories of ice skating on the pond. Does anyone else share memories of Wilson Pond?

# THE HENDRICKSON STORY

**JANE HENDRICKSON**

*FORREST DRIVE*

We moved to Richfield in 1968 when Larry accepted a teaching & coaching job. We bought a little 2-bedroom house with a big yard for our two big black labs. We were welcomed right away into the neighborhood: Ron & Lemme Graham, Bill & Meg Davis families, candy ladies & Bob & Sue Wagner. Bob was on the Richfield School Board & both he & Sue always took an interest in all matters regarding education here plus Dr Bob delivered all 4 of our children that came ever after: Christine Darby Danny Julie. Many happy events through the years. Lots of after game parties with teachers, coaches & administrators. & Now a Wednesday coffee group & birthday club going on 50yrs…From

Christine Hendrickson Krsnik: fond memories of belonging to the Richfield Figure Skating Club! I loved every part of practicing, competing & outing on the end of year show. I signed up for as many numbers as allowed. One year I had 6 costume changes. It was so great!...From Darby Hendrickson: Best day ever when my mom dropped me off at Woman Lake with a bag lunch early & picked me up late afternoon. I maybe only caught a couple of fish but that was ok…From Danny Hendrickson: Everyday was a great day in Richfield hopping on my racing bike & tearing around the neighborhoods. Sometimes I didn't watch for cars & riding across 76th St a car came off the exit ramp & hit me. The driver felt terrible, picked me up & brought me home. Green stick broken leg with a cast all that summer long! But I got a new bike out of it & an annuity settlement thx to my dad & attorney Priscilla Lord. So, I guess it was all worth it…. From Julie Hendrickson Oss: I loved growing up in Richfield! The parks, the games, the friends all over town. I especially loved participating in Community dance & Barbi Lee's dance lessons & the recitals at the end of the year. My campfire leaders gave me a stage name: "Julie Margo" which I wanted to take on the road to Hollywood. Long story short; it wasn't to be! But what fun every day we had! The Richfield community has always responded to our family to make us feel important & appreciated. My adult children & 15 grandchildren are all close by Julie in Bloomington, Danny in Shorewood, Darby in Deephaven & Christine right here in Richfield. After my husband Larry passed in 2018; Christine & Renato offered to take over my house, remodel it & make a place for all of us to live together. That is exactly what we did. They did a beautiful job & we are all living happily on Forest Dr forever with Family gatherings around the pool, sauna & hot tub talking hockey, real estate & as long as we don't discuss too much politics Life is good in Richfield!

# COMING TO RICHFIELD 1959

GINNY KIRKEGAARD LEPPART
*72ND AND GARFIELD AVE. SO.*

Our family of four moved to Richfield in January of 1959 from south Minneapolis. It was quite an upheaval for me as a recently turned 5-year-old. I had loved my former bungalow home and neighbor friends, and I had begun school in Minneapolis, where they started some children at age 4 at that time, depending on their birth month. I was not able to continue with kindergarten in Richfield as I had missed the required cut off of being 5 by the previous September. So, I ultimately had the privilege of going to kindergarten twice! In the meantime, I was a witness to all the remodeling and change as our new home was transformed during that first year. My parents had wanted more space and found the perfect "fixer upper" in west Richfield. Our new house was very unique for Richfield, as it was not a rambler or Cape Cod style. It was a full two-story cubical shape, sometimes referred to as a Craftsman Foursquare style. It was built in the 1920s and must have stood by itself "out in the country" for years. It was never a farmhouse, as I understood it. The price was right at $13,000. However, the home's interior was unlivable. The woodwork was dark, bordering on black, the living room walls were bright red, and the carpet was very old and smelled to high heaven! My parents spent well over a year fixing it up. When I picture my dad that year, I see him on a stepladder with a trouble light, painting walls and ceilings each evening after putting in a long day at work. Such motivation. They did hire some of the work to be done, and there was one man in particular who did the carpentry. He took one large bedroom upstairs and modified it into two smaller rooms, so that my brother and I could each have our own space. Each day I would eagerly await lunchtime, as this sweet man would open his lunchbox and give me the cookie his wife had packed for him. In the end, we had a remodeled kitchen, new carpet, fresh curtains, lots of tasteful paint color on the walls and white wainscoting throughout. The home was quite charming, and our family occupied that cherished dwelling for 30 years. My parents eventually moved to a more typical Richfield rambler on the east side when it became difficult for my dad to get up and down the stairs. The home looks inviting and well kept up to this day and has been redone to keep up with current tastes. One evening I drove by on my way home from an event in Richfield, and I could see the light of the TV flickering in what had been my parents' front bedroom. I became nostalgic, imagining my mom and dad in that room watching *The Tonight Show with Johnny Carson* as they always did. Great Richfield memories.

# SNEAKING OUT

**MARK SANNES**

*69TH AND 14TH AVE. SO.*

We were sneaky kids, my brother Jon and me. We'd have a night in the back yard, camping in the tent, watching TV via the extension cord. Monster movies were pretty darn good. Our monster movies were Frankenstein, the Wolfman and Dracula, all from the 1930s. Those were and still are the best! But our mission came after that. Our mission was to steal golf balls from the Richfield Airport driving range. Sometime around 2 am, we'd hop on our bikes, empty pillowcases in hand, and scoot to that driving range. We 'golf ball burglars' would then scoop up all the red striped balls we could and then scurry on back to camp. What a sight that was, stupid kids, riding our bikes through Richfield at 2am with sacks full of stolen golf balls! We almost got caught one time. The lights came on for the range and we ducked down low. Made it out with our full pillowcases of red striped balls. Range balls were used at any golf course hole where a water hazard presented itself. They always found the water and that was a good use of those red striped balls. We also used them for practice. Our backyard led into Christian Park, and we'd tee them up and try to hit the pond. Every so often, one would fly past the pond and somewhere into the houses beyond. We scampered back into the house! I used to keep my red striped balls in my top dresser drawer. Always had an ample supply! Well, for a while anyway. There's probably still a bunch in the Christian Park Pond and the water hazards of Normandale golf course. Those were good times for us golf course burglars ...Nuff said!

# REMEMBERING BILL DAVIS

**STEVEN O. LINDGREN**

*72ND AND HARRIET AVE. SO.*

Living in Richfield nearly my entire life gave me the opportunity to know, work with and develop friendships with many remarkable people. One of the most significant and lasting relationships started on a baseball field in Richfield when I was only ten years old and lasted until January, 2023. Much has been written and said about Arthur

Willard "Bill" Davis, Jr. I think it is fair to say I had a hero at a young age. Numerous stories have appeared on the sports pages in Minnesota (and elsewhere) about Bill's life growing up in Richfield, being a two-sport star athlete at the University of Minnesota and in professional baseball. My respect for him exceeded all expectations beginning in 1990 when we became founding members of the Richfield Spartan Foundation, Inc. along with five others. Building on what I received from knowing Bill by looking up to him on the baseball field at an early age, evolved into something even greater. Perhaps it was his commitment to the youth of Richfield which took on a different form than coaching, being a mentor, or serving on Boards of various entities. The creation of a Foundation enabled Bill to demonstrate an even greater understanding and empathy for the young people of Richfield. While two of the founding members of the Spartan Foundation Board of Directors preceded Bill as President, it was his thirteen years at the helm which game him the opportunity to demonstrate how much his philanthropic spirit extended into Richfield. His leadership style was inclusive, visionary, and remarkably effective in transforming an entity into a uniquely valuable Foundation for the Youth of our community. The entire Board greatly appreciates his leadership. In my humble opinion, he will be remembered for his contributions and mentoring to an extent not matched in Richfield. When Bill stepped down as the President of the Foundation and turned the reigns over to another generation of leaders, the Board suggested to Bill the idea of a scholarship in his name. True to his humility, he declined the idea initially. Fortunately, he was willing to give it further consideration and eventually agreed to a Bill Davis Scholarship Fund as part of the Foundation's Legacy, or Endowment Fund. He suggested as the cornerstone to the scholarship a commitment to community service as demonstrated by applicants. The Spartan Foundation Board of Directors honored him with the title of President Emeritus, as well. If you are a reader of this tribute to Bill and want to assist in furthering his legacy, please consider viewing the spartanfoundation.com website and click on: Donate to Bill Davis Scholarship.

# MY STORY OF GROWING UP IN RICHFIELD

**MIKE LYNCH**

*LAKE SHORE DRIVE*

If you ever watched the old ABC show, "The Wonder Years," starring Fred Savage, it really parallels life growing up in Richfield in the 1960s. They really were the wonder years for me! I was exceptionally fortunate growing up in a classic neighborhood just across the street from Wood Lake. It was an actual lake back in the day but when 35W was constructed its underground water supply was cut off. By the mid 60's pretty much all the lake was gone, and cattails completely took over. Before that happened, I remember sitting on my front lawn watching sailboats in the gradually shrinking bodies of water. Even though the lake was gone the woods around it survived. In fact, we referred to it as "the woods," and we sure had some good times there. If the big trees could talk the stories they could tell! We created paths in the woods that still exist to this day. Off those paths we built "forts" and dug deep holes where we would hang out at night and drink "beverages" that weren't legal for us back then. None of us were ever caught though. The Woods shielded us from the authorities! There was also the day when my next-door neighbor and buddy Don Falenczykowski and I almost changed the history of Wood Lake. Don and I were in the "woods," and he was helping me try to earn my Boy Scout Second class cooking badge. We came very close to starting a major fire! By the grace of God and just enough dirt and water, we managed to extinguish the flames. Another couple of minutes and the woods would have gone up and we would have been in so much trouble! In the '60s, adjacent to Woodlake, Richfield maintained a skating rink, hockey rink, and warming house. I spent many winter hours skating and watching the older boys play hockey. We drove the warming house supervisor's crazy with all our antics, especially playing Crack the Whip with extended lines of skaters. Just off Lake Shore Dr was one of the best sliding hills in Richfield that led down to the banks of the skating rink. If you could get a running start, you would be able to slide down the hill with enough speed and momentum to launch your sled or toboggan over the banks and onto the rink. It was a lot of fun but a hazard to unsuspecting skaters. Fortunately, there weren't any major incidents. The city quickly got wise to us though and put up a fence ending our sliding adventures. They also planted trees and shrubs that have really grown up and spread since those days. Before the city closed down our hill, we used it in the summertime to race our very poorly constructed go-carts. We also had the bright idea that if we attached homemade wings to the carts, they would get airborne. It never happened but give us credit for trying! In the early '70s, Woodlake became the Woodlake Nature Center, and I worked there as a part-time maintenance in High School and part of my college years. I also fell in love with telescopes and amateur astronomy at the nature center after attending a "Moonwatch" program conducted by Wensell Frantzich. I'll also remember the first time I looked at the Moon with his large telescope. I was hooked! He took me under his wing, and soon I started building telescopes and assisting him with his Moonwatch programs. After Wensell moved to Florida, Randy Hughes, the nature center manager at the time, asked me to develop and teach a stargazing class. Fifty years later, I'm still putting on my Starwatch programs all over Minnesota and Western Wisconsin.

I truly lived the "Wonder Years" growing up in my part of Richfield!

# FORE!...
# OR THREE SIDES OF THE INFAMOUS GOLF CART INCIDENT

# SUBJECT: 74 GOLF CART INCIDENT

**BRAD PERLICH**

*73RD AND COLFAX AVE. SO.*

"Someone" came to me and asked if I could help get a golf cart in the school. I said I think so, get me some golf cart measurements (width and height) and I would see what I could figure out......I figured it out - and told him how long it would take, and which door would work. A Day and time were agreed upon. I arrived a little early to school that day, took the center post out, chocked the doors open, then went to class…or maybe not? I laughed when the golf cart drove through the door and down the hallway. You'll have to get the rest of the story from...

# GOLF CART SEEN CRUISING IN RHS: I CAN'T BELIEVE THOSE GUYS DID THAT!

**MIKE RYMAN**

*73RD AND PARK AVE. SO.*

It was the Spring of 74. A group of high school seniors decided that Fridays were golf days. Gathering at one classmate's house became a Friday ritual as they all called the attendance window at the same time to call in sick for the day. As more Fridays came along ,conversation turned to "Hey why don't we drive a golf cart up to the attendance window Instead of calling in sick and asking for an off grounds pass for the day." Now the challenge... who's got a golf cart and how are we going to get it into the school? Well, it just so happened that a former graduate of RHS had a cart. The Plan was beginning to come together. Now the Tough part how do we get the cart into the high school? We then had to find an an engineer who could help us with our entry into the high school. That engineer from the class of 75 knew how to dismantle the door frame that would allow us entry into the high school. We gathered at 6 AM that Friday to trailer a golf cart to the school and then took apart the door on the North end of the building by 1st floor. Once the door was dismantled the game was on. Four classmates jumped on the cart and started their journey down the 1st floor hallway making a right-hand turn in order to get to the attendance window. We gathered quite a crowd of followers on our way to the attendance window. Once in front of the window the attendance staff started laughing when we requested sick day passes as we were going to play golf. Well, the attendance staff could not be outsmarted so they alerted Principal Olive that a golf cart was in front of the attendant's window. Olive scrambles and gathers his deputy Principals Stoecz and Hardy to head off these pranksters. The getaway was on, and the golf cart moved past the office for the escape door. Unfortunately, as it may seem, the pranksters were apprehended by the Principals. Once apprehended suspensions were filed, diplomas pulled and threats of summer work duty as punishment was threatened....To this day the story circulates within the Olive family. More to be told...

# OFF GROUNDS PASS

**ANNE BUDROE BENDA**

*65TH AND IRVING AVE. SO.*

It was early morning, on a weekday in late May 1974, at Richfield Senior High. Just a week or so before my class, the RHS Class of 1974, would be graduating. It was a typical scene in the 1st floor main hallway of RHS, several minutes before the first bell rang; full of seniors hanging out, talking and goofing off.A year earlier, on June 1, 1973, the state of Minnesota had changed the legal age of adulthood to 18. That meant that any RHS senior who had turned 18 during the 1973/1974 school year now had the legal right, as an adult, to excuse their own absences from school (no more forging parent's signatures on notes). Back to the main hallway that morning before the first bell rang...We heard a growing commotion coming towards us—laughter, clapping, cheers and another sound never before heard inside the school. The commotion emanated from a group of three senior guys approaching the Attendance Window in the 1st floor main hallway, right next to the school office. When they arrived, they requested Off Grounds Passes for a "college visit". (Off Grounds Pass was an excused absence for a few hours or the entire school day.)Since they were adults at 18, their requests for excused absences to visit a college were perfectly legit. The only thing a bit off with their request is the fact that they arrived at the attendance window in a golf cart, dressed in golf gear, clubs secured in the cart. The serious looks on their faces were priceless. As it turns out, the guys, Bill King, John Mullen and Steve Stewart, did NOT receive Off Grounds Passes that day. The trio were later called into a meeting with RHS Principal, Gene Olive. After explaining the consequence, they each received (probably detention), Mr. Olive laughed and laughed, and told them it was a brilliant stunt (he also instructed them to never tell anyone he said that).How did they get a golf cart into the school? And how were they able to drive it through the school, without being stopped? Their friend, Jerry Larson, RHS class of 1973, helped them plan and execute the stunt. Most importantly, Jerry's dad owned a golf cart. The guys, along with several helpers, swiftly removed the center pole from the double doors at the north entrance to the high school, near the industrial arts classes. The golf cart easily made its way into the school. Once they were in, and loaded onto the golf cart, no one stopped them. They drove through the main hallway, encountering hundreds of stunned and delighted students as they made their way to the Attendance Office. It is a sight I will never forget.

# THE NIGHT I MET MY GUARDIAN ANGEL

**RICHARD WIEGAND**
*74TH AND GIRARD AVE. SO.*

It was late in the summer of 1959. I lived near 74th and Humboldt on Richfield's west side and, all year, I watched the construction of what was soon to become West Jr. High School and Donaldson field. Interstate 35W had not been built yet so I could see it was an easy 'hump' to just walk there from my house. Being young and curious, I found myself more and more interested about the goings on there so, one evening when my folks were out, I talked my little 8-year-old brother to come with me to "scope things out" over at the site. As we slowly walked closer, we could see the beginning assembly of what is now the West Richfield water tower, which is on the West Jr. High School grounds. Also were many different construction vehicles and tools. Wow! At some point my curiosity got the best of me so, I had to 'investigate'. I wanted a better look at things, so, when I saw a rope dangling down from a scaffolding I began 'shinnying' up. About 40 feet, or so. After I struggled to get to the top, and out of breath, I momentarily found myself watching an absolutely stunning view of Richfield from that angle. Then, suddenly I became dizzy and fainted. I fell off the scaffold and fell the whole 40 feet, or so, to the ground. My 8-year-old brother saw me come down and said I landed in a pile of sand and "hit and flipped like a pancake"! In my unconsciousness I just remember a big FLASH and a long period of time, eventually waking up on the ground. I must have been out quite a while because when I 'came to' there were emergency vehicles, flashing lights, sirens, and people everywhere. I was rushed to the hospital. After some examination, they found no broken bones or anything else seriously wrong with me. The sand pile must've saved my neck. Later that week I'd worked up enough nerve to bravely revisit that construction area again in the daylight with a couple of friends. As I bravely showed them the 'accident site' where I landed in the sand, I suddenly noticed something. And what I saw has shocked and stayed with me since then. Less than a foot to one side of the sand pile I fell in was a five-foot-tall stack of concrete blocks, some broken. On the other side, less than 18 inches, was a giant pump engine with a long pipe sticking out of it. Had I fallen just a bit either way, I would not be writing this story.

# WAITING IN LINE FOR LICENSE PLATES AT REITER REALTY

**RICK REITER**

*304 72ND ½ STREET*

You are truly a Richfield old-timer if you remember waiting in line to get your license plates. In the early fifties, my dad, John G. Reiter Sr., was appointed by the Minnesota Secretary of State to be Motor Vehicle Deputy Registrar #56 which was designated to serve Richfield, South Minneapolis, and surrounding areas. At that time, all license plates expired at the same time, November 1st of each year. So human nature being what it is, many people would procrastinate and arrive at the license office at Reiter Realty, 6538 Lyndale, at the last possible day and time, resulting in long lines stretching out the door and down the street as far as the Heidelberg Restaurant on 66th Street. This of course, was in pre-computer days, so all paperwork had to be written by hand or on one of the old Remington typewriters Dad had bought second-hand, thereby delaying the line even more. For many years, the prefix "3K" indicated that the license plate was issued in Richfield. My brother, John Jr., sisters Mary Jo and Lucy, and I all helped part-time during these rush times, along with other clerks hired to do our best to serve the public and keep the line moving. (Many times, there would be ten or more of us serving the public at the license counter). We had to figure the cost of the license plate based on the weight and year of the vehicle, on a little cardboard chart, then fill out the application by hand. Dad was very fussy and insisted that we print everything neatly and legibly. We would look forward to lunch breaks when we could walk across the street to the Lynwood Cafe for their famous "commercial special", hot beef sandwich with mashed potatoes, or over to Nelson Drug for a hot dog and a cherry coke at their "soda fountain/lunch counter." On special occasions, Dad would take us all to the Heidelberg for a full German meal including those famous, delicious hot popovers. Meanwhile, the line of procrastinators would continue to grow at the license office and at times, we needed help from the Richfield Police Department for traffic control and to escort one of us as we walked over to make bank deposits at the Richfield State Bank several times a day. (This was in the pre-credit card era; all payments were made by check or cash). The ever-popular Sergeant Floyd Roman would help with this and/or assign his officers to the task. A few people would get impatient and become frustrated - or even irate - at the long waits and breezy November weather but my recollection is that most people were friendly and considered it an annual event that actually brought people together; many good conversations - and even friendships - developed while waiting in line. This arrangement lasted throughout the fifties and sixties until the law was changed and the Deputy Registrars would now be assigned to government offices such as city halls or county court houses, and the license plate expiration dates would be staggered according to the date the vehicle was purchased, thus preventing the infamous Reiter Realty Last Minute Rush.

# BOB TAIT-TAIT'S SUPER VALU

**MIKE TAIT**

*76TH AND DUPONT AVE. SO.*

I'm supposed to write a story about my father, which is very easy to do. Whether it's talking about what a great promoter he was, or just how he ran his business, there is plenty to talk about. He always had something going; it could be a mountain of pennies in sawdust for the kids to scramble through, a trolley to give customers a ride home with their groceries, a boat giveaway, Santa sharing time with kids, or my dad just at the service counter greeting customers. The store was also way ahead of its time from the service we provided to the scratch bakery or to the fact that we made our own ice cream right in the store. The store had a great meat department, and a deli that was top notch! But I'm going to tell the story about the time around Christmas when he would bring Rudolph the red-nosed reindeer into the store. We're talking about a real-life small reindeer that had a red nose. I was about twelve years old, and I was put in charge of this reindeer: I mean feeding, grooming, and you can guess the other duty. It was about day two and I came home full of red blotches all over my body and sneezing like I had the worst cold of all time. It came to be that the great promoter found out that his twelve-year-old son was very allergic to deer. Well, we made it through the holiday season, and once again my father was a hero to so many kids and families.

# RICHFIELD 1950'S

**SHEILA MATTILA FLANDERS**

*65TH AND SHERIDAN AVE. SO.*

Our home was built in 1954 on 65th and Sheridan in West Richfield. Mom loved pink. The house was painted pink with white trim. We had a pink and white tiled bathroom, a pink and white 1958 Chevy two-toned Belair sedan and a pink and white travel trailer that took us on many summer vacations. Our block had about twenty plus kids. We were the baby-boomers. I remember the Kreager's, Mattila's (us), Roy and Alice Anderson, Grindy's, Nelson's, Andersons, Bakers, Larson's, Gunderson's, Bryants, Kerpatrick's, Holloway's, and Mrs. Anderson. The "backyard" families were the Crosby's, Addis's and Budrow's. There was always someone to play with. We lived down the street from Sheridan Elementary School. It went from Kindergarten to Sixth grade. I was a walker and would go home for lunch most days. Out the school back door, I would take-off full speed across the playground, through the field where the school kids would play a pick-up game of baseball or football, running pell-mell up Sheridan Avenue until I reached our back door. Personally, I was glad to be home and not in school. Mom would have a bowl of bean soup, a bologna sandwich, and a glass of milk with a few slices of apple waiting for me at our Dutch style kitchen table. The walk back to school would have me pushing the late bell almost every time. I was a clock watcher. Two o'clock seemed an eternity away. When the time came to go home, there I went, running pell-mell again towards home. After homework was completed and piano was practiced, I was free to go outside and play. Wow! There was always something to do and someone to do it with. The Sheridan Pond with the old Weeping Willow tree was a great one to climb and sit upon its big wide overhanging branch. It was so large it could easily hold three of us at the same time. After supper and when dishes had been washed, wiped and put away, our games were more towards staying near home. Red Rover Red Rover, Statue, Chinese Jump-rope, Tag, Hide and Seek were the typical games we played. Maybe it was to help get the rest of our energy out before going to bed, but we had so much fun all while watching the sunsets from our front yards. Sheridan Pond was the best skating rink in the whole wide world! And there was a warming house with a wood burning stove and wooden benches that our boots would tuck under. The best time for ice skating was after supper. Jane and I would walk down Sheridan Avenue, turning left by the pond towards the warming house. After Thanksgiving many houses were decorated with multi-colored Christmas lights and with the new fallen snow, it made everything look so twinkly! I loved those walks to and from the warming house. Everything was so quiet and beautiful. Skating at night seemed so magical to me. The crispness of the air, my ice skates slipping over the frozen pond, with my best friend and I just being, was a time I will always treasure. Richfield during the1950's and 60's was a wonderful place to grow up. We witnessed the building of Southdale, Southtown, the pool and I remember the small hoop-la that happened when Richfield had grown from a Village to a Township and now to a city. With party lines, adding Area codes (ours was Union-9), and the development of the freeways, time was changing our small town to something that was exciting and new. What freedom we had as kids. I will forever cherish those times.

# RICHFIELD- A SPECIAL PLACE IN MY HEART

**CAROL BRANDBERG BURNIECE**

*63RD AND 15TH AVE. SO.*

My parents moved us to Richfield about 1951. I didn't know it then, but it would be the best place in the whole world we could have wished for. I attended East Elementary school. A wonderful old building with a huge playground filled with hazardous equipment most parents today would cringe at. The thrill of sledding down the steep street off 63rd and 15th Avenue....icicles forming on nose and lips and hair...as we screamed with delight. I went on to junior then senior high school. A scary event in 9th grade to be learning with seniors. Of course, some attachments evolved, and I had a flirtation with a senior until my dad put a stop to it. I was given a clarinet at that time, so I joined the band. It was the most important decision of my life where I met lifelong friends and my future husband. Oh, the fun we had in band.... marching in parades and playing at all the athletic events. Mr. Lundahl was the absolute best teacher of all time.... teaching us music and values and how to be decent human beings. Each of us could write a whole book about life in Richfield. It will forever remain a special place in my heart and thanks to all the Richfield people I still talk to on Facebook. May we ever fight fight fight for Richfield High....

# TEN-YEAR-OLD GETS WHAT SHE WANTS FROM THE RICHFIELD RECREATION DEPARTMENT

**PAT RICKERT**

*67TH AND GARFIELD AVE. SO.*

When we, the Rickert family, first moved here from Sioux Falls in 1970, the Richfield Recreation Department's summer park program was morning only at Little Bob's Park. We had four children then, three boys, Mike, Tom and Bill and our youngest, our daughter, Susan. The summer program was well attended by the neighborhood children. Susan joined in later even though she was not old enough to be eligible to attend. However, when she became of the age to join into all of the activities, they cancelled the program. Susan felt that was not right and found out what she had to do to reinstate the program. They told her at City Hall that she would have to canvas the neighborhood with a petition to get that done. She made up the wording of the petition, made the calls throughout the area getting the needed signatures of support from the parents and children. Frank White, Richfield Recreation Director was so impressed with the efforts that he came over to Little Bob's Park and met with Susan and reviewed the petition and decided to reinstate the program, which is what we all know that it is sometimes hard to resist the wishes of a ten-year-old.

# RANDY SOHN – RICHFIELD AVIATOR

**SARI L. SOHN HUGHES**

*63RD AND GIRARD AVE. SO.*

Randy Sohn was a resident of Richfield from 1960 to 1980's. During those years he acquired a world-wide reputation as a pilot of WWII aircraft for the Commemorative Air Force out of Texas, the EAA in Wisconsin and original Planes of Fame North out of Flying Cloud Airport, among other organizations. For a period of years he was also the FAA Designee for authorizing licenses to US pilots wanting to fly these aircraft. He wrote for numerous aviation magazines, and his technical manuals are still requested and referenced today by WWII aircraft owners and pilots. Randy learned to fly on a grass strip in Worthington, MN. He began his flying career in the Air Force, flying and instructing in the B-25. He was hired by North Central Airlines in 1960 as a line pilot in DC-3's and moved his family, JoAnn, Sari (RHS Class of '75) and Mike (RHS Class of '77) to a house on Standish which backed up to the MSP Airport. The family moved to 63rd and Girard Avenue in 1963. Randy transitioned to the Flight Training Department. This led to enduring a two-year stint in Bolivia when the US State Department contracted North Central Airlines to assist the Bolivian government. Bolivia wanted to improve the safety record of their state airline, Lloyd Aero Boliviano. North Central had a route structure and the aircraft types closest to LAB, not that North Central's flights were at all similar to flying over the Andes. He was with the airline as it became

Republic Airlines, and then merged with Northwest Airlines, retiring as a 747 pilot. Randy helped start the Southern Minn. Wing of the CAF after convincing many Minnesotan pilots of the desirability of winter flying time in South Texas. He was chosen as Chief Pilot to fly the CAF B-29 Fifi out of the China Lake, California desert in August 1971. It had been one of many decommissioned "target practice" aircraft for years and after 9 weeks of maintenance it flew to Texas. He told his family about the trip after it was over. Fifi's first summer tour around the USA began in St. Paul, MN due to Randy's lobbying for the Twin Cities as her official debut. In 1980 Randy joined a West Texas friend in celebration of the 75th Anniversary of Naval Aviation. The crew of eight flew a restored PBY Catalina across the Atlantic Ocean from Newfoundland to the Azores to Portugal, reenacting a flight from 1919. Randy started the Captain Sohn's Chili Club at Broadway Pizza, where pilots, police, hardware store employees, mechanics, general aviation pilots and retirees could share Pilot Soup and coffee on Saturday mornings. Few knew that word of that gathering circulated worldwide on aviation websites, and many people from out of state planned vacation activities to allow a chance to rub shoulders with the famous and infamous, notorious and experienced pilots of WWII, Korea, and Viet Nam. Randy was licensed by the FAA to fly "All Makes and Models of High-Performance Piston Powered Aircraft" in addition to "All Airplane Single and Multi-Engine Instrument Aircraft". His FAA license and Letter of Authorization ceased to list aircraft types because there wasn't room for all the types. He was inducted into the Experimental Aviation Association Hall of Fame in 1998 and the CAF Hall of Fame in 2011.Randy "Flew West" in April 2020. In April 2023 Randy was inducted into the Minnesota Aviation Hall of Fame, when his contributions to Minnesota aviation were recognized and rewarded.

# HALLOWEEN

**PAUL HARDT**

*62ND AND SHERIDAN AVE. SO.*

There were so many holidays to celebrate at home or at school when we lived in Richfield. We had holiday parties in school, we had Christmas programs at our church--Church of Peace on 64th and Xerxes. We went to the parking lot at Southdale or to the Edina Pool (eventually the Richfield Pool) to see 4th of July fireworks. One of my favorite holidays was Halloween. We lived at 62nd and Sheridan, and in that part of Richfield, we had long, double blocks that went north and south.... Russell, Sheridan, Thomas, Upton, Vincent....and so on. The long, double blocks were ideal for Halloween candy-gathering. We would start out at our home, dressed in our costumes.... I was dressed as Zorro, one year. And we would start going up and down the streets. It was so easy! And safe! We just kept going up one side of the block and down the other. We would start on Russell and move west. When we ran out of room in our bags or pillowcases, we would go back home, dump our candy, and go out again. It was so fun. We would get enough candy to last us well into the new year!

# CHRISTMAS AT FREMONT PARK

**ERNIE LINDSTROM**

*74TH AND FREMONT AVE. SO.*

For over 25 years, the neighbors surrounding Fremont Park celebrated Christmas every year at the park with a decorated Christmas tree, a bonfire, Santa Claus, and the Salvation Army Band. Candy canes were provided for the kids, and cookies and hot cider for everyone. The old garage on the premises was used for the refreshments (while it might seem unbelievable, it is the same garage on the premises that Bob Dylan practiced in!). Various individuals served as Santa Claus, including the mayor, John Hamilton, and the skinniest Santa according to the kids, Ernie Lindstrom. Gratuities to the Salvation Army Band were always very generous!

# I JUST WANT TO CHECK IN...

**MEG SKOGLUND JOHNSON**

*70TH AND LOGAN AVE. SO.*

Richfield was original suburbia!

I remember walking to Southdale....first shopping mall!

I remember riding my bike on the Interstate before it was done!

I remember walking to several ice rinks with warming houses...froze my feet!

The airport was tiny....

# THE 35W ENCHANTED FOREST AND HIDEAWAY

**LINDA PETERSON**

*64TH AND HUMBOLDT AVE. SO.*

When my brother Billy and I were little kids there was a forest two or three blocks behind our house full of wildlife - (saw my first caterpillar turn into a butterfly there) and a great place to collect beautiful rocks - I think they were agates and other gorgeous rocks. It was where 35W now is. Later, when they were building 35W, Billy and I would go sit at the top of the ramp under the bridge over 66th street and while away the time watching the cars go by and naming the different makes of the cars. Hope this makes you smile. It's a fun memory for me!!

# THREE ON THE TREE

**MARY CATHERINE MCKENNA**

*LYNDALE AVE. AND OAK GROVE BLVD.*

Back in 1969; I wanted to learn how to drive a "three on the tree" vehicle. I had not gotten my license yet and was supposed to drive with a licensed driver. My dad said to jump in the driver's seat, and he jumped into the back seat. I didn't even know how to start a car much less know how to shift gears. With careful instructions I was taught how the clutch worked and the configuration of finding the gears. When it was time to hit the streets; my dad would say "clutch" and he reached over me to shift the gear. We made it several blocks before shifting to gear 3. I prayed we would not stop on a hill. My dad told me the secret to the gears was to "shift when the hood shakes". His hearing was enhanced by the fact he was 100% blind! I said I was nervous about driving with an unlicensed driver. My dad said, "hey I had a valid license before WWII" We continued around local roads learning the gears and the fine art of shifting. Dad said, "the only thing to worry about would be Sargent Roman stopping us!" To this day; if I drive a vehicle with a manual transmission I think about "shift when the hood shakes" Thanks for your wisdom dad.

# SHERM BOOEN

**AL MALMBERG**

*66TH AND KNOX AVE. SO.*

For those of us who grew up in Richfield, as part of the "baby boom" generation, it wasn't hard to miss the home at 6711 Nicollet Avenue that had the tall "ham" operator's tower in the back yard. What many didn't know is that an aviation and broadcasting legend lived there. Sherm Booen and his wife Mavis were long-time residents of Richfield. Sherm learned to fly in Albert Lea in the Civil Pilot Training Program before World War II. In 1942, he was assigned to the Air Material Command at Dayton, Ohio, where he inspected and trained flight crews on the Honeywell autopilot system. In 1945, Booen began his radio and television career. He created The World of Aviation, a program that aired on WCCO-TV for 28 years, making it the longest running, locally produced TV program in the country. After receiving his Marine Corps commission, he went to Korea as an air traffic controller and retired with the rank of Colonel from the United States Marine Corps Reserves. During the 1960's, he founded the Minnesota Flyer magazine and would fly his Beechcraft Bonanza to points across the U.S. to report stories for his magazine and to film footage for The World of Aviation. He was instrumental in founding the Minnesota Aviation Hall of Fame and published a book, Minnesota Aviation History. Sherm and Mavis were members of Richfield Methodist Church located in south Minneapolis. Sherm Booen was inducted into the Minnesota Aviation Hall of Fame in 1995. He was inducted in the Minnesota Broadcasters Hall of Fame in 2002.Colonel Booen passed away in 2011 at the age of 97.

# 1960 BOYS BASKETBALL TOURNAMENT

**DOUGLAS "ACE" BARTON**

*66TH AND EMERSON AVE. SO.*

Not too many people today know what it was like to play in the Minnesota Boys State Tourney back in the '50s/early '60's. Here's some background: The only pro sports team was the Minneapolis Lakers. Gopher football and basketball was popular, but the biggest, most attended sporting event was the high school basketball tourney. Three straight days of 18,000+ attended this spectacle at Williams arena on the U of M campus. It was a one class tournament which made it more meaningful compared to the four-class event of today. Hockey took a back seat to basketball probably because of the Lakers influence and the total dominance of the northern Minnesota schools. Richfield being quite new as a school, meant the city was ripe and ready for a successful team in the highly competitive Lake Conference. We began the season by beating the '59 champs – Wayzata – at home. (One of my highest scoring games before breaking my arm at practice two days later!). In my absence, new student Bob Sadek took my spot and our team just kept on winning. After starting 7 – 0, the Richfield community became very involved and excited. It was a magical time to be a player! We won the conference with a 14 – 2 record and were ranked #1 in the state entering the State tourney. Now, one of the most popular elements of this tourney was the prospect of a small town "Cinderella" team beating the dominant, big metro schools, which up until 1960 just didn't happen. Enter Edgerton – a very small school in a little southwestern Minnesota town of people of Dutch ancestry. We faced them in the semifinal game, a game we will never forget; and a game that made tournament history in more ways than one. I remember the moment while we were down in the catacombs of Williams arena getting ready to take the floor. All of a sudden, the walls started rumbling, dust was actually flying off the walls. It felt like an earthquake – what it actually was: the Edgerton team was taking the floor! Then another thing we never forgot was the reception we got coming out of the tunnel: maybe 16,000 of the 18,000 people booing lustily – quite a lasting impression on a bunch of high school players. Did the crowd affect the outcome? Well, back in the day fans could become quite rowdy and sometimes violent: basketball teams were commonly called "cagers", referring to the fact that early on in the'40's teams played on a court surrounded by chicken wire fence presumably to keep the ball from flying off the court but in reality, to keep fans from attacking players! Were the refs influenced by this crowd? One of the records that stands until this day is the most free throws attempted and made in State tourney history – guess who holds that record: yes, the 1960 Edgerton team. We played in the very physical, competitive Lake Conference. What was normal defense to us was a personal foul in the Edgerton game. One could say that's no excuse as a good team adjusts to the way a game was being called. But we were just kids trying to do our best in a building where 90% were against us! We outscored them by 20 points from the field, only to lose to a record number of made free throws. Edgerton prevailed while we won the Third-Place game by over 25 points. In hindsight it was a lifelong memory for us, the players. We played in an historic game that became Minnesota's version of the movie Hoosiers. Most of us – except Bill Davis – would never be involved in a spectacle as big, as grand or as popular as was this tournament for the rest of our lives. But in closing, here's an interesting perspective from a father of a friend who played on the great state tourney winning Hopkins team of 1952: he said for most of his teammates it would have been better had they lost. To them they had already reached life's pinnacle, and the rest of their lives, sadly, were downhill from that point on! I think there is some truth in that.

# THANKSGIVING IN RICHFIELD

**DON WOLPERS**

*64TH AND RUSSELL AVE. SO.*

We are often asked, "what is your favorite holiday?" For me it is Thanksgiving for a number of reasons. There was one in particular that happened in my youth, probably about 1964. Not positive, for that was a long time ago. While relatively new to my Richfield neighborhood near -- Sheridan Elementary School, Thanksgiving that year was very cold with hardly any snow on the ground. Perfect weather for water to freeze clear and smooth on the local Sheridan Pond on about 65th and Thomas. The ice conditions were PERFECT! Back then Sheridan Pond had very few weeds. While the Turkey and fixings were in the oven, Mom and Dad always encouraged us to get out of the house for some fresh air. *(And don't come home until your cheeks are nice and rosy)* So, my brother Dale and sister Maribeth and I grabbed our skates and went to the pond to skate with seemingly 100's of other kids from the neighborhood. We put our skates on in the snowbank *(no warming house at this pond, No Helicopter Parents either – They weren't invented yet) Lots* of hockey skates on the boys, figure skates on the girls and speed skates on the speed burners. Plenty of games going on like; pom-pom pull-away, some true pond hockey, and my favorite: Crack the Whip… Hang on!! If there was a bonfire, I don't remember one, but if there was – it probably was burning newspapers in an outdoor incinerator. *Love that smell. As* I remember it, it was a scene out of a Norman Rockwell painting. Plenty of long stocking caps, scarves, mittens, and jackets that got cold, wet and heavy as the day wore on. We knew when it was time to go home. When you can't feel your feet or fingers and when your cheeks are nice and rosy. Yup – Back home to warm up…our cheeks now sufficiently rosy, we were just in time for some Hot Chocolate, warm up by the fireplace smell the smells of our family Thanksgiving Dinner. Looking back on it – I loved it. It's not always cold enough to freeze the ponds and lakes at Thanksgiving, but when it is I long for Holidays in Richfield with memories just like that. Favorite holiday?... I choose Thanksgiving!

# THE JOY OF SPECIAL NEEDS

**GAYLE M. SKLUZACEK**

*64TH AND 19TH AVE. SO.*

I was in third grade when my brother Joe was born. The next day my grandmother came to stay with us. There was a lot of whispering about my brother, but my grandfather was shouting that it was my father's fault. My mother did not come home for several days. The whispering continued and talk of my brother never coming home was stated. We experienced lots of whispering neighbors and looks of pity when we returned to school. Eventually my mother and Joe came home from the hospital. Joe did not look like most babies as his eyes were almond-shaped and he had a flat nose and tiny ears. We were told he was special because he had an extra chromosome. Joe was born with Down Syndrome. In The 1960s, a disabled child was a curse. Our family doctor told my mother not to bring him home as he would ruin our family's life. A number of our relatives and her friends also encouraged her to abandon her baby. Instead, my mother made it her mission to give him as normal a life as possible. She became active in Minnesota Association for Retarded Children (MARC) and eventually mentored other families in similar situations. When Joe was about two, my mother found a day school for him in West Richfield, The Louise Whitbeck Fraser School (63rd and Penn). My parents enrolled both Joe and my sister Missy who was 16 months older than Joe and diagnosed with some type of brain damage (which my parents found out a few weeks before Joe's birth). The school was very expensive, but one of the best in the country. (Hubert Humphrey's granddaughter was one of Joe's classmates and she was in Missy's Girl Scout troop). My father worked two extra jobs and my mother sold Avon to afford the tuition. My father also did janitorial work at the school to work off part of the tuition. My sister, brother, and I walked to school instead of taking the bus (to St. Kevin's); we brought our lunches to school instead of getting hot lunch; and we did without a toy or two. We pulled together as a family and found joy in both Missy and Joe. Missy was a beautiful blue-eyed blonde child - sassy and confident. Joe was cute as a button with curly hair and always smiling. They became poster children for MARC in the 1960s.Missy and Joe grew up as normal as possible. They learned to read and write; they did chores, they learned kindness, and the importance of being a part of community. They also learned to accept who they were and to stand up for themselves. In return, anyone who knew our family had a tremendous sense of loyalty to Missy and Joe. I recall a 6-year-old neighbor girl invited Missy over to play with dolls with her friends and another friend called Missy a retard. The neighbor girl would not stand for such bullying and punched her friend in Missy's defense. My friends got used to having to bring Joe or Missy with us to drive In movies at France Avenue or shopping at Southdale and even Valley Fair amusement park. Boyfriends had to pass the Missy/Joe test as I often took them on outings with a new boyfriend. If the boyfriend balked, I dumped them! As the years went by, Missy and Joe, became active adult members of the community. Joe was an usher at St. Richards Church, a member of the Knights of Columbus, and a busboy at the Thunderbird Hotel for 25 years before working at the Embassy Suites until the Pandemic. Missy was active in Girl Scouts into her 30s and worked at several senior homes in the area. Not only was my parents' goal of normalizing Missy and Joe achieved, but Missy and Joe touched the life of many through the warmth and acceptance the community extended to them. Missy passed in 2007, but Joe is going strong and still smiling.

# MIKE WAGGONER AND THE BOPS

**MIKE WAGGONER**

*65TH AND 22ND AVE. SO.*

**I graduated in '58** and was already in the early stages of having a band and playing local gigs with The Bops. My last Richfield High School Variety Show was around February of '58; I was 17. Wes Kohl was the teacher in charge of the shows and Mr. Kohl had a certain amount of show biz in his blood; a 'ham' if you will. Wonderful fellow and, regarding the Variety Show, he was always focused on all the participants being treated equal as far as creating the showcase, stage presence, opportunity to perform, etc. Therefore, no special billing, staging, or lighting for any one act. I had two friends, Mark Mack and Paul Mattison who were the stage crew and lighting guys. Un-announced to me they had a plan of which I wasn't aware. During my appearance in the show, at an appropriate moment in my song, they killed the stage lights and simultaneously turned on the large spotlight, which was in the catwalk of the Richfield High School auditorium! I wasn't sure what was going on and the crowd reacted in a split second. It was quite a moment! I found out later that Mr. Kohl wasn't happy and after the show he privately told Mark and Paul that that was 'showbiz' and don't let it happen again. End of conversation.

**In 1961, I purchased a house in East Richfield** near the Little League fields on the East side of Cedar Avenue just North of 66th street. I would have "The Bops" band practice at my house on Wednesday evenings getting the band ready for the weekend gigs. We'd review some tunes and work on two or three new ones and would set up all the band equipment including amps and sound. During the warm months of the year, we decided to set up and practice in the garage. It soon became a neighborhood event for neighbors and friends to gather for the band practice. Soon the street was full of parked cars, folks on our lawn and neighboring lawns, my driveway full, etc. Of course, not all the neighbors were happy and understanding. In fact, after the first few weeks the cops showed up and warned the band that we had to do this and that and that people needed to stay out of the adjoining yards, or we'd get shut down. Luckily, one of the officers who showed up was Officer Ray Nelson; his son Roland was a good friend of mine and I had met his mom and dad a number of times. We continued to have our Wednesday garage sessions, people continued to show up, Officer

Nelson (and his squad car) made himself available every Wednesday night and it became a sweet neighborhood event, well attended, and very enjoyable for many. Even some of the neighbors who had voiced concern would show up with their lawn chair in THEIR yard and enjoy the music and the evening.

Thanks to all who remember the wonderful era we grew up in and shared in Richfield, Minnesota.

# RICHFIELD'S FIRST CONSTABLE AND POLICE CHIEF

**LINDA MAHER**

*68TH AND PENN AVE. SO.*

My Grandfather, my hero…George W. Brening was born in Motley, Minnesota in 1891. Little is known about his childhood, but I know it wasn't an easy one. As a young man, he migrated to what is now known as Richfield and worked as a farm hand. Here he met his wife, Christine Boeser, and they married very young. In 1928, he was elected Richfield Village Constable. At that time, Richfield was a dumping ground frequented by all types of criminals from Minneapolis and St. Paul. Grandpa had stories about Baby Face Nelson and the like. Moonshiners were prevalent. One time when responding to a car accident he found over 100 gallons of alcohol. Examiners determined it was some of the best grain alcohol they had seen. Stories told include my grandparents housing "criminals" overnight in their basement giving them a meal and place to sleep since there wasn't an official jail house. After being re-elected Constable four times, he became Richfield's first Chief of Police when the force was founded in 1938. In 1942, he lost his position due to politics. At that time, the Mayor could hire or fire you. His job wasn't then considered Civil Service. As a result, in 1954 at the age of 62, he was assigned to Beat Patrolman covering Holy Angels Academy and the Hub Shopping Center (66th & Nicollet) on the afternoon shift from 3 – 11 p.m. He held this position until his retirement in 1961. He got to know a lot of the students at Holy Angels and they considered him a friend. Besides his Police career, he also worked as caretaker of the Jewish cemeteries on 70th & Penn with his sons. He worked every morning preparing graves, mowing, and maintaining the cemeteries before going to work on his beat patrol. Grandpa was a hard -working man and he only missed work once in 33 years when he had cataracts removed. I loved going to the Hub Shopping Center and running up to him and giving him a big hug, saying, "Hi, Grandpa!" loud enough so everyone close by could hear. He was a fun-loving person always telling tall tales. He used to tell me that he just made a batch of shortbread that he mixed with his feet and I should try some! He taught me about sharing when he bought me a sweater and bought one for my best friend, too. And, he would hand deliver ice cream cones to me regardless of the weather being a stifling 90 degrees or a frigid 30 below, on request. That is, until I got in trouble for calling him saying, "Grandpa, It's a good day for an ice cream cone. Grandpa often sang his rendition of songs to his grandchildren. He claimed he could play the fiddle, but stopped after the dog ran away. Every year on December 6th, he was "St. Nick" and would visit each grandkid's house, knock loudly on their door, and leave a brown sack full of nuts and hard candy without anyone seeing him. This was our reminder that "St. Nick" was checking up on us to see if we were behaving. We used to watch Hop Along Cassidy and the Lone Ranger on Saturday mornings. Grandpa loved watching the Roller Derby, too. Grandpa and Grandma lived on the corner of 69th & Penn. Their house stood proudly on the corner until the land was purchased and condominiums were built not so many years ago. Grandpa was a remarkable man that I will always remember with great pride. I was lucky, being the oldest grandchild and living just a few houses away on Penn Avenue, I was able to spend a lot of time with him. He passed in August 1970 due to heart complications, just two months before my daughter and his first great-grandchild was born…He's forever in my heart.

# A COUNTRY BOY IN SOUTH RICHFIELD

**DAVID L. TURK**

*76TH AND 5TH AVE. SO.*

I feel privileged to have been born in the United States and raised in Richfield. Both of my parents served in the Pacific Theatre during WWII and purchased our newly built house on the corner of 76th and 5th in 1951 when I was two. For the first ten years of my life or thereabouts 76th Street was a dirt road that did not pass through to Portland Ave. but rather dead ended on 5th Avenue. I believe the strip of land that eventually allowed 76th to connect to Portland was at the time still owned by the Butells(sp?) whose house stood on the corner of 76th and Portland until it was razed to become part of Roosevelt Park in the early 2000's. Before becoming Roosevelt Park the fields south of 76th were farmed by Hank Ranft where he would grow corn, soybeans and asparagus. From time to time his horse or cows could be found grazing on our side yard after escaping their enclosures. Directly south of where 5th Avenue ends and across the field near 77th Street there was a small pond serving as a watering hole for Hank's livestock. It had maybe a foot of water and below as much black silt. There was a large boxelder tree which had grown bent over the pond on which my brother and I attached a rope and would swing out and drop into the water exiting as muddy swamp creatures. Hank never minded us and other neighborhood boys running wild and free in those "Rockwellian" days and even allowed us some old boards to build a clubhouse in my parent's backyard. One summer my brother and I along with the Scanlon's, Nistler's, and other neighborhood boys built a baseball diamond with an old rusty bedspring as a backstop on a piece of Hanks unplowed northern field near 76th Street where we honed our skills as team players and eventually became very hard to beat when we grew to play team sports for Assumption. Southern Richfield was a wonderful place to grow and prosper as a young man. Our youth was rooted in rural American values and as cars and girls became integral in our youthful development, urbanization slowly caressed our adventure and rounded us for the world to come.

# BUD GRANT'S WIFE

**TONY RIEMENSNIDER**

*66TH AND 5TH AVE. SO.*

It was the Fall of 1971 at Richfield East Junior High School and I was a dorky, dweeby looking 9th grader trying to survive. I had one thing going for me, I was on the football team! I never played but I was on the team. It was the last game and if I'm not mistaken a victory would give us a winning season. Unfortunately, we were playing Bloomington Penn Junior High and their quarterback just happened to be Bud Grant's kid. Bud Grant's. Assumptions were made that it was not going to be our proudest moment on the field. But the game remained to be played.

When Bud showed up, we all stopped our warmup and just stared in wonder. It was really Bud Grant, the legend! He stood on the Penn JH sideline, at about the 20-yard line, just a light jacket on and never moved. Not through the entire game.

Well for Richfield East it was the game of the year, we did everything right and Bloomington Penn did everything wrong. I even got to play, four plays at defensive end! Yeah, I was about 5 foot 4 and weighed in at about 145. Amazingly, I didn't get run over, ran around or hurt. I even made a tackle! When I tell this story to anyone who will listen it usually goes along the lines of - we sacked Bud's kid 11 times behind the line, blocked a few punts and won the game by 50 points. Sadly, not true. However, we did win by a touchdown or two at the most, we did block a punt and we did sack Bud's kid, maybe 3 times, maybe not. It was a long time ago.

Winning the last game of the season, winning against Bud Grant's kid, seeing Bud in the flesh, these were cherishable things to happen in a dumb young kids' life. But the bus ride home was the best fun we could have had without making it a DDS (drop, drink or smoke) experience! As we rolled down Penn Avenue toward Richfield someone yelled out "hey Riemo" (that's me, Riemensnider - Riemo, get it?), "why don't you hang a moon!". Well, never one to run from a dare, not really, I was kind of a wimp, but that doesn't go well with the story. Anyway, there was a little white car behind the bus with two women in it and I proceeded to show them the dark side of my moon! It was the subject of the discussion the rest of the way back to school and in the locker room until everyone cleared out. On Monday after school Coach Norm Overland called me into his office. I thought it might be to suggest to me that I do some weight training over the summer. NOT! Instead, he began to tell me the story of a little white car following our bus home on Friday night. Turns out some knucklehead stuck his "ass" out the window at the two ladies in the little white car. Another turns out is that one of those ladies happened to be Mrs. Christ, wife of Coach Christ, the assistant coach of our team. And if two turns out aren't enough, another turns out happened to be that other lady in the little white car. Turns out she was a good friend of Mrs. Christ but also, she was the mother of the quarterback for the other team which made her the wife of that guy on the sidelines, Bud Grant. Well, Norm reamed my butt for about an hour that day. He spoke most of the time. I asked how he knew it was me (for future reference) and he said that my jersey number, number 24 was in plain view for the ladies to identify. I quickly told him that my number was number 44. And then he told me he talked with Brad Holt that day and he was told that Brad gave me his jersey on Friday (#24) because he wasn't going to be at the game and mine was dirty. Dang! Sadly my 'rep' at that age was always the one that got caught. No more football for me.

# THE NIGHT HIGH SCHOOL SOCCER TOOK CENTER STAGE

**DAVE PHILLIPPI**
*62ND AND CLINTON AVE. SO.*

In the early sixties, most boys in Richfield who played sports dreamed about playing varsity football in high school. At this time, soccer was a fledgling secondary club sport in the state of Minnesota. However, under the tutelage of coach Rudy Martingnacco, the soccer program began to gain traction as a viable high school sport. Through his constant efforts to develop the sport not only at Richfield, but throughout the state, soccer finally became a varsity sport in the mid-sixties. The Lake Conference added soccer shortly thereafter, with Richfield, Edina, Bloomington Kennedy, Bloomington Lincoln & St. Louis Park. Although soccer provided new opportunities for those not interested or too small to play football, it was still considered a minor fall sport compared to the mammoth football program at RHS. Coach Martingnacco was always looking for new ways to promote soccer at both the participant, as well as the fan level. In the fall of 1968, Rudy persuaded the athletic Director to allow the soccer team to play an exhibition during the halftime of one of the home football games. It was his first major step to expose the sport to the huge student body at RHS. That same fall, Rudy scheduled three of our home soccer games to be played under the lights on the football field. The highlight game featured

Richfield vs Edina – a great conference rivalry. Edina was heavily favored since we had yet to defeat them in soccer. It was a clear, crisp autumn evening. We all felt an extra charge that night running out onto the field to warm up before the game. Playing on our home turf, on the converted football field, under the lights, with several hundred fans watching. We usually had less than 100 fans come to watch our games. Being at night, many of our parents were able to come to see us play. And, unbeknownst to us, the game was being covered by the Minneapolis Star! Maybe due to the extra spark in our efforts, Richfield dominated the game, winning 4-0. Our goalie, Junior Chuck Scanlon was spectacular. Three of our four goals were scored by underclassmen. There was an article on the front page of the sports section in the Minneapolis Star the next night, along with photos, covering our game. This game seemed to set the stage for the future of soccer at RHS. Two years later in the fall of 1970, Richfield went 11-0, winning the Lake Conference *and* MN State Championship!

# A BIT LIKE MAYBERRY

**LARRY HERMON**

*72ND AND STEVENS AVE. SO.*

I would just like to start by saying that growing up in Richfield could not have been better, kind of like Mayberry. The fun, the lifelong friends, I don't know how many places are like that, but I wouldn't think too many. I think I'll just make a sentence or two about a whole bunch of stuff. The neighborhood, mine was great, I still know people from there over 60 years ago. Playing games in the street was a blast, someone would yell CAR and we would pick stuff up, move to the side of the road wait for the car to go by and resume play. We still had vacant lots to play in, trees to climb and trees to steal apples from. When they would dig up the streets or build a house on a vacant lot there would be giant dirtball fights. My next-door neighbor Larry Dayton and I were always doing stuff together, not sure why but people always asked us if we were brothers, the answer was always" No, we're both named Larry, how could we be? Portland Elementary School, East Jr. High and the High School, couldn't have been any better, still have a ton of friends from school, some all the way back to kindergarten. Hope Church was a great place to go for Sunday school, Confirmation and Boy Scout Troop 370.Before Boy Scouts there was Indian Guides and Cub Scouts....Little League, I've heard that East Richfield Little League was one of the biggest in the country. What a great part of life, put on your uniform, slide your glove over the handlebars and ride up to the ballpark. Then a quick trip to the concession stand for a sleeve of grape bubblegum for the game. The coach would line you up and look in your eyes to see if they were red from swimming at the pool that day. Later that night maybe you would sleep out in a tent with some friends. Augsburg Park was my main park hangout. Year-round things to do, skating and sliding in the winter, fort building, sewer exploring, softball, fence walking, dog running, bike riding in the summer. The drinking fountain ran 24 hours a day on the side of the warming house, best water in the world, used to ride my bike up there just to get a drink. Then later a good place to go when skipping classes. Bikes, the main transportation for years, you knew who was where by the bikes that were parked, later it was the same story with cars. I usually had my transistor radio strapped to the handlebars playing WDGY. Going to the sand pits was a blast, that was a huge area to ride around in, even more fun when you got a little older going there with a minibike. Once Paul Ekholm and I were sitting on my steps, Mike Fossen was riding my minibike, he hit a bump, the throttle went full blast, and he disappeared into my neighbor's huge pine tree. I thought me and Paul would have to call an ambulance because we couldn't breathe, we were laughing too hard. Several seconds went by and a faint "help me" came from the tree.

# A SLICE OF NELSON'S FAMILY RESTAURANT

**GARY FISCHBACH**

*63RD AND 1ST AVE. SO.*

Nelson's Family Restaurant indeed, was a family restaurant. Most of the employees of Nelson's were family members. Not just the families of Harlow and Delores, or kids Lee, Dave, and Kay, but many families from Richfield and south Minneapolis. I worked there in the mid 80's as well as my brother and sister. Most employees had a brother, sister, kid, or parent worked there. That's what made it so special. I'm still in touch with and still friends with people I worked with 40 years ago. From its days as a drive-in restaurant, to a sit-down restaurant, Nelson's was a great place to eat. In the 50's and 60's cars would cruise between Nelson's to Curran's restaurant at 42nd and Nicollet. Oh, yes, before my time. Every February, Nelson's strawberry pie made its debut. It was a big deal. The amount of pies sold in February and March was unbelievable and continued until fall.

# GROWING UP IN RICHFIELD

**KARIN FURE**

*70TH AND PARK AVE. SO.*

Richfield was sort of an idyllic place to grow up. With the booming of houses being built in the 50's and the families growing in the 50's 60's, we just had to walk outside to see some neighborhood friends to play some kick ball or Anny Over. We were able to walk to school with our friends without worrying about the safety of it all. We held Kool-Aid stands where we could just sit outside on the sidewalks waiting for the next customer. Richfield had both a swimming pool and a hockey rink. As a little girl, my mom would take my sister and I to the softball parks to watch my brothers play baseball. I can still remember my sister and I frequenting the concessions stands there to get some treats while watching my brothers. Growing up, during the summers, we would walk or ride our bikes to the swimming pool. Such great memories of going to the pool. We would be there all day lathering on our Cocoa Butter Tanning Oil. I can still hear the clanking of the baskets that we would put our clothes in before walking out to the pool area. The aroma of the popcorn at the pool's concession stand would never disappoint. The diving boards were always full of divers and jumpers and sometimes the lines went down the stairs to the sunbathing area. My dad was a cement contractor, and he laid a sidewalk shaped in an oval in our backyard that circled around two apple trees and our swing set and as kids, we would use our trikes, skateboards and whatever moving thing there was to ride around that oval in our backyard. In the winter, most kids would walk up to the nearest ice rink to put on their skates to skate. The warming houses were there and open for most of the days. But, even if the warming houses were not open at the time we were there, we would just sit outside on the bench, put on our skates and skate away. The winter weather wasn't an issue for us youngsters. There were many elementary schools where once we "graduated" to junior high school, we made more new friends. Anyone who played on sport teams played sports against other elementary teams and then got to play together with them through the years. One time, when East Junior High had a day off, a friend and I took the bus to West Junior High. We were walking around the halls and talking with the kids that I had in my confirmation class, and seeing the other kids, too. We were then called down to the principal's office where we were told to leave the school. Once we "graduated" to high school, we found some more new friends to hang out with. At Richfield High School, there were many sports teams to be a part of along with the teams who would cheer on our Richfield Spartans. In high school, we had cheerleaders, flag twirlers, and the Tapaires (Richfield's dance team). Being a Tapaire created many forever friendships for me and oh so many fabulous memories. It was wonderful to perform our dance routines for football pre-games and half-times, basketball games and to cheer on our Richfield Spartans throughout the year for football, basketball, and hockey games. As Tapaires, we also competed. During my sophomore year, we competed in an Aquatennial dance team competition. After that competition, a couple dance team advisors got together and decided to start what's called the Minnesota High School Dance Competition where the judging was more attuned to the dance routine and skill. The Richfield Tapaires won the first ever Minnesota State Championship in 1975. In my senior year, Richfield High School decided to create a sophomore dance line for the 10th grade girls. This allowed more girls to be involved with being on a team - specifically the dance line. The sophomore line was called the Tapettes. While I was in high school, we had strong sports teams and it was such an enjoyment going to the games and tournaments and supporting the Richfield Spartans. The area of Richfield was nearby with so many attractions. We were close to the airport – just a couple of minutes away. We had the Southdale shopping mall many years before the Mall of America. We were close to Lake Calhoun, Lake Harriet, and Lake Nokomis where we could ride our bikes and spend the day. We were close to the Metropolitan Sports Center, which was an indoor arena and Met Stadium, which was an outdoor sports stadium. Back "in the day", we would go to the Met Stadium to watch the Twins baseball games and the Kicks soccer games. The Met Stadium was also used for concerts and tailgating, of course. The Met Center was where the North Star hockey games were played from 1967 – 1993 and was also designed for other types of attractions and events like trade shows, conventions, and concerts to name a few. But nothing would compare to the Richfield High School graduating classes having our commencement ceremonies held there and trying to find all our friends after the ceremony. Richfield was a great place to grow up in and with all the connections through Richfield, it seems like someone usually knows someone who knew someone in Richfield. Happy days!! Go Richfield!

# STUDENT LIFE AT RHS

**JEANIE JOHNSON JOHNSTON**

*70TH AND HARRIET AVE. SO.*

Student Life was a non-denominational Christian group that was involved at RHS in the 70's and 80's sponsored by Campus Crusade for Christ (known today as Cru). You may remember us as the kids who carried their huge Bibles around school all day.... yes, we were the Jesus Freaks! The group started up when Campus Crusade contacted Oak Grove Lutheran Church (the closest church to the high school) about getting Student Life started. Several kids from the youth group there were instrumental getting the group going. When we first started meeting it was in houses once a week on Tuesday evenings. Eventually, when we got to the point where there were about 60 kids smashed into small Richfield style living rooms or basements, we moved to the basement of the old Richfield Library on 70th and Nicollet. Dave Johnston learned to play guitar by leading singing, as well as Bruce Christopher, Sue Thomas, Jon Schneider, and John Hedrix. We sang Christian songs and prayed for our school and fellow classmates. Some of the songs were "It's a Happy Day, and I Praise God for the Weather", "Oh, How I Love Jesus" and "Pass it on". One aspect of the group I really liked is that we came from every group at school: jocks, band nerds, cheerleaders, loners, partiers, and we found community. We also met before school every day in one of the classrooms to sing together and pray for each other. One time we had Barry McGuire (lead actor from the Broadway musical "Hair" and amazing Jesus Freak) join us before class to sing Christian songs for us. The room packed out at over 200 kids with others standing down the hallway. Such a fun, unique experience! The girls and guys were broken up into Action Groups that met separately with an adult group leader to study the Bible and go out witnessing to others. The main message was "God loves you and has a wonderful plan for your life"! Something I will never forget was the opportunity to travel to Dallas, Texas and experience the "Christian Woodstock" EXPLO 72, sponsored by Campus Crusade for Christ. It was so amazing to gather together with 200,000 people our age to sing songs, witness to others our faith and hear amazing bands playing Christian music…including Johnny Cash. We were so excited to be part of the Jesus Revolution that was taking place across the county and to be at the start of the Christian contemporary music scene. Student Life impacted me in many positive aspects. I am so thankful I was a part of this amazing group!

## IT'S A DRAG!

**GENE MILLS**

*69TH AND 3RD AVE. SO.*

I moved to Richfield in 1956 and am in the same house today. When our family (wife, mother in law and daughter) moved in there was no city sewer and water and the road was dirt. I am across the street from Norby's Pond and when we moved in there was a park surrounding the pond and it was a beautiful view. A few years later after they installed the city water and sewer I realized that the designated parkland was on the West side only. Homes were quickly built across the street backing up to the pond… One story I recall is that at the time the streets were dirt there were some young guys who decided 3rd Ave. So. was a great place to “drag race”. I stopped them a number of times to say there were children on the street and that drag racing was illegal. The racing continued and finally I called the police department to report the issue. Well of course this did not go over well with the racers and the following morning I awoke to discover they had filled the gas tank of my car with sugar. Thankfully I discovered this before I started the car. I had to drain all the gas out of the car. Retaliation came in simpler forms in those days.

The Richfield Road Ramblers

Jim Ondich

Bloomington High School

71st and 2nd Ave. So.

In 1951 Richfield 9th grade students' choices of high schools were Bloomington, Roosevelt or Washburn. This forced us into riding the school bus to school. It was also the time teenagers were getting their drivers licenses (what a liberation) get a car and drive to school. Some (most) cars needed lots of work but they were "our cars" and with the era of customizing we did our best with what we had to work with. Mud flaps, spotlights, taillights, wax and shine and wax and shine some more. We could be called a group but became a Club after attending a car club Road Rally in Colombia Heights. That's another story.
As the Richfield Road Ramblers we met at the police station where we formed a greater respect for police and they of us The news article tells the story much better than I can, but the memories for me are timeless and I got to live them…"The Fifties"

**The Richfield News**

PAGE ONE THURSDAY, JUNE 24, 1954

## Teen Age Drivers Working for Others

### City Woman Praises Road Ramblers As 'So Helpful, Cooperative and Kind'

**The Richfield police department last week received the following letter from a Minneapolis woman who was helped by road rambler Dave Hawkinson recently.**

**"Gentlemen:**

**"We want to express our heartfelt gratitude and thanks to the Road Ramblers. They assisted us on our way to Mankato in putting a new fan belt on our car.**

**"They had no thought for the time (It took a couple of hours) taken from their Memorial weekend holiday, or the dirt they got on their clean Sunday clothes.**

**"We can't say enough for these teen-agers who were so helpful, cooperative and kind!**

**"Sincerely, Mrs. Louis Brown, 4138 Quincy St. NE."**

Some South Hennepin boys are effectively proving to themselves and a number of stranded motorists that there are careful and considerate drivers in their age group.

With the help of the Richfield Police department, the boys have formed a Road Ramblers club which meets each Tuesday night in the police station.

Purpose of the organization is to "promote interest in the improvement of their automobiles, and of their driving habits, and to create an attitude of good feeling between teen-age drivers and the general public."

**Police officers are present at all the meetings to answer the boys' questions and help in any way possible."**

Most recent activity of the group was a "test run" at Augsburg park, where the boys tested their cars with help from the police department.

Richfield chief of police Cyril Johnson emphasises that the boys aren't "hot rods."

"They all have clean cars," Johnson says. "In fact, all cars are checked by the boys' own safety committee."

Johnson says each boy must have a valid driver's license to be a member, and any member tagged for a driving violation is automatically suspended.

The boys have special made-to-order license plates hanging from their back bumpers, Johnson says, and they all recently purchased identical jackets.

**EACH BOY** has a number of cards which are carried at all times and given to motorists who have been given assistance.

On the front, the card reads: **"You have been assisted by a member of the Richfield Road Ramblers, Inc."**

**The back says: "If you have appreciated this assistance, please mail this card to Richfield Police Station, with any comments.**

Johnson says the program has received many favorable comments, both from other law enforcement agencies and motorists who have been helped.

The group—which was organized last winter—is patterned after similar successful ventures in other communities.

The Road Ramblers Get Ramblin'

(photo by Gopher Studio)

Mayor Fred Kittell and Richfield Police chief Cyril Johnson drop in on the organization meeting of the Road Ramblers, club of teen age car owners and drivers whose purpose is to improve their own driving. David Hawkinson is president of the Ramblers; Bob Bode, vice president; Jim Ondich, secretary; and Ronny Trafton, treasurer. All members must have their car, insurance, and have a driver's license. Cars are checked for safety conditions before applicants are admitted for membership. The entry fee is $1, and members have to pay $1 in January and $1 in June of each year, plus 25c each meeting. Funds go for jackets and bumper tags indicating membership.

## The 71st and Nicollet Champs

Jim Ondich
71st and 2nd Ave. So.

The 71st and Nicollet Champs ball team and parade float...
About 1944-1945. We played at the now location
of World Harvest / Resurrection Churches across from
Augsburg Park. (Formerly Wooddale Baptist) I was about 10 years old and these photos are from about 78 years ago. My dad coached the neighborhood kids and he also set up games with about 4 other teams. I do remember playing around 58th and Nicollet in the Windom area and we also played on a field near 60th and Cedar.

THE MINNEAPOLIS

Richfield Policeman
Killed by Burglars

PHOTO 1

Minneapolis Tribune Fred Babcock killing headline

PHOTO 2
Cloverleaf Motel

PHOTO 3

Co-Captains Barry and Bob Bishop

PHOTO 4
Miller's Fireside Pizza

PHOTO 5

Mike Edberg as LeRoy Howe in
The Immaculate Deception

PHOTO 6

Finian's Rainbow advertisement

PHOTO 7

Float plane on Wood Lake One

PHOTO 8

Float Plane on Wood Lake Two

PHOTO 9

Float Plane on Wood Lake Three

PHOTO 10

Softball Marathon for the Heart Association One

PHOTO 11

Softball Marathon for the Heart Association Two

PHOTO 12

Augsburg Park warming house

PHOTO 13

Otto Hardt's Automatic-tees at his driving range

PHOTO 14

Bruce and Paul Hardt with their first set of clubs

PHOTO 15

1963 Lake Champs

Gunmen hold hostages at store in Richfield

[illegible]

GRAPE-FRUIT

99¢

PARTY DIP

[illegible]

PHOTO 16

An Evening unlike any other at Country Club Market

PHOTO 17

Al Payne No Hitter

PHOTO 18

The Peterson Family 1964

PHOTO 19

Willie Peterson in the Twins organ suite

PHOTO 20

Billy Peterson watching Twins game from organ suite

PHOTO 21

The Peterson Family 2007

PHOTO 22

Mark Foster with Santa, Skip and Jimmy Reed

PHOTO 23

Ticket from Shawn Phillips Concert

**Shadow's New Victim Happy Teen Club Fan**

**Eighth Grade Ideals**

SMILE

EYES

ENERGETIC

HAIR

SENSE OF HUMOR

CHARM

ARTISTIC

**Drama, Speech, Debate Summarized; Year's Activities Rated As Success**

PHOTO 24

Mr Duane Wold

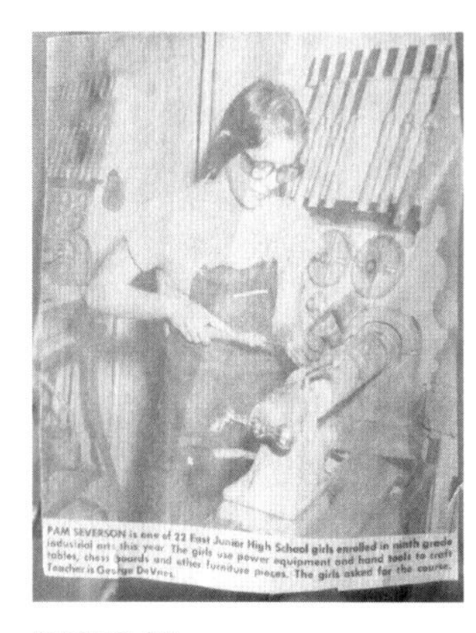

PAM SEVERSON is one of 22 East Junior High School girls enrolled in ninth grade industrial arts this year. The girls use power equipment and hand tools to craft tables, chess boards and other furniture pieces. The girls asked for the course. Teacher is George DeVries.

THE RAVE-ONS, pictured from left to right, are Larry Wiegand, Dick Wiegand, Lowell Knight and Skip Kovacs. The group performs both in Minnesota and Wisconsin. Just recently they were featured at the Prom ballroom in St. Paul.

★ ★ ★ ★ ★ ★ ★ ★ ★ ★ ★ ★

**Richfield's 'Rave-ons' Rival Beatles**

PHOTO 25

Pam Syverson-Girls in Boys classes

PHOTO 26

The Rave-Ons taking on The Stones and the Beatles

PHOTO 27

Bill Davis 1960

PHOTO 28

Mr Bill Davis

PHOTO 29

Reiter Realty

PHOTO 30

Boat giveaway at Taits Super Valu

PHOTO 31

Sherm Booen

PHOTO 32

Edgerton versus Richfield

PHOTO 33

Mike Waggoner and the Bops

PHOTO 34

A Country Boy in Richfield's view of Hank Ranft's Farm where Roosevelt Park is today

PHOTO 35

Nelson's Pie Tin

PHOTO 36

Nelson's Drive in Restaurant

PHOTO 37

Mike Fossen and his 6 tickets

PHOTO 38

Leffler's Dairy Store

PHOTO 39

Deb Browning and her Sunflower

PHOTO 40

The Food Fight

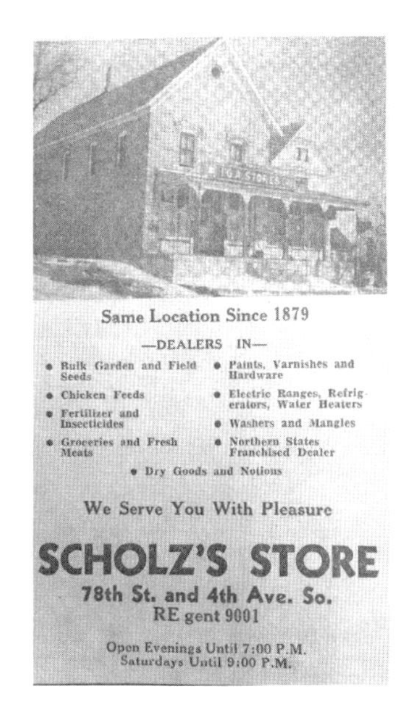


PHOTO 41

Scholz's Store

PHOTO 42

Our Love for our Neighbors.
Looking west towards Edina from 66th and Emerson during 1955 July 4th parade.

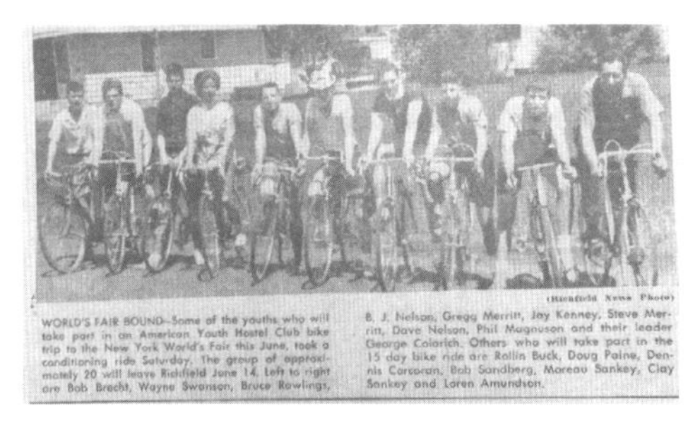

(Richfield News Photo)

WORLD'S FAIR BOUND—Some of the youths who will take part in an American Youth Hostel Club bike trip to the New York World's Fair this June, took a conditioning ride Saturday. The group of approximately 20 will leave Richfield June 14. Left to right are Bob Brecht, Wayne Swanson, Bruce Rowlings, B. J. Nelson, Gregg Merritt, Jay Kenney, Steve Merritt, Dave Nelson, Phil Magnuson and their leader George Colarich. Others who will take part in the 15 day bike ride are Rollin Buck, Doug Paine, Dennis Corcoran, Bob Sandberg, Moreau Sankey, Clay Sankey and Loren Amundson.

PHOTO 43

Bike Trip to The World's Fair

PHOTO 44

The Richfield Pool

PHOTO 45

Dennis Dietzler and Mike Fossen at the Augsburg Park annual hockey game

PHOTO 46

Becky Bingea with her sister and a Patrol friend

PHOTO 47

The Bingea family and the building of House of Prayer Church

PHOTO 48

American Legion Post 435

PHOTO 49

Circus Came to Town One

PHOTO 50

Circus Came to Town Two

PHOTO 51

Circus Came to Town Three

PHOTO 52

David Nye and the Iron Cross

PHOTO 53

Tom-Tom Drive In

PHOTO 54

Tony O

PHOTO 55

The Christian Farmhouse

PHOTO 56

The Magnuson Sod Company

PHOTO 57

The Granary House on Emerson Lane

PHOTO 58

Duell's Café

PHOTO 59

Richfield High School Baseball Field

PHOTO 60

David Waller and the Morris Nilsen Boys Choir

PHOTO 61

Sara and Dave's Dream House on 73rd and Lyndale

PHOTO 62

Tom "Tank" Christensen and his low-cut spikes

THE RICHFIELD NEWS

Assassination Stuns U.S.

Councilmen Mourn J. F. K.

PHOTO 63

The Richfield News

PHOTO 64

Miles Lundahl

# SUMMERTIME FUN

**JEAN GRANT RHOADES**

*66TH AND 16TH AVE. SO.*

Many Saturday evenings, I'd babysit for a neighbor's child. Vivid babysitting memories happened in the summertime. When I was needed to babysit Kristi during afternoons, I'd have her over to my backyard. There were very unique activities we would do. Here is a list of our choices: My father brought home three DC 9 airplane inner tubes, from North Central Airlines where he worked. We'd jump on these and try to do flips. Plus, we'd stack the tubes three high and hide in the center. Another activity was creating adventures in my playhouse. This playhouse was made from a large appliance packing box. There was an appliance store nearby on 66th Street. I walked there with a few of my girlfriends and upon request, the owner gave us huge boxes to take home. I can't image what drivers thought as we lugged these to my yard! My girlfriends and I would decorate our playhouses by lining the interior with wallpaper, the cut-out windows were adorned with curtains, and carpet scraps placed on the floor. We loved our 'personal neighborhood'. Other summertime activities were playing croquet, throwing Jarts lawn darts, setting up a screened tent with a large hammock inside, so to have space away from mosquitoes to play cards. My parents inspired creativity which helped me be resourceful with my free time. I am blessed with groovy summertime memories of growing up in Richfield.

# RICHFIELD HIGH SCHOOL – PLANTED SEEDS THAT GREW ALL MY LIFE

**BOB STRANDQUIST**

*66TH AND 17TH AVE. SO.*

**Springtime in America was baseball.** In the mid-1950's Richfield's recent war veteran fathers formed a Little League located east of Cedar Ave on Wold- Chamberlain airport vacant land. These dads became dedicated builders, coaches, and umpires. Hundreds of baby-boom boys ages 9-12 showed up for tryouts. I was number 353. The dads put us through skill tests of fielding fly balls and scooping grounders, pitching, running bases, hitting bunts, and swinging hard. Then we were chosen one-by-one for either the clinic, the minor league, the association league, or the majors. At 9 years old I was picked for the Association on a team sponsored by Red and White grocery store located at 7138 Chicago Ave So. Our coach Bob Lambert put me at shortstop and lead-off hitter. He built our team on his encouragement and positive reactions. "That-a-way". And "Get a little bingo, now' was his bunt signal to the batter. That year we won the Association championship. As a reward, our whole team was moved up to the majors for the next season. After Little League, I played more baseball in junior high, but in high school I rode the bench. So, I quit. Fortunate to be in a school that offered choices for us, I went out for the golf team and played on the RHS varsity for 3 years. Years later I became a high school golf coach in Roseau. In 1972 a girl tried out and made the team. Next season we formed a girls' team and they won the region and played in the State tournament for the next 3 years. I continued to play golf on my own. And, in 2013 I joined the Richfield Spartan Foundation that raises scholarship funds to support 25 RHS seniors through an annual golf tournament. So, from age 14 at RHS to age 76, I continue to play golf thanks to the seed planted by RHS Coach Jim Carlson at RHS.

**Field Trip to the Guthrie:** My RHS 11th grade English teacher, Mrs. Hendrickson joined with 12 grade teacher, Mrs. Ford to organize a field trip in May of 1963 to see its very first play, "Hamlet" at this new place in Minneapolis called the Tyrone Guthrie Theater. We sat in the top rows but actually were not far from the thrust stage. I was shocked to see the characters costumed in modern clothes rather than puffy sleeves and sweeping gowns. 'This is fake,' I thought. But the actors were amazing, agile and even funny. This experience brought words in a book into real life and not on TV. That was magic for me.

The next year, I entered college intent on a chemistry major. Disillusion soon followed when the professor kept forcing us to memorize chemical formulae. Bah. I quit and soon found that English classes were more interesting due to the wide range of locations, of eras and characters that inhabited the assigned novels, plays and poems. These seeds from RHS and from college grew into becoming an English teacher and in my first year my seniors read, re-scripted and staged "Hamlet" in front of an audience. This seed planted in RHS sprouted in 1969 and grew for 37 years.

Next week, we have tickets to see "Hamlet" on the Guthrie stage as a celebration honoring its 60th anniversary. Thanks, Mrs.Hendrickson, my RHS English teacher your brave vision inspired me for the rest of my life.

# GROWING UP ON LAKE SHORE DRIVE

**DON FALENCZYKOWSKI**
*LAKE SHORE DRIVE*

My Richfield story begins in 1955 at 6615 Lake Shore Drive. The address is still there, but my house isn't - it's now a high-rise senior apartment building. The three oak trees that my dad planted, however, still remain. It was a great neighborhood to grow up in, sandwiched between Lyndale Avenue and Wood Lake, with Graham Avenue in the middle. Graham Avenue no longer exists - it succumbed to the sprawling high-rise buildings that went up around it. My playground growing up was Wood Lake, a forgotten mud hole that was part of the Lake of the Isles chain. It became a swamp when they built the 35W Interstate Highway. It was surrounded by woods that, for the most part, was no man's land. We kids from the neighborhood would build forts and treehouses, and have adventures in the woods. Before the lake deteriorated into a swamp, my dad and some of the neighbors would go water skiing (I don't think you were allowed to but nobody ever cared). The only official usage of the lake and woods were for two skating rinks, with one being a hockey rink with a cinder block warming house on the northeast corner, plus an "unofficial" sledding hill. The sledding hill could be dangerous as the Park Department would pile snow onto the bank after they plowed the rinks. You would go down the hill, up the bank, and nosedive straight down into the rink! There was always some kid's blood frozen into the ice from the sled hill! In the mid to late 60s, there was talk of turning my beloved playground into a golf course. Thankfully, saner heads prevailed (my dad being one of them), and the lake and woods became the wonderful Wood Lake Nature Center that we have today! And now about the great families in my neighborhood: Living across the alley from us were three elderly sisters and their brother. Bun, Lois and Fawn performed Vaudeville with Irene Ryan (Granny from *The Beverly Hillbillies*). Next door to us was the wonderful Lynch family. Their son Mike was my best friend growing up. Mike became a meteorologist for WCCO, and an avid astronomer. There were many other interesting families in the neighborhood. At the east end of the neighborhood was a small mom-and-pop grocery store - it had a house attached to it where the family who owned it lived. To the north, along Lyndale Avenue, was Snyder's Drug Store complete with a small soda fountain and grill. Across Graham Avenue was Stillman's Grocery Store that later became the Sveden House Smorgasbord. Also, on Lyndale Avenue lived an inventive man named Fred Bergholt. His house was known as the "Tree House" because at one time it supposedly had a tree growing out of it. His house was full of interesting things - from airplane parts to a car he built from scratch called the Bergholt Streamline. One of my passions in life is aviation, my dad being a pilot for Northwest and living so close to Wold-Chamberlain Field (as Minneapolis–Saint Paul International Airport was then known, and less commonly known as today), so it was heaven with constant airliners and military aircraft flying overhead. I always had to look up whenever a plane flew over - and still do to this day! One day in December 1966, I was in our driveway after school when I heard an airplane going over 66th Street with its engines surging. I looked up to see an Aero Commander (I knew my aircraft) on fire, the flames engulfing the entire aft fuselage. The pilot tried to land on 35W but hit a car heading northbound. The pilot was the only occupant in the aircraft and was killed in the accident, but the driver of the 1963 Impala jumped out of his car when he saw the fireball coming at him and survived! Needless to say, life in Richfield was interesting So, that was a glimpse into my life at 6615 Lake Shore Drive from 1955 to 1974. Richfield was a great place to grow up and a great city to live in!

# MY EARLY RICHFIELD RANDOM MEMORIES

**DICK PACHOLKE**

*70TH AND LYNDALE AVE. SO.*

I remember the Tornado of 1951. It took out a dozen columnar poplars in the backyard. Mom and Dad were out for the evening, and we were with a babysitter hunkered down in the basement. There were trees down across Lyndale. Daylight revealed quite a mess...I remember Street Cars on Lyndale Avenue...I remember walking to Central Elementary School on gravel roads. I think at that time only the main roads like Lyndale, Nicollet and 66th streets were paved...I remember sliding down the hill off Lyndale and Lake Shore Drive in Winter and skating at the rink at Wood Lake taking advantage of the warming house...I remember the worn wooden steps leading to the basement of Lyndale Hardware. If they didn't have what you needed, you didn't really need it...I remember sitting at the counter of Nelson Drug store having a strawberry sundae and reading a Hot Rod magazine…I think these are accurate, but as I get older my memory is sometimes sketchy!

# RICHFIELD: OUR OWN CAMELOT

**KENT PETERSON**

*68TH AND KNOX AVE. SO.*

While growing up in Richfield in a family consisting of Mom, Dad and their four boys, our middle-class existence was akin to Camelot. Sure, none of us were going to rival the wealth and material things acquired by the Buffets, Gates, and Musks of today, but we were happy and most of us weren't wanting for much more. Dad worked an accounting job for Standard Oil and our Mom was a "stay at home mom". This was typical of most families that I knew. We moved into our house at 6830 Knox Avenue in 1954. Our Dad, like many WWII vets, put in a tremendous amount of sweat equity into the building of our home. He built the garage, finished a portion of the basement to add a bedroom and an additional bathroom and later put on a three-season porch on the back of the house. I have always regretted not learning the skills to be adept around a toolbox like my father. We had the best lawn on the block and Dad's Garden was the envy of our neighbors. Our house was just a block south of Fairwood Park, where the Peterson boys spent most of their waking hours in both the summer and winter. It consisted of a warming house, a softball field, a basketball court, two tennis courts and numerous deadly accoutrements like monkey bars and merry-go-rounds. Summers were occupied by pick up softball games, box hockey, ping pong and the like. We rode buses to the Navy Pool and later to the Richfield Pool for swimming lessons. My oldest brother, Tom, played a lot of tennis with the Stark family and good friend, Jay Marsh. We only went home for lunch and dinner. During the winter, Fairwood once again was our focal point for entertainment. Pom Pom Pullaway and taking the hats from the cute girls occupied most of my time. We ventured to Donaldson Park to play hockey. Some names you may recognize from the Fairwood community were Malmberg, Thorberg, Maxon, Stark, Dougherty, Schlemmer, Haws and many more. Though I cannot remember what I had for breakfast yesterday, I can recall 19 family names that lived on the 68th and Knox block! In college, I had both a summer and winter job at Fairwood through Richfield Parks and Rec. The Peterson boys matriculated through Woodlake Elementary, West Jr High and Richfield Sr High school system. Woodlake was a unique campus where 1st grade was held in a "portable" building, 3rd grade was held in the original main building and all other grades were housed in the new building along with offices, lunchroom, and the gymnasium. Most of my grade schoolteachers are memorable to me, most specifically, Mrs. Bingham and Mrs. Haug. Though my Jr High teachers aren't quite as clear in my mind, I owe a lot of my athletic success in High School to the mentorship of my basketball coach, Mike Plinske and baseball coach, Dewey Marcus. Like many boys in Jr High, I had a good many crushes and unrequited "love" interests. Sock Hops weren't the most comfortable environment for me. High School was a lot of fun for me, but I focused mainly on athletics. I wasn't the best athlete on my teams, but I know I was a damn good defensive guard in basketball and an excellent outfielder. I was a little better than average student, but you wouldn't find me on the Dean's List. Favorite teachers were Ms. Skala, Mr. Doss, Mr. Slattery, Mr. Hendrickson and Mr. Oberstar. Jim Hare was my baseball coach and a great mentor. He honored me giving me lifelong leadership skills, making me a co-captain my senior year. I give most of my success in baseball to my father, Cliff. He coached the West Little League team of all four of his boys! Growing up in Richfield has given me a great foundation in my life and I credit much of my personal and professional success to my family, friends and education. I wouldn't trade it for a life anywhere else, even Edina!

# GROWING UP IN BLUE BIRDS AND CAMPFIRE GIRLS

**CINDEE HENDRICKSON FORBY**

*68TH AND 11TH AVE. SO.*

At Elliot Elementary school in East Richfield, we were given presentations from the Girl Scouts and from Campfire Girls. Both organizations are for young girls to learn new skills, work with others and to have fun after school. There was not a lot of extra money in the budget at home to buy a uniform, so my option was Blue Birds/Campfire as my neighbor decided she wanted to pursue the Girl Scouts instead. So, I got Linda's cap, skirt, vest and was off for adventure as a Blue Bird. Besides, I liked the uniform better than the Brownie uniform and we got to sell Fannie Farmer Candy instead of stupid cookies. Nothing beats a French frosted mint!

Mrs. Ruth Pansch was my Blue Bird leader. We met at her home that was on the next block from where I lived. We toured the Richfield Fire and Police Departments, made tray decorations (aka nut/candy cups decorated for Christmas) for the nursing home on Portland Avenue and sang Christmas Carols there as well. We also learned and memorized the Blue Bird/Campfire pledges. It was so fun to make the cake every year for the anniversary of Campfire. We worked in teams to do it. We baked the cake, frosted it, and decorated it using tootsie rolls for the logs and red frosting for the flame. We got to share one with each other and then one was donated to a nursing home. I think I outgrew my group in the 7th grade and transferred into Mrs. Lois Terry's group from Portland Elementary. Mrs. Terry interviewed me to make sure my intentions were genuine in changing groups. She didn't want any hurt feelings with Mrs. Pansch. It was in her group that we went on nature hikes, taught basic camping survival building shelter and fires, we cooked over a campfire, made "hobo" dinners (meals cooked in the fire wrapped in foil). Over Christmas vacation the moms drove all the way out to Chaska to go to Camp Tanadoona for some winter camping. (In an old lodge), cross country skiing and snowshoeing. It took FOREVER to get there. The Moms slept downstairs by the fire and us girls upstairs where we relied on the heat rising notion. We took a trip to South Dakota and ended up surviving the worst flood that has hit Rapid City thanks to our bus driver Gene. On this same trip we went to the Passion Play of the Black Hills. We were supposed to do a sewing project and sew an outfit in matching material…did no one tell Mrs. Terry that I couldn't sew? My Mom made my vest and I think I punted on why I didn't bring my pants with me. I stood in the back for the picture. There was nothing better than getting back to Richfield that June. Back in the safety of our community…and the pool, but that's a different story.

# SWAMP MONSTER

**MIKE GRONLUND**

*63RD AND DUPONT AVE. SO.*

Our yard was ground zero for all activities in the neighborhood it seemed. One day in the late 60's a bunch of us were playing in the yard. We had a double lot so there was plenty of room. I kept noticing that it appeared that one of the old, galvanized garbage can lids must have blown off a can and was in the corner of the yard. No big deal we were having blast. Every time, over about an hours period of time when I glanced over at it, it seemed to have moved. What the heck, it was not windy. That was odd I thought. So, I went over there to attach it back to the garbage can it had blown off of only to find out it was not a garbage can lid at all, it was a giant tortoise. This thing was huge!! Where did it come from? We assumed the "the Swamp" but had no idea. We went and got Mom fearing it may be a snapping turtle and we chose to keep all of our fingers. Dad had come home soon after and they had noticed there was paint on the underside of this creature. It was what appeared to be a phone number. Mom called and got a hold of a person and found out this monster was stolen from a college. If I remember correctly. They came and picked it up... And we went back to being kids.

# FOSSEN AND BANE – THE RECKLESS RIDERS!

**MIKE FOSSEN**

*72ND AND 2ND AVE. SO.*

The block I grew up on was 72nd and 2nd. We had 60 kids on our block, from infants, to late teens, to early 20's. There were 12 kids my age alone. It was a great time to be a kid growing up in Richfield....I have chosen a story about a sunny day, July 27, 1971, to be exact. I was 15 years old. I went over to my friend, Dan Bane's house. We decided to go to the Richfield pool but had some time to kill before it opened. Dan's parents weren't home, so we decided to use a screwdriver to start Dan's dad's motorcycle, a 305 Honda Scrambler. Neither of us had a license, but we went tooling around East Richfield for about 30 minutes. About then, a Richfield cop pulled up behind us and flipped on his red lights. I was on the back and asked Dan what we should do, and he said, "Hang on", and opened the throttle. The cop chased us for a few blocks and was able to force us off to the side of the road. Dan immediately flipped a U-turn and headed the other way. Officer Sanke swore at us and jumped back in his squad car to continue the pursuit. He must have radioed for help because a few blocks ahead, on 74th and 11th, we ran into 2 squads and a roadblock. They threw us in the squad and took us to the Police Station. Then they called our parents to come and pick us up, and handed each of us 6 tickets:

1- no driver's license

2- no motorcycle endorsement

3-illegal U-turn

4-driving on wrong side of road

5-speeding

6-failure to stop for an emergency vehicle

Needless to say, we never made it to the pool that day!... I still have my tickets as a keepsake.

# MY SUNFLOWER

**DEB BROWNING SHAY**

*64TH AND THOMAS AVE. SO.*

I grew up around flowers and gardening as my mother was in the Richfield Garden Club. She, in fact, helped design the Richfield Wildflower Garden at the pond across from Sheridan School. (a story for another time) One year, Richfield had a contest for "The Biggest Sunflower in Richfield." Of course, I had to plant one. I never thought I would win the award for growing the biggest sunflower in Richfield, but I did. I had to write an essay on how I took care of my sunflower. The essay is attached for your giggles. I was quite shy back then (not like now, LOL). The coolest thing was that I beat a guy!! LOL!!

Debbie Downing

# My Sunflower

In taking care of my sunflower I mixed bone meal in the dirt that I planted the seed in. I watered it just a little so I wouldn't flood the seed. Then I watered it mostly every day. Finally in a couple of weeks I saw a sunflower coming up, then I started to water it more. Then finally it reached the point when it started to hang over. Then I staked it up and tied it with a old nylon. Every once in a while I put bone meal on it. Finally I noticed that a flower was growing on it, it got bigger and bigger. Then I started to pour buckets of water on it. We tried to measure it and we had to get on a high ladder to reach it. This is how I took care of my sunflower.

# THE DAIRY STORE

**CINDY LEE MOIR**

*74TH AND 17TH AVE. SO.*

Growing up, one of the places we used to go on a regular basis was Leffler's Dairy Store on Cedar Avenue. It was owned by a woman named Delores Leffler and she lived kitty corner from her store and took care of her mother. I used to walk her dog, Freckles, which was a very hyper springer spaniel, and we developed an apparently trusting relationship. She seemed to like all of us kids from the neighborhood quite well. The boys in the neighborhood were allowed to use the store basement to play poker and hang out. Whenever she had to go and fix her mother's lunch, she would allow us to watch the store for her (she was only ever gone about 10 or 15 minutes, but it made us feel important just the same. If I walked up there with my dog, she would always give him a popsicle as a treat on those hot summer days. One day I went to the store with one of my friends and when we left my friend took off her jacket and the sleeves of her jacket were full of candy bars!!! We were short so you had to step on the bottom shelf below the candy to reach it, but she was stuffing the candy down her jacket sleeve. One day I was a bit mad at my friend and told Delores that she had been stealing the candy that way. Delores told me she knew that, but because my friend came from a big family that she let it slide. She said with her having so many brothers and sisters at home, she wasn't getting nickels and dimes from her parents like I was and that eventually she would just stop taking it and it was never spoken of again. After it closed, we had to walk all the way up Cedar to the bigger store for our candy, it wasn't the same and those trips to the store didn't happen as often.

# THE BIGGEST PARTY IN RICHFIELD

**DEB CHIMZAR THORNEY**

*73RD AND 14TH AVE. SO.*

Where do I begin?... How about Richfield May 1975. My parents Frank & Lee Chimzar were out of town in California, and they trusted me to be in charge of our house at 7310 14th Avenue South right off of Diagonal Boulevard by Wilson Pond. (BTW, Steve Christoff a student at Richfield High School and a member of the Miracle on Ice Hockey team lived 2 blocks from me. Very exciting!) Getting back to the story and the day Richfield saw the biggest party ever... I had no idea this was even planned until someone asked me what time they should show up? What!!?? OMG. I did some investigating and found out Brad Perlich had organized a big party at my house for Deb Ashmore and Scott Coughlin and that people would have to give $2.00 to come to the party to raise money for the happy couple who we found out had just gotten married that day. To this day they have been married for 48 years with 3 Beautiful daughters and a lot of grandkids and are so blessed! There were tons of people there and I remember that the party was a huge success. We raised hundreds of dollars for them.If you had to use the rest room no one could go into the house, so they went down to the gas station and came back. My parents never found out about the party until many years later! My next-door neighbor was Patti Soderberg, rest her sweet soul, she and her friends were all there too. That's my story and I am sticking to it. What an amazing memory, especially for the Class of 1975. I believe that all the kids that were there had a fun time and that if you just close your eyes you'll be brought right back to The Biggest Party in Richfield!

# SCHOLZ MERCANTILE CO.
# 336 EAST 78TH STREET

**RANDY BUCK**

*75TH AND STEVENS AVE. SO.*

Back before there were convenience stores, food gas stations and Roy and Bob's Milk house on Nicollet Avenue there was a post war subdivision in the first suburb in Mn, called Richfield and it was full of little kids wanting to venture out into the wilderness of the cornfields, soybean fields and woods. The only place they could buy paper candy dots, candy cigarettes, other bars, bottled soft drinks and things their mothers sent them up to get was a two-story store called Scholz's Mercantile. Scholz Mercantile was a store built three years after the Battle of the Little Bighorn. For locals, Farmers, Travelers and as far as we were concerned for us, it was an amazing place. Friends and neighbor kids, Dick Borst, Ken Hoffert, Barb Fritz, Pat Butel, Mike and Kerry Jaeger, the Buck boys, Kellogg kids and so many more all went there. It was a meat market, grocery store, clothing store, seed store, hardware store, shoe and boot store, fishing gear store. You could even buy shotguns, all kinds of ammo, blasting caps, dynamite fuse and even dynamite! If you could not find it there you did not need it…Reflecting on those days, none of us could have imagined that the steps we climbed at Scholz's were the same steps that veterans from the Civil war had used.

# GARAGE BANDS

**PAUL MCINERNY**

*73RD AND 17TH AVE. SO.*

I suppose they've always been around. I mean, bands must start somewhere, so why not a garage? I know Richfield had its share of wanna be superstars honing their skills and vocals in mom and dad's garage. I was one of those wanna be's and had the wonderful experience of playing in garage bands in Richfield. We moved from Minneapolis to Richfield when my parents bought their first (and only) house in 1956 near 73rd & 17th Avenue South. Back in time when our phone number started with Union 6, and when you first picked up the phone, you had to listen to make sure there wasn't another household using the line. It was called a party line, and sometimes we would eavesdrop on the conversation. And we had a garage. I was fortunate enough to have parents who were very tolerant of my love for the electric guitar, for the guitar played an integral part of my musical development. My first electric guitar was a Silvertone, solid body 6 string guitar purchased via a Montgomery Wards catalog. Playing the guitar in the house was restricted to the hours when it would not disturb the other seven members of our household, which really meant plucking and fingers to chord practice was done in muffled silence. I took a few lessons at

Trestman Music Center, when it was located at 6503 Nicollet Ave. So., near the Richfield Theater. Of course, I had to let my friends know I had an electric guitar and had written a couple of songs. It was then I found many in my circle of my friends were also learning to play musical instruments. Bill Kephart (Richfield Class of '68) could play guitar, but his forte was the organ. Kevin Fox (Benilde High School) played the piano and guitar. Dick and Randy Pacholke (Richfield Class of '64 and '69) played multiple instruments and wrote songs. Lance Grande (Richfield Class of '69) was a song writer and played drums. Craig Blubaugh (Richfield Class of '69) played drums. These were just a few of the Richfield guys I had the pleasure to jam with, and jam we did in someone's garage. In junior high school, I was part of a band called the Herdsmen. We developed our repertoire by practicing in our garages. Sometimes we would leave the overhead garage door open so neighbors for blocks around could hear our vocals and music. We practiced in garages because they were large enough to hold our equipment, small enough for the intimacy of focused work and private enough where we wouldn't get in trouble or bother anyone. We must have been doing OK, because nobody called the police on us. We did, however, receive one complaint from a high school classmate who lived across the street from a garage practice, who informed us she was sick and tired of hearing "House of the Rising Sun." Eventually our garage sanctuary allowed us to learn enough songs for a respectable repertoire, and we began to play junior high school dances. One performance has remained with me, even after all these years. The Herdsmen were hired for a Friday night dance at East Junior High School. I was nervous, because in the audience was my sister, Jenny, and a group of her friends. I thought the band was good, but playing before Jenny and her friends had me anxious and it was certainly different from playing in a garage. For me, East Junior High was playing the big time. The band gathered on stage behind the closed curtain, and we took our positions. Amplifiers were on, the drummer was ready and then somebody from the school stepped up to a microphone, gave a brief introduction and yelled, "The Herdsmen!" As the curtain opened, we went right into our first song. Although I cannot remember the song, I *do* remember about fifty junior high school girls screaming as if we were the Beatles. I'm not sure how much my sister paid her friends, but it was such an incredible experience and confidence builder. Our garage is now empty of guitars, drum sets, amplifiers, and broken drumsticks and guitar strings. Gone are the microphones and endless yards of extension cords. Yet, I wonder...on a warm, summer day in Richfield, is it still possible to drive through a neighborhood and hear the distinct sound of a live band practicing in the garage? A tip of the hat to all the garage bands of Richfield and their accommodating parents!

# THE STORY OF THE VANISHED CHICKEN

**MEL JACKOLA**

*CENTENNIAL ELEMENTARY SCHOOL*

Long ago when I was an active sixth grade teacher at Centennial School in Richfield, this interesting event actually occurred. Each year my class would prepare and display Science projects at our wonderful Classroom Science Fair. One year a student of mine created an excellent project of body skeletal formation. Chris purchased the carcass of a whole chicken that he cleaned all tissue from and glued the bones to the form of a standing chicken skeleton. He did an excellent job. Mr. Vern Ratzloff of East Elementary became aware of our chicken skeleton and asked if he could borrow it to use as a model in his class's study of skeletal structure. After using the model for several weeks, I received a surprising and shocking call from Vern telling me something terrible had happened, the skeleton was gone, vanished. During a weekend break, pet white rats escaped from their classroom cage and made a meal of mounted chicken bones. Chris was told what happened and handled the incident with understanding maturity. Many lessons had been learned plus two white rats really enjoyed their weekend.

# OUR LOVE FOR OUR NEIGHBORS

**CHUCK STRAUCH**

*66TH AND EMERSON AVE. SO.*

It was the winter of 1966. Although it was a gamble to date out of your school system, I had scored a date with a very lovely young lass from Edina. To make matters worse, we decided to go to a hockey game at Braemar Arena where Richfield was playing the insects from Edina. Richfield had tied Edina earlier in the season, and both teams were high in the rankings. I played on the 'B' squad and would not consider missing this game. This was an era where the rink had no glass barriers, just chicken-wire behind each goal. We were sitting about 10 rows from the ice right on the blue line. I remember seeing Dick Erickson against the boards right in front of me minding his own business after a whistle. Without provocation, an Edina player skated over to him and 'cold-cocked' him. This did not sit well with the rest of the Richfield hockey team and all hell broke loose. In addition to the players, fans were jumping over the boards to join the festivities. The crowd's mood was getting ugly, and I decided the best thing for us was to get the hell out of there. Most of the fans were under control, but there was a lot of tension in the air. There was an abundance of yelling and trash talking in the parking lot, so I left as soon as possible. I dropped my date off and headed for Richfield's local hot spot; Burger King on 66th Steet. There were a few Edina kids there which made a few fisticuffs unavoidable. Some of the Richfield crowd drove over to Embers on 494 and 100 to see if they could cause any trouble at Edina's hot spot. All in all, the battle concluded with no gunfire, bats, knives, chains, death, or serious injury. That night was the turning point in Richfield's intense hatred (rivalry) with Edina. It took 2 years to get a small amount of payback, when the 1968 Spartans crushed Edina in basketball 81-75, and stopped Edina's state record 69 game winning streak!

# LIFT HIGH THE CROSS

**MICK SCOTT**

*76TH AND 13TH AVE. SO.*

I'm Mick Scott and I grew up on the corner of 76th and 13th. I've always been on the short side, especially in Jr. High. I was an Acolyte at House of Prayer Lutheran Church. As an Acolyte I would often lead in the worship participants by lifting high the processional cross. That was quite a feat as it was made of oak and large polished brass end plates. It looked great but it was really heavy. Each time I'd Lift it high above my head to place it in the stand I flirted with tipping over backwards. It became a matter of faith and prayer. As a member of the church's Boy Scout Troop #443 I was working on my "God and Country" badge and had to come up with a church related service project. My dad had the great idea that we construct a new processional cross that we all could safely carry. Dad was a great craftsman, and we made an exact copy of the cross except with brushed aluminum instead of brass. It was welcomed by all the Acolytes as it was so much easier to carry and lift. That was in 1973 and from the wedding pictures I've seen since, it was still in use some 20 years later.

# BURN, BABY, BURN

**TODD OLSON**

*67TH AND ELLIOT AVE. SO.*

I guess that lots of kids have an interest in fire. I suppose I did too. Once I had mastered starting one safely (I don't recall passing a test to that end, but that's another story) I was given the chore of burning the family trash. Just the burnable stuff of course, the rest was either hauled away by the "garbage man" or Dad and I included it in a trip to the dump in Burnsville. We had a fire "can" in the corner of the back yard on our street on Elliot Avenue. This is before any city ordinance prohibited such activity and before we understood the detrimental effects of such burning. Not to mention the unpleasantness to our downwind neighbors. But it was the late sixties and lots of us were doing it. This chore provided me time to contemplate life's challenges as well as a lesson in building a good fire. Who needs the Boy Scouts. Dad eventually erected a privacy fence that blocked our view of the fire can from the house. I'm not sure if I took that opportunity to do nefarious things in that privacy, but as I noted previously it was the late sixties. I don't recall when we halted that practice of burning trash, but it likely overlapped with the burning of another substance in the front yard. More specifically, on the curb in the street in the Fall. Again, no city ordinance yet, so why not burn leaves instead of bagging and hauling them away or composting. Late sixties burn baby burn. Unlike burning trash, burning leaves has a more palatable aroma. At least, that was probably one justification. Maybe it was also an extension of our rural agricultural roots. Perhaps our prehistoric ones. What I do know is that it created much fun for the neighborhood kids. No one got hurt as I remember and it engendered neighborhood comradery. Kind of an early version of National Night Out. Which brings me to the next chapter in this story. No, I didn't become an arsonist. Well, not a textbook case, at least. At the end Elliot Avenue was Legion Lake. Known to the kids as The Swamp. Now it is called Veterans Park. Back then it was undeveloped, save the new pool which had been built, and it was source of endless exploration and fun. Some may recall the "sludge pond" behind the water works on Portland. You couldn't ask for a better way to spend your day. Unless you were in a mischievous mood. My friends and I decided we would build a small fire in the long grass along 66th Street. A small fire, just for fun. We were masters of fire, mind you, given our trash and leaf burning skills honed just up the block. What we didn't pay mind to was the lethal combination of dry grass and wind when it met fire. Unfortunately, none of us were Boy Scouts. A match was struck, the long dry grass was fluffed up to create better tinder, and the flame emerged. And then the wind made its appearance and we had a raging blaze. One of my courageous (albeit foolish) friends did a tuck and roll across the growing blaze in an effort to snuff it out. No luck, it was off and running. Fortunately, the wind was blowing in a direction that took the fire towards the unoccupied center of the grassland. Our attempts to contain the fire at its edges were futile. We were concerned, not so much for what the fire might damage, but for the potential trouble we were in. Before long, Richfield Fire arrived. I'll never forget the fireman with his portable extinguisher and the cigar in his mouth. We could see that they would soon be able to tame the fire but of course we didn't admit to anything when he asked us who started it. We blamed a fictitious malcontent. He didn't buy our story. But he didn't arrest anyone either. We were admonished and released back into the wild. Fall was coming, and we had quality leaf burning time coming soon.

# RICHFIELD BASEBALL LIVES ON IN COOPERSTOWN

**CHIP SHARRATT**

*64TH AND 13TH AVE. SO.*

Chip Sharratt, RHS 1970, here. Ever since high school graduation in 1970, I'd spent 20 years living in 7 different states and traveling throughout the world on two Navy aircraft carriers and one surface combatant ship before returning to Minnesota and family in 1991. Within only a few months' time I'd be sitting in the bleachers of East Richfield Little League baseball park watching youngsters play ball on the very same fields my passion for baseball had grown decades earlier. The four Sharratt brothers enjoyed competing at and learning to love "the game of baseball", with over 20 individual summer-seasons of playing on those same fields. But in 1992, I also quickly learned that those 12 ballfields would soon be torn down for MSP Airport expansion and to add a new N-S runway. It broke my heart! Then, after tracking down the Little League President at the '93-season closing ceremonies, he told me that the baseball complex would be completely bulldozed and hauled away the next summer. I asked if I might be able to gather some remnants to take for building some new baseball fields near Cooperstown, NY. (?) An enthusiastic nod was all I needed and received! My next-youngest brother, Dwaine, had been living with his wife and family near her Massachusetts roots for years, but they had recently bought a 150(+) acre Campground in 1997 near Cooperstown NY. And, of course, it's the home of the National Baseball Hall of Fame. He then quickly decided to expand his business model and build two premier baseball fields right there near "the Birthplace of Baseball", to replicate our family's own baseball-learning experiences. I called Mitch Hale, an RHS '74 classmate of Dwaine's and a great family friend, and we went to work collecting cherished treasures from the rubble of those fields. Dwaine planned to take as much as possible back to Cooperstown. We gathered rolls of chain-link fence from several ballfields; hundreds of baseballs that had been jammed into the cinder-blocks of every dugout (set-free by the bull-dozers), press box artifacts, bases and home plates, pitching rubbers, the flag pole, and multiple sets of bleachers where our parents had rested their bottoms for years - watching their kids play on those fields that our dads helped build in the late 50's and early 60's.. We even laid claim to the big steel V roof-supports at the front of the concession stand! The one thing we most desired was the electronic scoreboard from Field One. Sadly, somebody had ruined it before we got there by using a blowtorch to cut out the electronic lights in its middle. I could never figure why (?)!) So, all these new baseball "treasures" were then stored in my parent's East Richfield garage until Dwaine could come back to MN to get them. (I'm sure our mom was thrilled by the new acquisitions!) Since Dwaine would return to MN with his family every winter for the Christmas holidays, he dragged a trailer back to MN for two consecutive years to haul his trove of "Richfield Baseball memorabilia" back to Cooperstown. He then quickly started restoring items, and then commenced building his Little League and Major League fields in the summer of '95. His fields are now considered some of the finest baseball diamonds in the Cooperstown area, even comparable to Doubleday Field! His fields are used by players of almost every age, including fathers teaching their toddlers and early elementary schoolers to throw, catch, or to hold/swing a bat. On the other end of the spectrum, the senior tournaments hosted at Dwaine's fields include players of all ages - from 18 to the oldest at 93. And they come from all over the world, including Canada, Europe, Russia, Japan, the Caribbean and Central America – to name a few. Our oldest player, George Goodall at 93 his final season, had played in the minor leagues with Satchel Page and Dizzy Dean. He could still turn a ground out at second base! Plus, he was a switch hitter at the plate! Incredible – and totally fun and engaging! Dwaine also hosted the only youth instructional baseball camp near Cooperstown for nearly twenty years, up until COVID in 2020. His head coaches for almost ten of those years were Hall of Famer Orlando Cepeda's two sons, Ali and Malcom, who'd both played in the SF Giants Minor League organization. Fantastic players, superb role models and great teachers for the kids! Since Dwaine had piggy-backed his instructional camp over Hall of Fame Induction Weekend, a few of the Hall of Famer's were known to stop by his camp to meet the kids and even sign autographs. That included the Giants Orlando Cepeda (of course), and Canadian citizen and Chicago Cub's pitching great, Fergie Jenkins. The stories those men shared about their baseball passions and careers in pros were truly inspirational for all! So, the legacy of East Richfield baseball now lives on near Cooperstown NY. To top all that off, Dwaine's wife Juli was ahead of her time and quickly laid claim to the domain name: cooperstownbaseball.com – much to the chagrin of the Cooperstown Hall of Fame, and Doubleday Field. Check it out, however, for some great looks at Dwaine's "Fields of Dreams";

historic Richfield Baseball now preserved near the National Baseball Hall of Fame!

(Footnote: Dwaine Sharratt sadly passed in Nov 2023, but his baseball legend and legacy lives on.)

# BUDDING AVIATORS

**KEVIN GILMORE**

*LAKE SHORE DRIVE*

I was 8 years old when our family rented a home for one year on Lake Shore Drive in Richfield in 1965. My dad's job had our family moving back and forth between Minneapolis and Detroit several times in the span of as many years. We never seemed to stay anywhere very long and when we'd move back it would always be to a different neighborhood and school district. It was never fun being the new kid in class but after a couple of weeks, it really didn't matter I suppose. There were four of us guys who used to hang out together: Mike Lynch, Steve Casperson, and Don Falenczykowski. Don's older brother Bob played in a band, The Delcounts, and they'd practice in his garage. The band stayed together for years and achieved local success with some of their music getting airplay. Between the wildlife refuge across the street, the alley behind our homes, and all the shops along Lyndale Ave and 66th street, we had plenty to keep us busy. Don's dad was a pilot for Northwest Orient (as it was known at the time, later to become Delta). One of us four had the idea to build an airplane of our own. I'm not talking about a model airplane but rather, one that we could sit in and fly around the neighborhood. We spent probably the better part of two days cobbling together our plane with whatever wood and spare parts we could find in our garages. Don's driveway would serve as our hangar. How I wish somebody had taken a photo of our work, but none exists that I'm aware of. With the project completed, we rolled our plane across Lake Shore Drive and positioned it atop a hill overlooking a marsh (that years later would become Woodlake Nature Center). Don was our pilot. He climbed in while the rest of us looked on in excited anticipation that our two days of effort were about to pay off in a very big way. I never once doubted our engineering abilities. Don was about to soar off out over the marsh and I suppose I imagined him circling back overhead while rocking his wings at us. His pretty sister was there to help us send him off. Don began his takeoff roll down the hill and to be honest, what happened next is all a blank to me. I'm not sure our plane even made it to the bottom of the hill. Our dreams of flying met with unforgiving failure as Don climbed out of the cockpit. And that was that. Within the hour we were no doubt off to other adventures, just maybe not so grandiose. Don did earn his wings and retired a few years ago from his career as a pilot for Southwest Airlines. I would go on to become an air traffic controller; now retired as well. I have no doubt that Don and I spoke many times over the radio frequency without ever knowing it, and in a way, completing the adventure we'd begun five decades earlier. Our little neighborhood on Lake Shore Drive across from Bridgeman's Ice Cream shop (now Pizza Luce) where our family lived for one year was the source of many fond memories of mine. How I would love to go back and relive some of them.

# SO MANY LITTLE MEMORIES

LARRY DAYTON

*72ND AND STEVENS AVE. SO.*

I grew up living next door to Larry Hermon. We did almost everything together, it seems through the Portland Elementary school days & a lot during Junior high. I was a year older, so we only had one year together at East Jr. High before I moved in with my dad in Bloomington. We were always on some kind of adventure though. Bike rides everywhere including the Hub, Southdale, Portland school, Como Zoo, Lake Harriet, Richfield Little League baseball which I never would have had the courage to get involved in had it not been for Larry Hermon's dad encouraging me to do so & working with us in the front yards playing catch & hitting baseballs. Richfield Little League had an amazing to me location on the east of cedar avenue on 66th St., near the airport with what seemed like many ball fields for different leagues there. A great concession stand with the best popcorn & grape bubble gum. Loved it. My first year in Juniors we won the championship. Cub Scouts was great. Bobbie Vickerman was our Den mother. Mike Fossen, Larry Hermon, Steve Hanson, Terry Bernier, Bill Vickerman, Hank Fisher to name a few were in there. I won the Pinewood Derby one year which was held at the gym in Portland. The cars were supposed to be built primarily by us however my dad got involved as I visited him once a week on Sundays. He ended up building most of the car due to the separation living in different homes although I was there for the shaping of the car at his buddy's house who had a wood working shop. There was a weight limit for the cars. His friend suggested adding weight which we did carving out a hole in the car bottom filling the hole with lead then smoothing it over with wood putty prior to painting it. Anyway, it kicked booty on that pinewood derby track & was still within the overall weight limits. We also added graphite to the axles/wheels as oiling was not allowed. Everyone (mostly Dad's) wanted to know why it was so fast taking home the trophy. My dad loved to brag so he spilled the beans on what we did. Needless to say, the next year the competition got smart & came prepared adding weight to their Trucks (they had everyone do trucks that year out of the same block of wood.) We got beat badly. LOL, It was fun just the same. I can't remember who won the overall that next year. I have lots of memories of playing outside in the neighborhood with countless kids who grew up there and summers at the Richfield Pool. Another thing that comes to mind was a walking field trip we did in fourth grade I think at Portland elementary school. Around 1965 perhaps. The entire class & other classes walked down to the house of Richfield resident & sculpture artist Donald Danielson (I looked it up. lol.) as he lived just several blocks from the school. He was commissioned to build the 25 Ft two headed fire breathing dragon for Howard Wong's Restaurant located in Bloomington off 494. I was in awe of the whole thing seeing this beautiful piece he had created & welded together in his garage. He gave us a little talk on the process answering questions from all the kids. It was placed in front of the restaurant in 1966 I think & breathed real fire from natural gas. Everyone likely remembers that as it could be seen well from 494 passing by. I read somewhere that it still exists as a college mascot in northern Minnesota. The memories of growing up in Richfield are awesome and will always be with me as they are with many.

# THE IVERSON FARMHOUSE

**LESLIE JULIEN MAYCROFT**

*64TH AND 17TH AVE. SO.*

While growing up, one hears passing half-stories, references to a history rather assumed that you know of. But you do not. You do not know how it all adheres, or its significance. So, it was with the story of the East Richfield home in which I grew up. I would not have known or integrated the history of my hilltop, 3-bedroom ranch on 64th and 17th Ave. if not for a former neighbor, who with intent came to my mother's funeral luncheon at Richfield's Mt. Calvary Lutheran Church. Somehow the deep feelings I'd always had for that earth-place made more sense as she spoke. Betty wanted me to know the history of that property that my mother had never told me. I suppose it was the "in with the new, out with the old" mentality that made the telling unvalued. But all that I'd experienced of living on that land HAD been unconsciously internalized somehow. Our 1954 house was built on the peak of a hill. In our back yard was a large, flat concrete circle, and in a rare moment, my mother told me that it had been the base of a silo. And when the large tree in our back yard was felled, the earth produced bones, especially a full horse jaw, with both upper and lower jaw teeth intact. So. Where did I grow up?? Betty told me. When Betty and her husband moved into their newly built house on 64th and 16th, the abandoned farmhouse of the Iverson farm still stood. Betty watched Richfield transition from farmland to suburbia. She impressed upon me that our house stood on the exact land of the Iverson's house. One day, around 1950, the neighborhood kids, including the daughter of Mt. Calvary Lutheran's pastor, Rev. Gaertner, explored and became dangerously trapped in the basement of the deteriorating, abandoned farmhouse. The parents panicked. Finally, police and firemen pulled them out. So, I grew up on the Iverson homestead. This meant so much to me to know. Now I can picture its history and understand the deep feelings I had for its place.

# MY EXPERIENCES WITH JAKE MCCOY

**STEVE SELCHOW**

*76TH AND 17TH AVE. SO.*

Jake and I first met at East Junior High. He was my Physical Education teacher and hockey coach. My first interactions with Jake were intense yet entertaining. When I moved on to High School, he coincidentally transferred that same year. Jake was playing the same roles he played at East Junior High. For those that took his Physical Education classes, you may remember the whiffle ball bat on your bare butt (that wouldn't happen today) if you misbehaved, however, it was effective. Playing hockey for him was an honor. He played on the 1964 Olympic hockey team in Innsbruck, Austria and was an All American at the University of Minnesota. He had many sayings such as Close only counts in horseshoes, Hand grenades and dancing, Katie bar the door and many others. During one summer break he asked to interview me for a Master's program he was enrolled in. We met at Augsburg Park and sat at a picnic table where he asked me questions. The questions were about life in general as well as my opinions of events of that time. It was nice getting to see a more personal side of Jake. Fast forward many years and we crossed paths at the Richfield Ice Arena. He was coaching in one rink, and I was playing on the other. I was able to get his number after the game. I called him up to see if we could get together. We met at Adrian's on 46th and Chicago which, unfortunately, is no longer there. My reason for wanting to get together was to tell him what a positive influence he had on my life and that he was a mentor to me. It was a great discussion and I'll always remember it. Sadly, Jake died less than one year after we last met. In my opinion the world lost a great man. I encourage everyone to reconnect with long lost family and friends. You will never regret it.

# MUSIC AND SIXTEEN CANDLES

**MOLLY MCGINNIS**

*69TH AND FIFTH AVE. SO.*

Growing up in Richfield as many baby boomers can relate, you reminisce and enjoy and reflect on the memories of your childhood, community, and friends. The neighborhood kids would gather for games like kick-the-can. Some summer nights the kids enjoyed eating rhubarb from the neighbor's garden too. Winter months were spent ice skating with friends at Memorial Park. The fresh snow and coolness of the air were refreshing as you skated around the rink. Summers were always a splash at the Richfield pool. I always enjoyed having a season membership. It was the summer hangout for so many. One of my favorites was celebrating my 16th birthday in the summer of 1972. A friend of mine Terry Ahlstrom, who I have known since our elementary school days, had formed a band and the opportunity to play live music was ideal. The perfect summer event for a 16th birthday party. And of course, my mom approved. The news of Terry's band playing spread throughout Richfield. This was going to be a grand event and great publicity for the band. The band members were Terry Ahlstrom (lead singer), John Savageau (bass), Tony Shields (drums), Jim Gardner (guitar) and Dwaine Sharratt. The band set up their equipment in my garage. Everything was set and the band was ready to play some great songs. The set of songs played during the evening was from the 50's, 60's and 70's. Many friends, classmates and relatives were there. Even my 84-year-old grandmother was there! There were over 100 people in attendance. It certainly was a fantastic evening as the music played throughout the neighborhood. As the band played on, we were certainly aware of the noise ordinance time cutoff at 10:00pm. Noting my mom had notified all the neighbors on our block prior to the birthday celebration event that there was going to be a live band. Close to the 10:00pm cutoff time a Richfield police officer arrives to remind us of the city's noise ordinance cutoff time. It truly was the best 16th birthday celebration a girl could ever ask for. To this day, each year on my birthday my dear friend Terry sends me a message saying the band is ready to play. Cherished and fond memories are everlasting.

# THE SKOGSTAD'S

**BERNADETTE SKOGSTAD AMMONS**

*71ST AND STEVENS AVE. SO.*

George and Bea Skogstad moved to 7145 Stevens in 1950 after living Northeast after Dad's Naval tour during WWII. At the time they had young twin girls and a young son, they lived and loved Richfield in that house until they died but not before adding another set of two girls, another boy and another girl, graduating seven from RHS over 20 years. We all attended Assumption where Dad coached baseball from 1960-1976, including both brothers, Jim, and John. Through the years his team's approximate win/loss record was conservatively 120-18. Every Spring I miss the sound of bats rolling in the back of the station wagon and his trusted assistant, Larry Matthews always at his side. Most, if not all of us still love baseball. Both of my boys played through college with the youngest finishing this Spring. Richfield is a place warm to our hearts still today!

# FATHER AND SON LIFE LESSONS

**MIKE WEBB**

*73RD AND PARK AVE. SO.*

As a teenager I had newspaper routes in Richfield during the top two snow years in state history. It was during the early 80's when you had to hand deliver papers to the front door (not the street boxes like these days in the burbs). It explains why my father taught me how to drive the 1978 Pontiac Bonneville at age 14. Some of those Sunday mornings you couldn't push the yellow 2-wheel paper cart through the deep snow down the street. But if you packed a car trunk full of Sunday newspapers your rear wheels on the car could get traction and it worked great. Not that dad didn't want to get up at 4am to drive and assist me to deliver papers, he was teaching me valuable life lessons in trusting your children with heavy equipment at a young age. Fortunately, nothing bad ever happened and when I went to take my driver's test 2 years later and got 100%, that was the proof… Going to Mr. Donut on 66th and Penn after my routes were done and ordering 6 donuts was my reward!

# HERE COME THE CHILDREN OF HOPE

**PATTY BOUCHIER NEHRING WILCOX**

*76TH AND BLOOMINGTON AVE. SO.*

I think that was the name of our first album. We ended up making two albums that we would sell at our concerts all over Minnesota, Wisconsin, and Iowa. We even went as far as Illinois and Nebraska occasionally on our weekend trips. And once a year we would go on a 10-day tour to Colorado, singing in small towns along the way. Singing at the YMCA of the Rockies was my favorite venue of all! A handful of us sang at the funeral of a six-year-old from Hope because we were his favorite singing group. That was a tough one. As far as I know, we were the only Christian rock group like ours. We were even invited to sing in Japan. We had some very talented members and leaders - some incredible voices and musicians including the state drum champ, and some that went on to lead churches of their own. We went to Iowa the most. Ron Davis was our Youth Pastor at Hope Presbyterian Church. Ron was born and raised in Iowa. He was also a youth pastor there before coming to Richfield. Because of Ron's love of Iowa, I think we all had a special place in our hearts for our Iowa trips. Ron has now written several amazing books that I highly recommend! We would sing at churches around the Twin Cities three weekends a month. Then once a month we would pack up the bus at the church on a Saturday morning and hit the road. Those long bus rides were a blast! We'd roll into Mt. Ayr or Clarinda Iowa, and head to our host church. We'd unload the bus and get the drums and guitars all set up in the sanctuary, then walk into town and explore. Those small towns probably didn't know what hit them when 20 or 30 high energy high schoolers showed up. The churches always had a potluck dinner for us before our concert. At the potluck we would be assigned to our host families for the weekend. Yep, that's right – we'd be in a town hundreds of miles from home and go home with strangers! This was the '70s so there were no cell phones or email. Our folks had no idea where we were & no way to get ahold of us. Crazy to think about doing that these days, huh?!I broke my foot when we were in Marshall, Minnesota so I had a chance to be in the audience that weekend. What fun - we were really good!! Coincidentally, the doctor who set and cast my foot was the family I had been assigned to that weekend. We'd start the concert with just the piano playing. Then one by one the drummer, upright bassist, and guitarists would walk in and start playing. Finally, the singers would come in as we started the concert with Oh Happy Day. We'd end the concert with Pass it On and pass lighted candles from us to our audience. The churches were always full for our evening concerts and when we led the services the next morning. We'd sing and Ron would preach. Then there would be another potluck in the fellowship hall before we packed up the soundboard, trumpet, flute, etc. and headed back to Richfield. When I listen to our albums now, I realize what talented members we had. We had some top-notch musicians and spiritual leaders. In high school it sometimes felt like I was giving up a lot of parties and other fun weekend activities. But over the years I've realized how fortunate I was to have been part of this amazing group. The fun, fellowship, travel and so much more added to my life more than I knew at the time and I was incredibly blessed to have been part of The Children of Hope!

# MESSAGES

**PAUL OBERG**

*71ST AND COLUMBUS AVE. SO.*

A distinct memory involves me when I was in my mid-teens (14-16 years old and 1960-62) in Richfield. My mother was the House of Prayer Church office secretary at the time, and I was in the church sponsored Boy Scout Troop working on a Merit Badge which involved service to the church. This required doing 100 hours of various duties ranging from shoveling snow, setting up rooms for Sunday school, etc. One of my weekly duties was to fold all the bulletins for the Sunday morning services. This was usually done Saturday mornings in the church kitchen. One Saturday, I thought it would be great fun to prepare multiple ice cube trays using dish washing liquid, the idea being it would be a great surprise to my mother and the other church staff when they were back to work Monday. I proceeded to replace all the trays with a wonderful soapy mixture which would surely get her attention on her first break. How was I to know there was going to be a wedding reception there that very same Saturday night? How was I to know that both my parents were invited to the wedding? How was I to know that the very ice I prepared was to be used in the punch that was to be served to all the reception guests? How was I to know that there was a snitch somewhere in my Boy Scout troop? I did not fully realize what had happened until Sunday morning after I had my breakfast. Upon taking the first gulp of my orange juice, it seemed that the glass must have never been rinsed. I said nothing and soon grabbed a piece of toast all covered with grape jelly. Wow! My tongue was aflame with a tremendous burning sensation, and I thought there may even have been bubbles exiting my mouth. I still said nothing but began to think it was all a very strange coincidence given what I had planned for my mother's return to work. The total realization came when I stuffed in a mouthful of scrambled eggs. My gosh, how could anything that looked so good taste so unbelievably awful? The same proved to be true of the bubbly bacon.... I still said nothing and to the day that we buried my mother, no word of what had transpired at the wedding reception that Saturday night was ever mentioned between us. There absolutely was no need to do so. We both knew. Message sent. Message received!

# RICHFIELD – OUR FAMILY ADVENTURE

**JOHN HAMILTON**

*72ND AND HARRIET AVE. SO.*

In 1958 Mom Dad, my sister Anne and I moved from Philadelphia to Richfield. Dad was transferred to Richfield when he worked for Timex Watches. Dad bought the house before we arrived. What appealed to my dad was the size of the backyard, Twice the size of the traditional backyard in Richfield. The basement also had a Rec Room. Both were to have extensive use. Baseball and football games in the backyard were commonplace. In the basement we had marathon pool games. We lived within walking distance of Central Grade School and Richfield High School, growing up with an easy walk to watch high School football and baseball games. Mom and dad wasted no time getting involved in their new community. Mom joined a bowling league; both were involved in the PTA. Dad became president of the West Jr. High PTA. Dad was a Rotarian and eventually president. Church played a major role in the family. We attended Richfield Methodist. Both Anne and I were confirmed there and participated in the annual Living Pictures during Lent. Dads' involvement in the city and schools would eventually lead him into the political arena. He won election to the School Board. I must state that during Dad's tenure on the board he served with some of the most dynamic civic leaders Richfield has ever seen. During this time my dad started to teach me rules of politics. Because dad was on the board, I was taught that you will be judged by who you associate with, character matters, and don't do anything to cause harm to the family. I kept these guidelines in tack with my own ventures into the arena. Dad believed in giving back to the community. Every holiday season, my good friend Scott Meyer, his dad, and I spent many cold nights and weekends selling Christmas Trees at the YMCA lot. Proceeds would go to assist disadvantaged kids go to camp. This was an important lesson that they wanted Scott and I to know. In January Scott and I were sent outside to go door to door selling boxes of candy so we could earn our way to camp. The lesson went for the importance of charity to the value of a work ethic. Dad believed the colder the better. Who will turn down a kid selling candy in the bitter cold. After a long stint on the school board Dad ran for mayor of Richfield and won. Participated in the 4th of July Parade. He often had his Granddaughter Erica in the car with him. My sister Anne and her Husband Russ often drove the car. Following being Mayor Dad announced the parade. Dad enjoyed being mayor and continued to visit schools, played Santa, and became very active in the Richfield Optimist Club. What dad couldn't account for was the great rain of 1987. Where a massive storm settled in over Richfield and Bloomington. 10 inches of rain in a few hours. The record still stands. The system wasn't built to handle such a deluge.

Despite the nay sayers he took every call. And was in constant contact with city staff. There is a political saying. Don't let a good crisis go to waste. His opposition, along with an unethical media, took advantage of an unfortunate situation and he lost reelection. Because of Dad's sense of a greater good, He didn't take legal action against the players despite being encouraged to do so. Dad continued to be a resource to the city and those seeking public office. Mom in her own right did not sit silently on the sidelines. She worked diligently with the Richfield Chamber of Commerce and Women's Club. And a strong influence with dad. All good things must come to an end and so it was with dad. In 2011 dad was diagnosed with terminal cancer. But he wasn't done providing life lessons. One night at dinner, his voice had become weak and his head was down. Suddenly he popped his head up, Pointed his finger and with that booming John Hamilton voice announced, "It's all Mental." During his service Anne spoke of his love of the ocean. I spoke of Dad's "isms." To note of few. * If you don't get involved, you don't have the right to complain. * It's not enough to do the best you can for yourself, you must do the best you can for your community. * Never compromise on your principles… Mom, who always remained strong and mom, passed away in 2021 with quiet dignity. Names like Hamilton, Karnas, Lindgren, Luttinger, Kirchner, Gunderson, Law, Sandahl, and Ludeman to name a few. These were individuals who had the leadership, strength and vision for a greater Richfield.

# BRRR, SWIMMING LESSONS.

**PHIL BATTAGLIA**
*APPLE LANE*

The year was 1967. Most Moms, the Apple Lane Gang's included, forced us to take swimming lessons. I remember many early June mornings, temperatures in the 50's, walking to the pool not so enthusiastic about having to jump in the water. That was, until... we met Kathy. Kathy was a lifeguard, and let's just say she filled out her swimsuit nicely. Of course, being stupid 10-year-olds, we would laugh and giggle about how cute she was. We even went to her house once and had popcorn, so she must have felt the same about us, right? Anyway, over the years, I had forgotten all about her, until 1993. 1993 is the year The Sandlot was released, and Wendy Peffercorn brought back the wonderful memory of Kathy. We were The Boys of Summer. One of the best scenes ever in a movie was when Squints faked drowning to steal a kiss from Wendy Peffercorn. If only I had been as smart as Squints.

# THE 1970 FOOD FIGHT

**JIM MILLER**

*75TH AND 2ND AVE. SO.*

It was awesome. It was planned for a week. White tee shirts were the dress for the day. Everyone knew about it. Our class was 900 plus. Not to mention the other two classes.Mr. Bartosh called for an emergency talk in the auditorium with the senior class. He told us how immature we would be if we went through with it. My good friend SB (my good friends know who I'm talking about) had a knack of yelling without moving his lips and yelled Bartosh sucks!!!. The whole place broke out laughing. Mr.Bartosh walked away... Fast forward to a packed lunchroom. People skipped classes to go. There were 2 tables of instigators, ours, and the table next to ours. It was quiet at first. The lunch that day was Chow Mein. All it took was one noodle to be tossed and all mayhem broke out... food, plates, tables upside down, BIG mess. Janitors refused to clean it up. Can't blame them. Only a few kids got kicked out of school. Made front page of Richfield news. Ahh the good old days. I had a blast in High school. Respectfully Jim Miller class of 1970.

# THIS WILL NOT HAPPEN AGAIN!

**ANNE WASICK HOLZ**

*72ND AND LYNDALE AVE. SO.*

A food fight in the high school cafeteria happened during the winter of 1964/1965. As I remember it was on a Friday because cheese sandwiches, carrot sticks, and milk cartons were flying through the air. Thankfully, I was eating at the far end of the cafeteria.... The next morning an announcement came over the PA system, it was stated "THIS WILL NOT HAPPEN AGAIN! Sure, enough on the last day for hot lunches that year, guess what happened?... I guess the announcement that came over the PA system was a challenge!

# A WALK DOWN FREMONT AVENUE

**CLARK HUGHES**

*75TH AND FREMONT AVE. SO.*

I'm taking a walk through my old neighborhood in Richfield...Where Fremont Avenue ended at 76th street was Berea Lutheran Church and our sliding hill in winter, the incline of the 76th Street overpass at 35W. All the local kids would gather at that hill and race downhill, spilling over before we'd hit the frontage road at the bottom. It was a great place, starting with a gentle incline at one end for the little kids and a terrifying, steep rundown next to the bridge and freeway fence. Sliding hill legend had it that one of my friends ran his sled under a truck rolling down that frontage road. On the other side of 76th Street was an old motel at the end of Fremont, surrounded by huge oak streets, and a lot down by the freeway where people would dump stumps and old brick and concrete. That's where I think Best Buy built their HQ eventually? Further north on Fremont were the Mormons who'd knock on our front door every year to do their church work, the home where a family from Turkey lived for a while, the Braniff pilot, our best friends the Groth kids, and then our home, one door away from the corner of 75th Street. It was a blue-collar neighborhood where you would fix your own car if it broke. We'd climb the giant blue spruce tree high above rooftops to shoot apples from my backyard using slingshots we made from old hockey sticks and bicycle inner tubes. Every vehicle going down that street was a target for our apples and snowballs! I remember once when a biker stopped and chased us kids when one of us shot an apple through his wheel spokes. What an explosion of juicy apple bits! What a grand chase! We didn't get caught because this was our neighborhood, and kids were in charge of every fence, shortcut, shed and unlocked garage. Our street smelled like hot tar in the summer, and its pavement smooshed under our bare feet. In fact, the periodic rebuilding of our street was a major event back then. Tractors would line up at one end and the word would go out among the kids, the street builders are back! They'd tear up, grind down, plow, spray liquid tar and mix up the mess and then at the end of a hot day, pack it down with steam rollers. Good times. At 75th and Fremont was the center of our kids' universe – Fremont Park, a triangle slice of land that at that time had a road on each of the three sides. There were the giant swing sets, the tall metal slide, the teeter totters and probably best of all, the game box and city rec. programs in the summer. We'd play pickup games of softball there, touch football, wrestle, fight, and line up for the buses to Central Elementary and to swim lessons at the community pool. I learned to skate by the headlights of my dad's car at the rink they used to flood there. Remember those bikers we'd peg with apples? They were headed down to 75th street, then down Girard toward 74th street, where a block from our house a rock and blues band would practice in the Wiegand's garage. They'd peg rocks at us kids as we sneaked down the street, through yards and under fences to spy on them as they practiced (thus the apple bombing up on Fremont). The Wiegand brothers and the other musicians would later become the band Crow, which cut an album and gained some fame with their song "Evil Woman". A couple blocks north was Wood Lake, then a marsh, after the 35W construction supposedly punctured the clay seal that held water in what used to be a place where boats and water skiers played. We'd go down there often to explore the sand trails on the edge, the thickets and to probe how far our little courage would allow us to go into the huge storm sewers that emptied into the marsh. This was before they put up a high fence, an offense to our neighborhood kids, and started to build a nature center. A lot of the houses lining Wood Lake on our end had garages or former boathouses, I suppose, down the hill near the former lakeshore. Once, a buddy and I were walking down Oak Grove when he said, "want to see the tunnel to Wood Lake?" He had a paper route on Oak Grove and said the owner of a big white house showed him the tunnel. So just after sunset one winter, we knocked on the door and asked to explore the tunnel. The old couple graciously let us in, showed us the door, and we marched down the concrete incline of that lighted tunnel, probably 100 feet or more down to a garage at Wood Lake. So cool! And ya, we actually would barge uninvited into the houses of people we knew and knock on the doors of those we didn't to ask a question or invite them to pay us a quarter to shovel their driveway. Finally, there was the neighborhood legend of the night the UFOs landed on 35W by the walking bridge at the Southwest end of Wood Lake. Apparently, a driver late one night claimed he stopped for a small spacecraft that landed on the freeway, and little aliens shaped like beer cans walking on three legs. Ya, beer can aliens. I spent way too much time later in life looking for the bar that driver was probably coming from.

# THE LUCKIEST GIRL ON FIFTH AVENUE

**SANDY AHLSTROM MAHN**

*75TH AND 5TH AVE. SO.*

My days in Richfield began in the middle of second grade at Elliott. On that first day, Jan Pulk shared her desk with me. We are still good friends. In third grade, at Portland Elementary, my teacher was Mrs. Arnold. I liked her, she reminded me of my mother. In Mrs. Dolmar's fourth grade class, my Dad came to tell me I had a baby brother and that I could name him. Terry Borman sat behind me and he was nice. I named my brother Terry. Mrs. Rye was my fifth-grade teacher. She wore clothes from the Southwest, colorful skirts that twirled when she walked and beautiful silver, Native American jewelry. I remember one day, Tom Day called her "Toots", I can't remember what happened, but she gave him quite a frown. I don't know if square dancing was in fourth or fifth grade, but Dick Hagen was my partner, and I liked him. In sixth grade I remember thinking Mrs. Hardwood was very large. We studied Minnesota History. I wondered what East Junior High would be like. East Junior High was fun, lockers and locks, many teachers, more new friends, slam books, learning how to outline, thinking Monica Schulz and Ted Schnorr were a really cute couple. Eighth grade. I can't remember if it was seventh or eighth grade that Bill Findlay sat right next to me in Miss Engedahl's English class. Whatever year it was, he was a nice guy and made the class fun. I had a science teacher with red hair and a green sport coat that he wore a lot, I cannot remember his name. Ninth grade meant we were the big shots. The day always started walking the halls with friends - Joyce Erickson, Sandy Munyon, Jan Pulk to name a few. There were Sock Hops, me hoping I'd learn to do the stroll and not fall on my face. Talking to Mary Jane Ward in the lunchroom about trying out for cheerleading next year. She had heard the West Side girls were good, and they were. I wondered what Richfield High School would be like. The only sadness I remember at RHS was on November 22, 1963. I was sitting in Mr. Curry's Speech class. A voice came over the loud speaker, President Kennedy had been shot. I shared that with all the others in the class that day. My years at RHS were just the best. I was so lucky to meet more good friends, lucky to be able to cheer for Richfield for two years and to do it with Nancy Andreotti and Meg Skoglund. The '63 football team was State Football champs, Bill Kendall and Jim Hanson, two really nice guys, made Homecoming '64 special. There was Tinsel Twirl, classes with friends, and just passing in the halls and seeing everybody was fun. The Class of '65 graduated on a beautiful June night. I remember wondering on that bus ride back from the Senior party, "what am I going to do with the rest of my life?"...At our Sophomore party, before the dance started, there was a program. Ten or so Sophomore guys were dancing across the stage in pink tutus, pretty funny! One of them asked me to dance later that night. We're still dancing, just slower.

# THE HALL PASS

**GREGG WALKER**

*62ND AND VINCENT AVE. SO.*

During my senior year I was Student Body/Student Council Treasurer. As a student body officer, one of my class periods was in the Student Council Office, along with the other Student Council officers. Some days we had things to do; other days we could use the time as a study period or just goof around. When I learned that some of my friends were helping in the Language Lab at the same time, I wanted to go there and hang out with them. This was not easy, though. A Hall Pass was required to leave a classroom during the school day. I solved that problem by grabbing a pile of hall passes from a teacher's desk and forging the Student Council Faculty Advisor's name. One day, while heading from the Student Council Office to the Language lab, a teacher stopped me. He asked me for my hall pass. I showed it to him, complete with the forged signature of Mr. Julian Ako, the Student Council Faculty Advisor. Suspicious, the teacher took me to Mr. Ako's classroom where he was teaching at the time. When Mr. Ako came to the classroom door, the teacher told him that I had been caught with this hall pass and had claimed that Mr. Ako signed it. When the teacher asked Mr. Ako if that was his signature on the pass, Mr. Ako replied – "that is the way I write my name." He rescued me from trouble. Later that week Mr. Ako took me aside and asked for an explanation. After learning that I used the pass to get to my friends in the language lab, he gave me a set of blank passes with his signature and told me to "use them wisely." I have been a teacher (high school and college) for fifty years and have practiced what I learned from Mr. Ako that day. Students need support and forgiveness, even when they do crazy things. I learned that from my cross-country coach – Paul Stambaugh – as well.

# AUGSBURG PARK ANNUAL HOCKEY GAME

DENNIS J. DIETZLER AND MIKE FOSSEN

For children growing up in Richfield in the 1960's and 1970's, one of the favorite winter pastimes was spending school day evenings, and all weekend, as well as winter vacation days and evenings, at the local skating rink for good old-fashioned games of outdoor hockey. One such rink was Augsburg Park located at 72nd and Nicollet. The boys (and some girls) would mostly play get-up games of hockey, but on Friday night the entire crowd would play the game of Pom-Pom Pull-Away. At times, more than 50 players could be seen at these Friday night games. As one can imagine, lifelong friendships were developed over the years by these activities. These friendships produced another long-lasting activity called the 'Augsburg Annual' which was created by Mike Fossen in 1999. Throughout the years Mike continued to organize the event, with Dennis Dietzler being instrumental in coordinating each year. It was to become a multigenerational tradition for many Richfield friends and families. Mike and three of- his siblings, along with their extended families, continued to participate over the next 20 years. The teams consisted of players from the 1960's, 70's, 80's and 90's. These games became so well-known that in 2016, the Richfield Sun Current heard about the event and sent a reporter to cover it, writing an article entitled 'Hockey Still Has Roots in Richfield' as a front page spread for the Sports section. The game was played fairly, with teams being chosen by players placing their sticks at center ice, then someone would split the sticks in half to make the two teams. The game was set up as a tournament with 3 games being played and the winner must win two of the three. It was always played for fun, but like most sports the players were competitive. Eventually a fun rivalry developed when Dennis Dietzler organized his own team out of the group. This led to some good-natured ribbing i.e., Dietzler Outlaws VS Fossen Fossils, or Fearless Fossen's VS Dietzler Degenerates. The ultimate prize of the Augsburg Annual was the Gordo Award. Named after Gordon Paulson, the longtime warming house attendant at Augsburg Park, the award was given annually, at the end of the game, by the previous recipient to the player that he/she felt most deserving. For example, Doug Wilton received the award for hitting his head on the ice, causing blood marks, a sign of a true hockey player. Another year, after receiving the award, the trophy traveled the world, being carried by Jon Schlegel in the cockpit of his international flights. There has been, and to date still is, much controversy over which team won the overall cumulative record. The controversy was always hashed over at the American Legion, where everyone met for some good camaraderie and libation after the games. Sad to say, due to old age, in 2021 the last game was played. As usual though, the stories of our athleticism continue to get better with age.

# FANTASTIC MUSIC AT THE RICHFIELD AMERICAN LEGION

**STEVE DEVICH**
*FORMER RICHFIELD CITY MGR.*

In the decade that proceeded the COVID 19 Pandemic, Thursday nights at the Richfield American Legion offered one of the finest music venues ever presented in the Twin Cities! It was on those special Thursday nights that the finest version of the Delcounts entertained the typically packed house with a song list of the best of Classical Rock for the ages. Of course, those evenings included the Delcounts performing their 1960's hits, 'Let the Good Times Roll" and "What is The Reason". Charles Schoen, the founder and original member of the Delcounts was surrounded by guitarist Bill Davis, bassist Bobby Jones, keyboardist and vocalist James "Owl" Walsh, and drummer Jerry Archambault and occasionally "Chico" Perez on percussion. The band members, with the exception of Charles Schoen, were also current members of the legendary Twin Cities rock group "Gypsy". The musical talent assembled in the Richfield Legion on those Thursday nights was nothing short of spectacular. The music, which seemed to transcend time and space, could bring you back for a minute or so to your fondest moments at the high school prom. Some Thursday night regulars went there to hear the great R & B singles and rock anthems of the 60's, 70's and 80's performed live. Other folks went to have the opportunity to dance with friends in an environment that brought back treasured memories of the Marigold and Prom Ballrooms or the dance floor of Mr. Lucky's. A few, like myself, were able to recall memories of an earlier time playing many of those same songs on stage in a Battle of the Bands or Home Coming Dance. No matter why anyone frequented the Legion on those wonderful Thursday nights, one thing was for certain. Everyone had a great time and left at the end of the night anticipating the following Thursday night and the Richfield American Legion, where it could happen all over once again!

# OH, MY LOLLAPALOOZA!

**SHELLEY CLARK PRESLEY**

*74TH AND 10TH AVE. SO.*

Such great memories of a group of us after Friday Night football games walking over to Bridgeman's. Who didn't love Bridgeman's? Everyone ordering their burgers and fries or tackling that famous Lollapalooza. I do remember sharing with friends. After all the fun calling one of our parents from a pay phone to come and pick us up. It was so much easier when one of us could drive, and who didn't love Broadway pizza? It seemed we went there after hockey games. And they still have the same great pizza 40 some years later. Whenever I pay a visit to Richfield from Kansas City Broadway is a must stop. I now have my daughter, son in-law and granddaughter stopping there when in Richfield. I had a great childhood in Richfield. My parents purchased their home there because of the AAA rated schools. I am still in contact with some of my neighborhood kids. One being a very close friend over 50 years! Wonderful memories for sure!

# TRESTMAN'S MUSIC STORE MEMORIES

**LOREN STILES**

*75TH AND SHERIDAN AVE. SO.*

It was 1968, and I was a very young and enthusiastic kid looking for my first drum, and the closest music store was Trestman's. I believe my father knew the owner fairly well having done plumbing work for him periodically. I was just getting involved in school band and had never owned any type of percussion instruments; all I had were telephone books to beat on, and that seemed to aggravate my dad since he often needed to look up customers names and addresses from them only to find pages missing or beat to shreds. So, the day finally came when my dad drove me to Trestman's to purchase my first drum and later a cymbal. It was truly a kid in the candy store experience for me; there were so many beautiful shiny instruments to look at. I found a wonderful Ludwig snare drum and accessories to get me started. Drum lessons followed shortly after this. It wasn't long, and I became bored with one lonely snare drum; I needed more. It was back to Trestman's again for a small Ludwig drum kit; I was really off to the races now. Eventually, I found that I needed a ride cymbal, as I was taking an interest in Jazz; it seemed any drummer worth his salt had a ride cymbal. Time to go back to Trestman's. This time I was met by a short balding man with the biggest toothy smile you have ever seen; it was the legendary percussionist, Elliot Fine. Elliot was principal percussionist for the Minnesota Orchestra and well-known jazz drummer, educator. I told

Elliot I needed a good ride cymbal to go with my drums kit; he smiled and walked away; he came back a short time later with a beautiful 18" Paiste ride cymbal with rivets covering the whole circumference of the cymbal. Elliot held the cymbal in one hand and struck the cymbal with a drumstick using the other hand. He said, "You like?" Again, he had the biggest friendliest smile. I said yes, and my dad paid him for the purchase, and then we were off. So, Trestman's was where it all started for me, and I am sure many other young aspiring musicians have similar stories of a wonderful music store with amazing staff as well. Oh, and I still own the 1968 Ludwig Snare drum; the other instruments are long gone to new homes and hopefully still being loved.

# MOON OVER THE GYM

**TODD PETERSON**

*74TH AND GIRARD AVE. SO.*

I played varsity basketball at RHS when I was a senior. More accurately I was on the team but did not play much. Like the tradition established a few years earlier by Corky Kuklinski I was what was known as a buffalo, a bench warmer. This story is about what happened one cold winter night at the Spartan Gymnasium. Since it was 46 years ago, I don't recall who we were playing or the outcome but the facts as I lay them out are unfortunately 100% true. That winter night there was a problem with the heat in the gym. Rather than call the game it was decided us buffalos would wear our warm-up pants while sitting on the bench. As fans of that era can recall, our warm-ups had a vertical stripe pattern to provide the illusion we were taller than we were. A definite psychological advantage over our opponents. Although they were not stylish, they were warm. As usual we went down to the locker room for the pregame pep talk and then came back up to the gym to the strains of the school fight song. After the pre tip huddle I took my accustomed spot at the end of the bench wearing those striped warm-up pants. The team was playing well and from my spot I could watch the game while at the same time scanning the crowd and watching the unattainable Richfield cheerleaders. Suddenly Coach Starner yelled my name. "Petersen you are going in". Now for a buffalo I had never heard my name called for first half action. If I got in at all it was a mop up roll either when we were far ahead or far behind. Imagine my surprise because a buffalo never sees first half action. I must have been in a daze because I did not move very fast after my name was called so he yelled it again. I sprung to action so I would get in before half time. I threw off my warmup jacket and then pulled off my warmup pants and this is where the problems started. You see I never tied the drawstring on my shorts because the elastic waist band kept things up. In my haste to get my warmup pants off I also pulled down my shorts. I quickly realized what was happening and pulled my shorts and pants up again hoping no one had noticed my full moon. In the meantime, the coach yelled my name again but this time louder because I was still not up to his spot on the bench. I became more flustered as I saw my chance at first half action slipping away, I pulled down my warmups again and had the very same result. Both pieces of my uniform came down again in unison. What seemed like an eternity only took about 20 seconds to transpire but I was mortified. Finally, I reported to the coach with my pants off and shorts up he never knew the difficulties I had encountered getting to him. Of course, the horn sounded for halftime, and I never saw first half action. I watched the rest of the game from my spot on the end of the bench. I replayed what happened over and over in my mind. I was worried about who had seen my full moon at a home game. Fortunately, no students or cheerleaders seemed to notice so I was in the clear. Later I learned my parents and my teammates' parents who were sitting behind the bench had seen it all. My mom even threw her hands over her eyes in embarrassment. My friend's parents shared the story widely and it was told to every woman who I dated by his older sister who was not even there. Quite an incident to live down. Over the past 45 years I have attended 8 class reunions and there has been no mention of this mooning. I believe the statute of limitations has passed. I feel very fortunate to have grown up in Richfield as many of my era would agree. My experience in Richfield and RHS helped make me the man I became. But in retrospect, I know the most important life lesson I learned growing up there was: ALWAYS TIE YOUR DRAWSTRING!

# THREE QUICK GRADE SCHOOL MEMORIES

**ANITA AGERLIE GUILLOTEL**

*67TH AND HARRIET AVE, SO.*

As a kindergartner at Central Elementary I took the bus from 72nd and Lyndale. We lived in a double bungalow there. One spring morning I walked in and saw kids coming out of the lunchroom holding their upper arms - shot day. I turned around and walked out and back home. I sat on my front steps until my mom got home from grocery shopping. Needless to say, she was concerned to see me there. The phone rang as we walked in the house. It was the freaked-out principal. I had been seen arriving at school, but I was not there... Grades 2-6 we lived on 67th and Harriet and I went to Woodlake Elementary. Winter afternoons after school kids around the area went to the Woodlake skating rink. I don't remember feeling too cold and I had to make myself leave to go home for dinner... One big snowstorm during grade school the roads had not yet been plowed early evening. My dad tied our toboggan to the back of our station wagon. My 2 sisters and I had a blast as he drove slowly along deserted back streets. I remember my mom was not too happy about it.

# WHAT WAS IMPORTANT IN MY LIFE GROWING UP IN RICHFIELD

**SUZI (SUE STORM) BLUMBERG**

*66TH AND COLUMBUS AVE. SO.*

I wasn't much a lover of school and learning. I preferred to play, so what was important to me was the fun programs I was able to attend every season of the year. These were all put on by the Richfield Recreation Department, which was run by my dad, Burt Storm, who worked for the schools. In the summer of my elementary years, I went to my neighborhood playground, Memorial Park, and enjoyed craft activities, sports and seeing my friends. I got involved in a turtle racing contest once and still have the medal I won!!! Swimming lessons were important, and I can remember freezing in the early morning in June at Lake Harriet, not so sure I wanted to go into the water! In the winter it was important to ice skate as much as possible at my neighborhood rink at Memorial Park. I can remember at home on the weekend we got phone calls all day long when the weather was bad, asking if a particular rink would be open. Sometimes I'd skate too long, and my toes would freeze and the warming house attendant would massage my toes near the heater that heated the room. Crack the Whip was a fun game we played, but I don't think we were supposed to. I got many concussions as a result of this game! I also remember the skating races we'd have on a Sunday. I never won those! As I became a teenager, it was important for me to earn money, so I worked babysitting and was always busy. I started when I was 11 and earned .35 an hour! At 16 I had my first real job at Donaldson Department Store at Southdale. I worked there through college, mostly in the Women's Hat Department. I could go on and on!! Selling Girl Scout Cookies door to door. The school banking program at Central Elementary. Church at Hope Presbyterian and the fun community it was. Having a great doctor who officed at the Hub. My bike that got me wherever I wanted to go—especially swimming at Lake Nokomis every day in the summer as a teen. The incredible way that I felt safe as a child growing up. Even playing after dark outside. Roith's Drug Store's ice cream cones every Sunday after church (on 71st and Chicago).

# A CONFIRMATION WAKE UP!

**JOY LUNDQUIST KENNEL**

*76TH AND PARK AVE. SO.*

I went to House of Prayer Lutheran Church most of my life. On Sunday's when we would go to church being that it was only 3 blocks away, my parents would want us to walk together. I sometimes felt a bit embarrassed, and I wished because many of my friends did not go to church that I could just go and play with them, but as time went on our confirmation classes, choir, activities and sock hops were fun......

For our confirmation we had practiced beforehand what to do at the large square altar, including kneeling together at a certain time. The boy next to me slumped over onto me and I elbowed him pretty hard to stop kidding around. I soon found out that he had fainted because he was so hot in the robes we wore!

# 1964 BIKE TRIP TO THE WORLD'S FAIR

**JAY KENNEY**

*69TH AND MORGAN AVE. SO.*

June 14, 1964, Sunday. Flag Day. 11 of us 16-year-olds and our families and our support vehicle gathered at the Hub parking lot to begin the adventure of our young lives. We were going to ride our bicycles to New York City and the World's Fair. We had trained for months getting ready for this day. Our goal was to average 100 miles a day. We said our good-byes to our families, and we were on our way. The trip was uneventful through Wisconsin. We would spend our nights at campgrounds or public parks after getting the OK by city officers. We ate lunch and dinner from our own food stores. Usually we ate at diners along the way. We had all earned money from jobs, paper drives and personal savings. On the fifth day of our journey we took a ferry from Manitowoc, WI to Ludington MI. Crew members asked about what we were doing, and of course we couldn't tell them enough about our plans. Well, apparently some of the crew alerted the captain about us and the captain in turn radioed ahead to the mayor of Ludington and let the mayor know what we were doing. When we disembarked, we were greeted by radio and TV news crews and the mayor. The city opened its doors to us. Dinner and breakfast was on the city and we were allowed to camp in the city park. We were also given a free viewing of Viva Las Vegas. The trip across Michigan was uneventful. The scenery was cherry orchards and sheep farms. You could smell the sheep farms from more than a mile away. Our typical day was up at 4am. Break camp and then have breakfast. We started biking at 6am or earlier. We would ride all morning and have lunch from our own stores or have lunch in a diner. No chain restaurants. We would then ride all afternoon and stop between 4pm and 5pm. All the while our support van would drive behind us with a sign, "Bikers Ahead." We would usually stay at a campground or public park. We would generally go to our tents and sleeping bags shortly after sunset. Of course sometimes we would lay in our tents and talk of things simple to our sixteen year old's thoughts of the universe. From Michigan, we took a few miles through Canada to Niagara Falls. The 10th day of our journey was spent in tourist mode in Niagara Falls. Now we were on our home stretch. We just had to finish our New York leg. It took us six days to cross the State of New York. We arrived in NYC. Stayed at an old army base on Long Island. From here on out, we were tourists. We did all the NYC tourist sites: Times square, Empire State Building, UN, Statue of Liberty, St. Patrick's Cathedral (Out of which we were thrown because we were wearing Bermuda shorts). And of course, we attended the World's Fair as much as we could. It was amazing. While we were finishing up with NYC, a few of our parents began arriving to get us back home. But the trip wasn't over yet. On the first leg of our return trip, we stopped in eastern Pennsylvania at an Amish farm for a traditional Amish dinner. From the Amish community, we traveled to Washington, D.C. We hit all the tourist spots: White House, Capitol Bldg. Washington Monument, Lincoln Memorial, Smithsonian Institute, Arlington, etc. We also took in the Gettysburg Battlefield and spent the remaining days just driving home. We returned home on July 11. Happy, but also sad that our trip was over. We had bonded as one only can on a trip like that.

# UNDER THE ALUMINUM TREE

**CHRISTINA CAVITT**

*64TH AND WASHBURN AVE. SO.*

Christmas 1960 was a time when bold colors were all the rage in American suburban interior decor. Our living room was painted a shocking mint, set against a dark green accent wall. The drapes over the picture window were forest green, splashed with yellow, watermelon and chartreuse highlights. The davenport was pink faux leather. The only gentle visual touch was a grey, fat weave wall-to-wall carpet perfect for camouflaging the antics of five rowdy children. Mom's annual tempera paint Christmas scene covered most of our picture window at 6404 Washburn Avenue South. The corner streetlight shone a stubborn dim hue through that year's nativity – a primitive manger scene with Baby Jesus at center stage. At dusk, my two sisters, ages 9 and 7, simultaneously yanked the short brass chains of the two living room lamps, plunging the room into eerie shadows. I was 4 years old and knew big girls weren't supposed to be afraid of the dark. Nevertheless, I was terrified. I sat frozen to my chair until one of them switched on the heart of the family Christmas tree – the color wheel. The wheel's motor slowly ground to life and whirred laboriously to turn a circle of red, yellow, green and blue lenses in front of a high-intensity sun lamp that spotlighted the tree and washed the rest of the room with warm colors. I accidentally knocked it over once, so forever after, it got caught at blue until the gears caught up and shot the wheel forward to red. Actually, the tree wasn't a real dead tree. It was aluminum, with metal branches jutting out of drilled holes in a tall stick. These were bound with hundreds of skinny aluminum strips and adorned with shiny glass ornaments, placed at random by us kids. The effect was magnificent. We girls scurried beneath the bottom boughs to gaze up at the enchantment overhead. When we squinted, the sparkling reflections became stars over a silver forest. This place was sacred. Grownups were not allowed. We lay down with our heads touching in a tangle of brown, red and blonde hair, a cluster of gigglers and a trio of brave explorers. That's when the magic began.

# GROWING UP IN RICHFIELD, "ALL AMERICAN CITY"

**BECKY BINGEA**

*64TH AND 11TH AVE. SO.*

In 1953, my parents and three of us five Bingea siblings moved to Minnesota from the West Coast to establish a new church, House of Prayer Lutheran (HoP), in the cornfields of Richfield. Although my parents both grew up in St. Paul, my father started his ministry in Olympia, WA, and spent eight years there. I was 2 ½ years old when we moved and, thus, began my childhood in Richfield. Like many of my Baby-Boomer peers, I went all through elementary (Elliot), junior (East), and senior high school in Richfield. I was a Spartan through and through! I grew up in two homes in Richfield, the first at 6739 Elliot Ave. S. (1953-1962), and the second at 6438 11th Ave. S. (1962-on).

Growing up as a local minister's daughter, fondly known as a "PK" (Preacher's Kid), I came to know many members of our community, as our HoP church membership grew to over 4,000 baptized members over the next 23 years. A funny PK story: Before the first unit of our church was built, the church council meetings took place in the basement of our parsonage home on Elliot. Like some other homes in the community, we had a laundry chute that went from upstairs to the basement. Although not intentional, council members were sometimes hit with dirty laundry! I remember "Released Time" religious education during the school day to bus to nearby churches, including ours. Like any good PK, I sang in the church choirs, including appearances at Southdale during the holidays. Our Youth Choir even cut an album in 1964, "Voices of Youth," which I still have! Summertime was filled with summer camp and neighborhood activities, including box hockey, Battle Ball, swimming lessons at the Navy Pool near the airport, and many fun hours at the then new Richfield Community Pool on East 66th Street. We neighborhood girls loved putting on backyard shows for our parents and neighbors, complete with swing-set "acrobatics" and enactment of songs in dress-up, such as "Ain't She Sweet" and "Hey, Look Me Over." In wintertime we loved ice skating at Christian and Augsburg Parks and playing hockey in our flooded backyards. Slumber parties were popular, as were shopping at the Hub and Southdale (the oldest mall in America!) and taking the bus to Dayton's in downtown Minneapolis. It was an easier lifestyle back then, and we were allowed to ride our bikes all over town and into Minneapolis; we called them "bike hikes." A coming-of-age event occurred in 5th grade when most of us girls got our first pair of nylons for the Minneapolis Symphony. Although some communities back then did not allow girls, I was a proud Elliot school patrol in 6th grade. While some friends were active in Brownies and Girl Scouts, I was in Bluebirds and Camp Fire Girls

– I liked the colors of our uniforms! Music was an important part of my life, even outside the church. Although my mom was the church organist, both my mom and brother Dave were accomplished pianists, accompanying school and church events and teaching piano lessons. I took piano lessons for ten years but, unfortunately, did not continue after high school. I also played the violin in grade school and junior high. I sang in The Madrigal Singers in high school and was fortunate to be part of the chorus in RHS's first musical, "Finian's Rainbow," in 1967.My activities in senior high also included *Aurean* staff, Debate, Pep Club, Y-Teens, Usher's Club, Counselor Aide, and National Honor Society. Our Senior Banquet was at the Thunderbird Motel, and our fabulous, parent-planned, all-night senior class party, "Italiano Exceptionale '68," was at the high school. Because of our ever-growing RHS class sizes, our Class of 1968 was the first to hold graduation ceremonies at the Metropolitan Sports Center. I now live in the San Francisco Bay Area (San Rafael), which has been home for 40 years. I love the weather and volunteer activities in my community and enjoy my retirement after 40+ years as an audiologist. Although my parents passed years ago, I am still close to my siblings in Minneapolis (Dave, RHS class of 1965), Phoenix (Rachel, 1970), Boise (Gretchen, 1974), and Seattle (Steve, 1980, in Seattle). Even though I don't get back to Minnesota often, I thoroughly enjoy my visits home to see family and close friends. But…my life really began in Richfield, a great place to grow up!

# MEMORIES OF PLAYING CUB FOOTBALL

**GENE JOHNSON**

*75TH AND CLINTON AVE. SO.*

My name is Gene Johnson. I was raised by my mother and father in Richfield on 75th and Clinton Ave. I have an older brother and younger sister. I attended Portland Elementary School and Richfield junior and senior schools throughout the years. I graduated from Richfield Senior High School.In 1957, the Richfield Jaycees put out a community wide notice that they needed players for the 1957 cub football team. Richfield boys who were at least eight years old and under 100 pounds were eligible. Football helmets and shoulder pads were required equipment. My desire to play football started when I earned my first five dollars by taking over my brother's paper route for a week. I bought shoulder pads with the money I earned. I then joined other friends with a desire to play on a football team. My parents bought me a football helmet, and I bought a football with the money I earned by babysitting. Football teams were selected according to school boundaries resulting in a ten-team league. The team I played on was the Portland Rams. In addition to our head coach, each team had up to four assistant coaches. Our head coach was Marshall Salisbury and Ron Johnson was his main helper. I viewed the football program as a very valuable experience, and I learned so much from our coaches about teamwork and sportsmanship. Our team practiced Wednesday, Friday, and Saturday evenings starting the beginning of August. Our first game was on

September 8th. We played against the Woodlake Gophers and won by a score of 27 to 0. All games that year were played on the ballfield of Richfield High School. As the season continued, I advanced to the A squad and played the left end position. Our last game was played in mid- October against the Assumption Saints. We ended the year tied for second place with five wins and one loss. In 1958, I again played on the Portland Rams cub football team. At year end, our team and the Assumption Saints, two high ranking teams in the Jaycee Cub Football league, climaxed our seasons with a visit to the Minnesota state prison at Stillwater, Minnesota. With three prison inmates officiating, our game proved to be a real battle, ending in a 7-0 victory for our team. Following the game, we enjoyed dinner at the officers dining room as guests of the Warden. Approximately 50 players, 10 coaches and sponsors, and 5 Jaycees were included in the event. Because of the positive responses on the part of prisoners, players, coaches, and Jaycee members, prison officials extended an invitation for a similar football event the next season.

# RICHFIELD FROM SIX SPARTANS IN VIEW OF HOLY ANGELS ACADEMY

**BILLY FINDLAY**

*67TH AND STEVENS AVE. SO.*

My parents, Don and Margaret Findlay, migrating down from NODAK bought their home in 1945 on 6700 Stevens Avenue by trading in their car for the down payment. They both resided at home until their passing, Mom in 1995 and Dad in 1997. Raised us six kids, four of us born in Minnesota, two older brothers in North Dakota. All of us went to RHS. Tom, the oldest would have graduated in 1958, but joined the US Coast Guard instead. Not uncommon for the 'fifties. Bob, was part of the Aurean editorial staff, graduated in 1959. WMF, me, graduated in 1965, with Steve, 1967, Carolyn 1969 and Diane 1971. All of us either entered the military, or our spouses were in the military. Bob elected to join the Peace Corps, following JFK's lead. Carolyn married her HS sweetheart, Dennis Knutson. After his first wife's passing, Tom remarried his HS sweetheart, Bonny Smith (RHS '58). We are all still living.

My jobs in Richfield:

| | |
|---|---|
| Ralph Hollenbeck Farm | 68th & Nicollet |
| Vaughn's Pure Oil | 66th & Portland |
| Clark Super 100 | 66th & Pleasant |
| Elsen's Pure Oil | 77th & Portland |
| Piggly Wiggly Market | Hub Shopping Center |
| Veteran TV & Electronics | 65th & 14th Avenue |

After 1965 graduation, five guys from Richfield ventured out to Phoenix, just to say we were there. Jim Koranda, Greg Springer, Gary Krueger, Bill Hulwi and WMF lived in a rental house, bussed dishes, cooked and caddied. Went broke, some got homesick and returned by Thanksgiving only to expect our local draft board notices any day.... While home on leave, brother Steve set me up with a nursing student attending the U of Mn. Even though Ann is from Edina (EHS '67), we hit it off great with our first date at Bridgeman's, now Pizza Luce. In 1970, after I wrapped up my hitch in the Coast Guard, we married on an early August morning at Minnehaha Falls. Ann, completing her Nursing at Northwestern and the University, we ventured east to Western Wisconsin, purchased land in the town of Rush River, near Baldwin. We built our home, raised our family and have resided here ever since. We travel back to the MSP area quite often as both our daughters reside in the Minneapolis and Robbinsdale area. After our son Mike retired in 2019 from the US Army, with his wife Katie and kids, reside out here in the area near us. Mike takes care of the home front and Katie is on medical staff at our local hospital. I realize this is more than a little narrative about Richfield itself, but the story intertwines, especially with us six siblings raised in Richfield, and our daughter Melissa returning to RHS. We all have warm memories of our childhood home and with our neighbors, what it all meant to us.

# CIRCUS CAME TO TOWN

**GEOFFREY GRUDZINSKI**

*68TH AND LONGFELLOW AVE. SO.*

Growing up on the frontage road of Cedar Highway at 68th and Longfellow in Richfield brought many wonderful memories. This was in the Rich Acres addition, just down the road from New Ford Town by the airport where there were 54 little houses in the middle of the golf course. Both Gorbachev and Shamu the killer whale drove by our home as we waved them on. One of the fondest memories was of the animals. Most summers when I was young, the Ringling Brothers, and Barnum and Bailey Circus walked the live animals past our home down Longfellow Avenue. This was to get the animals from the train station to the site of the old met stadium where they set up the large circus tent. It was easiest to just walk the animals and so each summer, we got a nice little show of the animals as they walked past our home. I remember the elephants, grabbing branches from the weeping willow trees, and ripping them off as they pass by. There were camels, zebras and elephants that walked freely, while lions and tigers were in caged trailers. Somehow my father knew the timing and would have us sit outside in lawn-chairs waiting for their arrival. This was a great childhood memory.

# MY NAME IS MOOSE!

**MIKE FLANDERS**

*65TH AND WASHBURN AVE. SO.*

I earned the nickname "Moose" around 1959. As a ten-year-old kid, I played Tackle in football. Sheridan School field was our home for most (if not all) the football games during the late summer and into early fall. We boys were full of "piss and vinegar" and roughing it up after supper was a great way to play this game. Coach Wes Haddlestead and Coach Jim Raymond were paramount in teaching us rowdy kids these new game skills. Steve Snobeck was one of my teammates and we have remained friends all these years. Many of us boys would play pick-up football and baseball games during the summer in Jack and Bobby Fifield's backyard, on 65th and Russell. No fencing in the backyards produced a big area for us to run and play in. One of the Fifield's backyard neighbors were the Mattila's (Emil and Alice, Sharon, Suzanne, Sheila and Richard). They had a large garden with a great patch of raspberries. Sometimes I would sneak into their berry patch, hoping the tall stalks would sufficiently hide me. Not so much, as the little toe headed Mattila girl would not only spot me but tattle on me to her father! Her dad would laugh and say, "let the boy eat, he's hungry!" I kept eating. (I married her in 1982 and we celebrated our 40th anniversary last November.) In 1961-1962, Doug Kingsriter and myself were the home-run hitters for the Babe Ruth Richfield Baseball League. I was about 12-13 years old. Arnie Smith was our coach, and he was a great encourager, especially during this time for me. We played our games in the fields behind West Junior High. The games were played during all kinds of weather on Saturday afternoons and weeknights after supper. How itchy those uniforms were since they were made from wool, especially when it was hot outside! I remember my dad Keith, telling the umpires to "punch another hole in those masks so they could see the game better." My dad. He always seemed to have something to say in such things. He loved sports and enjoyed watching his boys play in them. My two younger brothers, Mark and Pat, played football and baseball throughout their school years at RHS, as well. These sports were a big part of our school and home life. I was not so much interested in school but get me on a football or baseball field and I was all in!

# DRIVING PRACTICE AT SOUTHDALE

**JUANITA WASICK JOHNSON**

*72ND AND LYNDALE AVE. SO.*

My dad would take me to Southdale on Sundays to practice driving. The parking lot was big and was closed on Sundays. One day after I got my license my mom asked me to drive to Kennys Market near 66th and Penn and get milk. It was by a Quonset Hut type building. I happened to hit the side of the building trying to park. I drove home and put the car in the garage. A few days later, my dad did not say a word...He just presented me with a bill for $100.00 from a local Body Shop.

# A LOVE OF NATURE STARTED IN RICHFIELD

**DORIS RUBENSTEIN**

*RESIDENT SINCE 1984*

I had just moved to Richfield in July, 1984. I'm originally from Detroit and had lived in South America and then New York City for 10 years before moving to the apartments on 65th Street between the liquor store and Richfield Lake. After 10 years in New York, I felt totally divorced from nature. I hated having to go to a park to see a stretch of grass bigger than a postage stamp. I pitied the trees growing in a tiny patch of depleted soil in the middle of a sidewalk; they seemed to exist only as a place for dogs to pee. When I found my apartment in Richfield right next to Richfield Lake, I thought I was the luckiest person in the State of Minnesota. I felt even luckier that my apartment complex had a swimming pool on the grounds (it has since been cemented over). So, there I was, lying by the pool in the July sun, enjoying the good life before my new job (in Edina) started. Then, literally out of the blue, a large white bird came swooping down toward me. I thought it was going to spear me with its long, pointy beak! I rolled off the lounge chair to avoid the crash; the bird realized its mistake at the last minute, too, and made a quick turn, missing me by inches. Clearly, the bird had mistaken the pool for part of Richfield Lake. That experience changed my life. I wanted to know what kind of bird it was. I went out and bought a pair of binoculars and a birding guide. From then on, I seldom walked Richfield or Wood Lake without those two items in hand. Now, I've travelled the world to see some amazing, beautiful birds. And it all started in Richfield.

# SUMMER AT THE POOL

**ROLF FURE**

*70TH AND PARK AVE. SO.*

My Mom grew up in Bertha, Minnesota and when she was very young, one of her friends drowned so, she made sure we all went to swimming lessons! Now I grew to love the Richfield Pool and spend many summer days there but on those swimming lesson days, it seemed like the water was ice cold and it always seemed to be cloudy and windy!! An exaggeration, I am sure. As much as I hated them, I took them every year and ended up getting my lifeguard certification. The Richfield Pool became for my friends and me, one of our favorite hangouts in the summer. We'd ride our bikes there and be there most of the day!

# A SENSE OF FREEDOM AND LESSONS FOR LIFE

**JOHN SAVAGEAU**

*66TH AND ELLIOT AVE. SO.*

My time in Richfield, Minnesota began in the 1960s, ending in 1975. This was the age of the Vietnam conflict, Man on the Moon, explosive growth of suburbs extending south of Minneapolis, and a sense of freedom for children growing up in the city. For my friends and I that sense of freedom was limited only by how far we might be able to explore during the course of a day on bicycles. This range could include nearly any location in the city of Minneapolis, along the Mississippi or Minnesota Rivers, MSP Airport, what is now called the Hyland-Bush-Anderson Lakes Park Reserve, and many other locations in locations surrounding Richfield. Summer vacation at ages 9-15, before we transitioned to driving, was a three-month opportunity to explore, learn, get in a bit of trouble, and just have fun. My favorite spots to wander were around the airport and along the rivers from Minnehaha Falls to the area now named Mound Springs Park. Huge area, and during the 60s and early 70s almost entirely undeveloped, wild, and devoid of other people. This allowed my friends and I to indulge in absorbing nature and learning how the Mississippi and Minnesota River Confluence impacted much of the rest of Minnesota and perhaps the entire watershed of the central United States. Learning and looking forward to seeing migrating birds, hoping to have a beaver or muskrat sighting, and being exposed to the expansion of the greater Minneapolis and St. Paul metro area. All had a deep impact, driving much of my commitment to environmental and wildlife issues that have followed me throughout my life. In high school I developed friendships with Native Americans, after graduation lived with a Cree and Ojibway family for a couple years and lived in remote areas in both northern Minnesota and Canada. While I have only returned to Richfield a few times since leaving in 1975, the experiences and culture have stayed with me through a career that has brought me to more than 120 countries, and still influences decisions and professional activities. When planning infrastructure projects, I still use memories of my days exploring the wetlands and trails along rivers as a reference to ensuring sensitivity and awareness of the impact my actions may have on the environment, wildlife, and indigenous peoples or residents those projects may touch. It surprises me that nearly 50 years have passed since leaving Richfield, and I am still able to keep in touch with many classmates who are spread around the country and world, remember those who have left us, and remember nearly every street and park in the city. But my fondest memories always return to riding my bicycle to the river and wetlands below the Minneapolis Airport, riding past the Metropolitan Stadium, the Met Center, North Central Airlines hangers, and the 24th Street Bridge on the way to our private paradise. Maybe it is time to return one more time before those memories have a chance to fade with age.

# HOLY ANGELS AND ITS STRONG CONNECTION TO OUR FAMILY

**JULIE ELSEN TVETE**

*71ST AND COLUMBUS AVE. SO.*

Holy Angels and the surrounding area have strong ties to my family. Academy of the Holy Angels (AHA) was built by the Sisters of St. Joseph in the middle of an open field in Richfield during the great depression. My grandparents, Ralph, and Elsie Hollenback (Nani and Boppa to me) lived next door to Holy Angels during the early days of Richfield. Their daughter Ginny told me these stories of my grandparents and Holy Angels. Boppa became friends with the Holy Angels custodian and eventually the custodian offered him the opportunity of showering in the utility room as Nani and Boppa did not have running water in their home. In exchange, Boppa would bring fresh picked vegetables from his garden for the nuns and teachers. From 1936-1946 he rented acreage from the school to farm on the land that is now St. Peter's. My grandparents owned a vegetable market in Richfield located in various spots and finally on 68th and Nicollet in the front yard of their home. My mom and Aunt Betty and Ginny, took piano lessons on the 4th floor of Holy Angels beginning in 1939 from Sister Mary Alfred. Many years later my siblings and some of our cousins would attend the school and some of us continued the tradition and took piano lessons there as well. (My mom, Betty, married Don Elsen. The

Elsen's were a prominent family with a deep and rich history in Richfield. My dad's family has owned and operated Elsen's Service Garage since 1893 when it was first established by his grandparents as a blacksmith shop). My aunt Ginny recalled "Nuns in their flowing habits were given permission to take a leisurely walk around the land surrounding the school. They always went in twos and would stop at the Hollenback farm where Elsie would give them her homemade cookies and fudge "...I love stories of the first days of Richfield and the importance of family and education on who I am today.

# FROM SMALL TO BIG

**SANDY CHRISTENSEN SMOKSTAD**

*71ST AND HARRIET AVE. SO.*

In 1958, my dad got a teaching job at Richfield East Junior High. We came from a small town, Spring Grove, Minnesota. The population was about 1,100. Richfield, at the time, was about 50,000. Big change for me coming in at tenth grade. I was scared to death. My parents found a house right across the street from Central grade school which was right next to the high school parking lot. Nice, I never had to take a bus to school. In Spring Grove, we lived right across the street from our K-12 school. My Dad was a science, math and calculus teacher besides the coach of all sports such as basketball, football, track and field and baseball. Growing up with all these sports and even being in band, helped me to cope with coming to this large school. I joined the band in 10th grade but missed the cheerleading try-outs for this year. I had to wait till later in the year for 11th grade cheerleading. I tried out for my junior year and made it. I think I was the first one to do a flip in this big school! Back then 1959 to 1960 the five picked were cheerleaders for all sports. We had such a great time! In my junior year for basketball, we went to the State tournament and played against Edgerton. Got second. After two years I felt I belonged. Then before you knew it, my Senior year was here! So many great things had happened to me in such a short time, then it was Homecoming. I was chosen as one of the final candidates. No one knew this, but I was the only one with a borrowed dress. Mom and Dad wanted to buy me a dress, but I said wait, I'll only wear it once. Let me call the queen from two years ago to see if she would let me use hers. Her name was Janice, I believe. She had last used it the year before to crown the new Queen. She lived in Richfield, and she said yes, I could use it. It fit perfectly! It was the most exciting and most beautiful event I'd ever experienced! As we started the grand march I looked up and saw my dad. The school had called him to come watch the coronation and then he went back to the Junior High School. It was a good thing we had long dresses as my leg was like a jumping bean. It would not stand still as they walked back and forth to pick one of 10. The miracle was, I got it! Never in my wildest dreams did I think that could happen. I got the first dance with my dad at the Homecoming Dance which meant the world to me because a month after I graduated, he passed away at age 50. Mrs. "Gopher" made a picture book for Mom and Dad. After 63 years, It's still as fresh in my mind as that day. Great memories!

# A CHILDHOOD DAY ON CLINTON AVENUE

**CLARE SLANIKA**
*75TH AND CLINTON AVE. SO.*

Growing up on Clinton Avenue in Richfield, Mn. offered me exposure to security and simplicity, at least for a while, that is rarely found now. Richfield in the 1950s was a growing town and our street was surrounded by a farmer's field on the south side and growing urban housing to the north. My street was at the end of the development, so it was necessary to walk through the cornfield and bump into an occasional cow if we were to walk to the small playground or the church on the other side. On this particular day in June, of 1957 I was nearly 5, and one of my best play friends, Donna, who lived across the street from me decided we would sew some clothes for our baby dolls under the elm tree that was in our front yard. Donna and I had just finished kindergarten. We were born on the same day and lived across the street from each other. It was great! The day was hot and after my mother gave us some sewing scraps and two needles threaded, we began to cut out doll pants and skirts and stitched them together. My mother said we did a good job but in hindsight, it was a miracle the clothes stayed together. No matter - it was time for Donna to go home and I had to help my mom with laundry. I would pass the wet clothes to her and she would hang them on the line. It seemed most neighbors hung laundry on the line. One could always tell if there was a new baby in the house or if it was sheet washing day. just by what was hanging on the clothesline...When we were finished, we would stand between the sheets and drink orange juice. It was our secret. It wasn't long after the laundry was done that two friends and I walked through the cornfield and cows to play at the park. We were now almost 6 and we were allowed to go to the park by ourselves as long as we stayed together. What a thrill! We loved the old merry-go-round and had fierce monkey-bar competitions to see who could go the fastest across the bars. Unfortunately, one of our friends got stuck on the monkey bars and couldn't get off. Our friend was almost my age and was cared for by her grandma while her mother was at work. I ran home and didn't care if the cows chased me to tell my mother that our friend was stuck on the bars. My mother stopped everything, and we all went through the cornfield, passed some cows, and made it to the playground. Sure enough, our friend was stuck on top of the monkey bar and my mom climbed up to get her down. Once we knew everyone was safe, we headed for home and noticed that our pet ducks (small at Easter but now large in June) had followed us to the park. We all scrambled to pick up the ducks and walked home with the quacking birds in tow. That afternoon all the kids took naps. My mother had two more children at that time and in the future, there would be four more. For now, we were a manageable group. After nap time many of the neighborhood children would gather in the street to play a game of softball or kickball. Child leaders emerged to determine who would play what bases and who would be a pitcher or thrower. More than one time a ball would go through our front door or window. All the fun ended at 4 and most kids went home to clean up for dinner. When my father came home from work my sister and I would meet him at the door and my mother was all prettied up with curled hair and lipstick. After dinner, I helped a little with dinner dishes and on this particular day, my mother and I took a short drive to a plowed-up field near the Gem shopping store. At one time it was an asparagus field but now it had been turned over and readied for use as an asphalt parking lot. Somehow, renegade asparagus stems would poke through the torn-up ground, and my mother and I would pick the narrow, young, tender sprouts. When we had a basketful, we brought our treasures home, cleaned, chopped them, and packed the stems ready to use the next day. Already a long day, baths were in order and my sister, and I went to bed by 8, with fans blowing on us to reduce the heat. After a story read to us by mom or dad we were sleeping for the night. Once in a while, we could hear Mom and Dad chatting on the back steps or laughing about the simple adventures of the day before we drifted off to sleep, it seemed unassuming, ordinary, peaceful. The small, almost insignificant activities of those days on Clinton Avenue in Richfield now seem like a dream. How was it possible to be completely oblivious to what the future held for most of us? To be sure, there were difficulties, problems and challenges we were unaware of during those days that we were unaware of however, it seems that as children, we were sheltered, protected if you will, from harm or heartache that might arise in the future and steal from us the very simplicity and security that sewing doll clothes, helping with laundry, napping in the afternoon, playing kickball in the street or picking asparagus at dusk out of an old farmers field provided to us. Perhaps our ability to transcend the advanced issues of our present time involving rights, technology, changing social norms, and the rise of global understanding find their underpinnings in the security and simplicity of our early childhood experiences. To that point, it is wonderful to remain in contact, especially on our birthdays, and throughout the years with the very friends I grew up with on Clinton Avenue in Richfield Minnesota.

# THE BEAUTY OF SMALLNESS: GROWING UP IN RICHFIELD

**KIMBERLEY DOTSETH**

*77TH AND WENTWORTH AVE. SO.*

Even though I left Richfield in June 1981 for San Diego, it fills my childhood memories. Probably once a day or so I think of something from my days in Richfield. The small things occupy my thoughts. My most immediate small memory probably brings me the greatest joy. It was walking home from Richfield High School all the way down to 77th & Wentworth where my family rented a townhouse in New Orleans Court. We lived in two different townhouses there between the third grade when I started at Central Elementary until I moved to California in June 1981, a year after my high school graduation. Walking home from high school was great solitude for me and I loved it. I didn't necessarily love the walking, but along the Pleasant Avenue railroad tracks were walls of lilacs. I am talking about huge, high walls of green and purple, filling the space on the western side of the tracks. I would walk along the lilacs in the spring, on my way home, euphoric at the smell. Today, lilacs transport me to those railroad tracks. I have a few sad memories that make me who I am today. I won't share all of them from my Central Elementary years. If you were there, you know. But there is one later "sad" memory that made me the strong person I am today. It was the summer of 1979. I had been a Flag Twirler and absolutely loved it. I couldn't think of anything more fun than that, except for one thing: being a Tapaire. I wanted to be a Tapaire so badly. The costumes, the shoes, the hair, the fishnets, the dancing, the precision:

all of it. I decided to go for it before my senior year, foregoing the Flag Twirler tryouts on purpose. The day of the Tapaires tryouts, that summer, I was ready. I had practiced all the moves and was confident I could join the line and be chosen. We all had the same thing to practice: Jump, Kick, Jump, Splits. I had done it a hundred times. In rehearsal before the actual tryout, everything changed in a second. In one of my jump-kick-jump-splits, I leaned too far into the splits, leaning forward with my body. My hamstring tore in half. I remember screaming and blacking out. My stepdad, back at New Orleans Court, was at home when the call came in. Today you'd call 9-1-1. Then, someone called your house. My dad came to get me and I was taken to the Fairview Southdale Emergency Room. I was on crutches all summer and was neither a Flag Twirler nor Tapaire for my senior year. By the time our senior year started, I was off crutches. I don't remember anyone asking me how I was or what happened or anything. I was a good girl. I never skipped a day of class, ever. I was also never asked to any of our high school dances – not one. My husband and I talk about it occasionally, sort of laughing, but something like that changes a person. I was shy and needed to leave Minnesota to really find out who I was. I did that in California. We'll leave this positive. I loved the Dairy Queen on 76th & Lyndale, discovering Led Zeppelin on my friend's brother's attic record player, our Midwestern thunderstorms, LaBelles, Broadway Pizza, Bridgeman's, and the crazy HUB where I bought corduroy Levi's for $12. Taking the city bus everywhere from a young age. The Southtown Fair. Only lasting through one Girl Scouts meeting, because they said I was too independent. (Got that right!) I remember hitting tennis balls against the industrial building garage door on 78th and Wentworth. I remember the moment my brother told me Elvis had died. And I remember being by the pool in the summer of 1972 thinking to myself, as a ten-year-old, "This is really the best year for music." And it was.

# MEMORIES OF RICHFIELD

**NANCY SLOCUM HIATT**

*68TH AND GRAND AVE. SO.*

To me, Richfield Minnesota was the best place a kid could ever grow up in. I lived there in the 60's, just north of the high school. Times were simpler then – the neighborhood kids all knew each other and played together outside – Kick the Can, Tag, Red Light Green Light, etc. Summer days were spent on the playground at Bob's Park. I loved the box hockey competitions. We rode our bikes to the pool and spent all day there, ending with a treat at the Dairy Queen on 66th street. In the winter we skated and sledded at Woodlake and Augsburg Park. You could ride your bike just about anywhere – the Hub shopping Center, library, the parks, Bridgeman's. I loved it when Bridgeman's had their BOGO sale and my parents stocked up! Richfield schools were among the biggest and best in the state. Top notch education prepared me well for the size and academic challenges at Brigham Young University. Extracurricular activities provided great times with friends. I spent nearly every day after school in the "debate room" with Vicky Webb, Joe Kearny, Kris Harkness, Daryl Youngman, Dan West, Ken Lund, Mr. Seeden, and others. In the evenings we went to the University of Minnesota Library to get information for the debates. On Saturdays (and often during the week) we traveled to debate tourneys or hosted one at the school. Some of the most excitement ever came when Edina lost to the mighty Spartans. I'll never forget the basketball game where we stormed the court, and the excitement with a big football victory. I wish my children could have the experiences I did.

# CLIFF'S APCO AND TWO FROM RHS

**JAY BRENNER**

*73RD AND GARFIELD AVE. SO.*

I have fond memories of the two Cliffs Apco gas stations in Richfield. One was on 75th and Lyndale and other on 65th and Lyndale. Cliff owned both; I remember when dad would pull in there in winter (it was all full serve then). Cliff would come out and ask my dad "fill er up and do you want isopropyl alcohol as well"? Dad of course would agree, and I could hear the little glass bottle contents gurgling into the tank, by that time my head would be out the window smelling that wonderful petroleum product going in after the alcohol. I heard the rumor once that Cliff was bringing a cash bag out after he locked up one night and someone beat him fatally for that bag. I was very sad to hear of such a tragic ending to a hardworking man, who was making a positive living in our city of Richfield..... I remember being in gym class with coach Walker. The whole class would be down on the floor doing our fifty push-ups and I would see his shoes as he walked by all of us, and he would say "Great day to be alive gentlemen!" Several moans could be heard after that... I also remember having Daryl Doss right after lunch and I would always walk in with a six pack of Oreos. He would then say to me " gimme one of those Brenner" and every day I would. You really weren't supposed to have food in the classroom. It was kind of an unwritten rule between him and I, that if the one Oreo penalty was paid, the other five could be admitted for my consumption inside forbidden space.

# A BOY AND A DOG

**DUANE JOHNSON**

*63RD AND 15TH AVE. SO.*

A long time ago there was a farm near us, past the wheat fields called Bowman's farm, (approximately 64th/11th Ave S). To make way for new houses, blocks of wheat fields and Bowman's farm were destroyed. All that was left of Bowmans farm was the scar where the house and pig pens/barn once stood. Trees were uprooted and piled high in places on the frozen ground. I went there a few times though I was too young to remember much about the farm and the people who lived there. After the farm/buildings were razed, I was there and I saw a dog in the distance, looking at me. I called to it, but it was very wary of me...when I got home and told my mother, she said, "that's one of Bowman's wild dogs" I asked more about them and ended up asking her how I could get close to that one dog. She told me to take some food scraps with me tomorrow which she left out for me. I returned the next day and walked around the desolate landscape and there on a large, bulldozed hill was the dog...He came closer this time...I kneeled and called but he kept his distance so I threw the scraps to him and he ate them....then he wandered off in towards the swamp between 62nd St and 66th St. I left and came back the next day with more scraps. We met again and this time he let me pet him gently and I coaxed him into a spot under the huge, uprooted tree pile nearby. It was a cold March Day but we were warm in that sunlit sheltered spot and spent the afternoon together side by side. I went back the next day and the next but never saw him again. I wished I had been able to take him home and was going to do just that if Mom said OK. We always had a dog or cat around it seemed, but not at that time. I wished I had done so that day.... Much later in my life I rescued a dog in Pine Springs that was hanging around my brother's house. I enticed it with some hamburger...We called her Ayla and she was one of the best dogs I ever had ,though I always longed for my first 'friend'.

## JARTS AND DON'T TOUCH THAT ONE!

**KATHY JOHNSON MCNAMARA**

*75TH AND 4TH AVE. SO.*

I was very fortunate to grow up in Richfield. It was a time of innocence and a wonderful feeling of community. Playing outside from sunup to sundown was an almost everyday occurrence. Many summer days were spent playing in the back yard of the Scanlon family on 5th avenue. They were a very athletic family, and we used their yard to play baseball, kickball, capture the flag, hot box among many other games. They had all the equipment necessary to keep us busy! Jarts was a popular yard game to play. As it was bound to happen, I was hit in the head by one of the Jarts. Joe S. was the one who threw the Jart, and anyone who knows Joe knows he was a pretty good ball player. I am confident he had put a fierce force behind that throw! I was very lucky there was no permanent damage (those close to me might beg to differ!) Jarts were eventually banned due to being too dangerous.

To this day, whenever I run into Joe S, he asks me if I remember the "Jart Incident" … In 10th grade my Science teacher was Mr. Danielson. I remember that one day, our class went on a field trip to Woodlake Nature area. We walked the whole two to three blocks over there from RHS. Anyway, he was pointing out different plants on the walk through the park and he showed some of us a particular plant and said to us "don't touch that one!" Now being a very intelligent smart aleck, I of course bent over and touched it. Nothing felt weird or anything, so I thought he was just pulling our legs. It was not very much later that a red rash and blisters started to appear on my hand. It ends up that the plant in question was "itchweed." I will always remember this event as a "teachable moment!"

# TRAINING FOR AN IRON CROSS ON THE STILL RINGS

**DAVID NYE**

*67TH AND 11TH AVE. SO.*

Over the years many people have asked me "how does one train to perform an Iron Cross on the Still Rings?" First of all, I started gymnastics in tenth grade. That was extremely late as most gymnasts start at around age five, I was a wrestler all through Junior High and so I had some extensive catching up to do. About the only thing I had going for me was that I had rather formidable upper body strength. My swinging moves in tenth grade were feeble at best, so I needed to acquire a move that would get me some points. I had always admired gymnasts who could hold an Iron Cross, so after much consultation and research I found that the fastest way to gain that kind of muscle strength was to use an eight-foot 1/2-inch medical grade latex rubber hose by standing on the hose with my arms straight out to my side and pulling upwards stretching the hose until in a cross position. Also trying for an Iron Cross as best as I could day after day on the Still Rings themselves! All in all, it took about six weeks of intense work to acquire this move. Adding the "L" to the Iron Cross was fairly easy since I already had the "L Seat". It was just a matter of adjusting my balance. One of the hardest aspects is making sure that your shoulders are even with the center of the two rings, very often you will notice that, at the high school level of competition, the gymnast is not down far enough as to be even with the center of the rings. Actually, "Giants", (swinging from one hand-stand to another), was much harder for me to learn. By the end of my Senior year, I was extremely close to an Inverted Iron Cross, if only I had another year! Right? Richfield dropped boy's gymnastics in about 1977, I think! I will always have such fond memories of Richfield High and so many wonderful experiences.

# RIGHT ON TARGET

**DEBBIE NIELSEN PALM**

*64TH AND 17TH AVE. SO.*

My parents were living in their home in Richfield when I was born in Aug 1953. They had moved from Minneapolis to their home on 6445 17th Ave S, about 1 1/2 years earlier. My Older brother Dan, who was 2 years older than me (Aug 1951), was born in the Minneapolis home. Our family had 4 children each about 2 years apart, Paul was born June 1955, & Nancy Nov 1957. We attended East Elementary school on East

66th Street, across the street from our school was the church that we attended, Richfield Evangelical Free Church. My parents bought the model home for the area. Just a few blocks away on Cedar Ave they hadn't built anything yet, so that is where we hung out to play baseball or football. There were enough kids in the neighborhood to make up teams. Living close to the airport we got used to the planes flying overhead. If it happened during a time a teacher was talking or we were in church, we just put things on pause and continued when the noise died. Neighbors on our block owned a small restaurant called the Tom Tom. My mom worked there for a while so if us kids needed her, we just walked the 2 blocks to talk to her. We often had our lunch there. Our church started out in a home then for a while in a school. When the church was built, one of the members worked for the city of Minneapolis, & when they removed the cobblestones from the streets of Minneapolis, our members used them to build the church. My dad could walk around the church & tell you who built each area. We had cousins that lived in Illinois and when they came to visit, I would be in charge of taking them to Southdale to shop or just look around. Our parents gave us enough money for the bus and lunch at Woolworth, a slice of pizza & a pop. There were 7 girls, I was the oldest, so I was put in charge of the money. We also had a small amount of money that we could buy something that we found shopping.

The Target store that is located on 66 & Cedar has our home address:

6445 17th Ave S
Richfield, MN 55423

I hope they haven't received any mail for us, Haha !

# PUT ME IN COACH

KEVIN SHARKEY

*66TH AND PARK AVE. SO.*

We were a baseball family to say the least. I played, my sister played, my Dad umpired several nights a week and Mom worked the concession stand. Dinner was always early so we could get to the Little League facility on 66th, west of Cedar Avenue. The ballpark was huge, at least to us little kids. There were the little league fields, the girls' softball fields, a Pony League field as well as a Babe Ruth field. There was always something to do or games to watch. We would bike to the fields on nights we weren't playing and just hang out, watching other games and eating banana popsicles. Our bikes always had a baseball glove strapped to the handlebars just in case someone wanted to play catch. The season always started out with tryouts. We all had numbers pinned to our T shirts. We played catch, swung a few bats, fielded grounders and pop flies. The coaches wrote down the player's numbers they wanted for their teams. It was terrifying and exhilarating at the same time. I so wanted to play for Korner Plaza and wear a purple hat. Another dream shattered. The coaches then got together and somehow decided on who went where and on what teams. I'm not sure if money passed hands or how the decision-making process evolved, it was all very secretive. We were just a bunch of nervous kids hoping to get picked and didn't care how they did it. I turned out to be a pretty good player. I wasn't a consistent hitter but was on base a lot either by getting hit by a pitch (my specialty) or by getting a walk. Most of my hits were singles and to this day have never put one out of the park. But I was pure speed on the base paths. Like most preteens and teenagers, I had no fear. I'd run through the third base coach's stop signals and rarely got thrown out at the plate. It was during this time that I got the nickname "Skeeter" because of the way I would buzz around the bases. It was at this time I also discovered I was not very good at taking direction. There were several divisions that went bottom to top with T-ball, juniors, northern, minors, international, association and majors. Everyone wanted to move up to the next level every year, even then we were a bunch of overachievers. The epitome of our Little League career was making it to the Majors. The Major's field had a two-story announcement booth with the announcer in the top floor and the concession stand in the lower part. There was an actual scoreboard! Definitely every player's dream was to play in the Majors at some point in their career. The biggest thrill of playing in the Majors was when the announcer called out your name as you stepped to the plate. There was play by play commentary and the stands were always packed with onlookers. It was heaven on so many levels. There were so many great memories of growing up as a kid in Richfield, but Little League still stands out as one of the best.

# MEMORIES FROM A VEGETARIAN DEER KILLER

**KAREN I. SHRAGG**

*WOOD LAKE NATURE CENTER DIRECTOR 1991-2019*

I walked into the doors of the best job of my life in August of 1991. I was the new director of Wood Lake Nature Center and could not have been greener. There were two situations that the staff presented me with right off the bat. First was a need to build an amphitheater next to the building. The second was that deer were about to become a big problem. Why? Because for the first time in Wood Lake's history three deer had overwintered in the 150 acre natural area. Without wolves to keep them from eating up all of the shrubs and trees, those deer were going to multiply, and they did just that. In just a few years there were 45 very bold deer eating from the bird feeders, destroying the ski trails and worst of all, eating everything up to a browse line, six feet off the ground. The first problem was easily solved. One of our board members of the newly formed FOWL (Friends of Wood Lake) agreed to donate the $5,000 it would take to build the amphitheater. The second problem took us years to figure out. The choice was made after many community meetings, to set up traps in the center, so that the deer could euphemistically be 'dispatched' It was agreed that their bodies would be donated to the Hides for Habitat program of the Minnesota DNR. We had staff on hand who were proficient hunters, but this was still hard for them to do at such close range, but they knew they were saving the forest. The deer were over their carrying capacity, determined to be three deer, so that the woods and all it supports would be preserved. There was no other viable choice. Deer birth control not only didn't work, you had to kill pigs to make them, and moving the deer was prohibitive, and where would they go? The whole state is brimming with deer who can reproduce in their first year of life, often having twins. So here I was, a vegetarian who had never hunted in her life, in charge of a program to eliminate deer, the pretty lawnmowers of the forest. I had no problem, however, since my reason for being a vegetarian is all about helping to create a more balanced demand of limited resources on a more and more crowded planet. I realized that sometimes we have to make tough choices. Once the word got out the phone calls kept coming and there were even protesters who came with their banners, my favorite being: DOWN WITH THE DNR. I calmly explained that the DNR had nothing to do with our plan, only that we had to keep careful track of the deer we 'dispatched'. It came in handy to tell these friends of animals that I too was a vegetarian and asked them the profound question. "Are you a friend of ALL animals or just deer?" "ALL", they answered and with that I launched into the list of wild animals who couldn't live there anymore because the deer had altered their habitat. "If we don't do this task, we will only have geese and a few mallards here, I told them. Say goodbye to the ovenbirds and all other birds, mink, weasels and the rest who need ground cover to survive. There were some humorous moments along the way. It was my job to bait the traps every night for three weeks in that first year. I headed out in the dark with shelled corn in my backpack. I would usually coerce a friend to come with me. One night it was one of our councilmen. On one occasion, he crawled inside the 4 foot by 6 foot trap and SNAP he was trapped inside. I laughed so hard, well we both did, that it took a while to help him out. A not so humorous event was when we discovered that someone had sprayed the traps with a repellent. They had to be laboriously cleaned and our program was delayed. My initiation into being a director was an education in compromise and the realities of what happens in a fragmented habitat which can only support a few of these magnificent creatures.

# THE STREAK...

**CHRISTINE FRASER ESPIRITU**

*66TH AND 1ST AVE. SO.*

In the mid-1970's I witnessed a few "streaking" incidents. One was at a bowling alley, and one was at a baseball game, but the most memorable happened at school. I was a Senior at Holy Angels. It was near the end of the year and the whole school was in the auditorium to recognize staff members. The principal was about to give an award to a custodian when a streaker ran across the front of the room and down the main aisle to the double doors in the back of the auditorium. Father O'Brien and Father Powers were standing in the back right by those doors. They jumped out of the way and let the girl, wearing only a bag on her head, push out the doors and escape out the side doors of the building along 66th Street. A car was waiting to pick her up and drive her away. I think she got caught!

# HOW CHRISTIAN PARK GOT IT'S NAME

EDWARD CHRISTIAN

My grandparents, Frank and Theresa Christian, owned and operated a farm in Richfield, MN for many years. Their farm was from 66th Street on the north to 70th Street on the south, and from 17th Avenue on the east to Bloomington Avenue on the west. Their next-door neighbor on the west was Joseph Alt. Joseph Alt was a bachelor, never married, and my grandparents assisted him from time to time and they were very good friends. There was a slough on the south end of their properties where my grandfather and his dog, Max, used to hunt ducks. My grandfather passed away in 1942, but my grandmother lived until 1950. In between, the Village of Richfield expressed interest in that property on the south end of their farm and Joseph's farm for possible park purposes. On May 10, 1944, Joseph Alt, came to terms with the Village of Richfield and the property was deeded over to the Village, that being "The South one-half (S1/2) of the East twenty-five (25) rods of the West one-half (W1/2) of the Southeast Quarter (SE1/4) of Section Twenty-six (26), Township Twenty-eight (28), Range Twenty-four (24), according to the government survey thereof." When the property was conveyed to the Village of Richfield, Joseph Alt informed the Village that the property was being conveyed for park purposes only and on the condition that the Park be named permanently as "Christian Park" in honor of his friend and neighbor, Frank Christian. The park continues to be named Christian Park and the Christian descendants are proud to have it so named.

# RICHFIELD LESSONS LEARNED

**JUDY COUGHLIN**

*66TH AND 12TH AVE. SO.*

The place where we grow up shapes us in ways we don't understand until much later. It's a major character in the story of our lives. Richfield taught me some important life lessons. I lived there from age 9 to 19 in an apartment on 66th and 12th Ave. I went reluctantly from a house, all the other kids I knew lived in houses. Some kids thought it was cool as my apartment had a little balcony. They would say just like Romeo and Juliet. I knew how that story turned out... My mom worked so I stayed at my grandparents' house in Minneapolis. I went to school in their district. I was a student president and mature for my age. As a girl of 11 I was told I could be on my own and start school in Richfield. At East Jr. High I knew no one. No one knew I was new. To make Richfield friends, I used the fact I had no supervision to my advantage. Poker games were held at the Formica kitchen table until my parents got home from work. We played with real chips, potato chips, Fritos and Doritos they all had different values. I learned how to start over and go into new situations and adjust. This served me well in every job I started. My grandparents had a white Dodge Pioneer with cherry red seats. They were covered with plastic so that the back of my legs stuck to them on a hot summer day. It also had fins which I thought was beyond cool. As they drove me to confirmation, we all squished in the front seat without seat belts as was the custom of the time. Now my grandfather sat stunned at the corner of 66th and Bloomington. We had been T boned by a guy who jumped the light. My grandmother and I were gone, vanished into thin air. Later he would say "I thought you two had gone to heaven and I was in hell." My grandmother, thrown from the car, escaped with a few minor cuts. I sat in the middle of the intersection with one broken and one fractured collar bone. I remember thinking I certainly didn't need an ambulance! I was embarrassed kids from school might see me and still thought I could make it to confirmation class. At the emergency room my words came out in a jumbled mess. I didn't know I was in shock. When told not to talk, even more wild gibberish spilled out. I was sent home when I was able to form real words again. I avoided that intersection for years. The accident did get me out of softball. I'm a runner not a thrower. Every spring in gym I said, "I can't play softball I broke my collar bones." It wasn't a lie. I tried it for three years until one gym teacher asked how long ago it happened and I was busted. I learned we heal in time and can move past trauma. I work in a hospital clinic with a much greater understanding of our patients with trauma. The same teacher who busted me also taught us the stroll dance from the 50's. The movie American Graffiti was big the role model for us. Our 50's themed sock hops were like going back to a magical, much more innocent time. We loved cruising 66th street, it was the heart of the city. We hung out at the A & W off 494. Protocol was backing in to keep tabs on who was coming and going. One night it was my job to safely guide the end of my friends' parents' boat of a station wagon. She maneuvered into the stall, I got distracted and she plowed into a mint Barracuda. There were two cute Richfield boys inside which made it worse. My friend thought she would be grounded for life. I felt guilt beyond measure. The owner was quiet while his friend went on a rant. It turned out later insurance got the Cuda owner money to do some much needed repairs on the car. We ended with one double date out of the catastrophe. Final lesson - sometimes the thing you think is the worst turns out OK.

# THE MANN FRANCE AVENUE DRIVE-IN

**RON BERGLUND**

*68TH AND STEVENS AVE. SO.*

The Beach Boys published a song about "The Drive In" back in 1964. The lyrics included the following:

*Don't sneak your buddies in the trunk 'cause they might get caught*
*By the drive in*
*And they'd look kinda stupid gettin' chased through the lot*
*Around the drive in..."*

During the summer of 1967, several of my knucklehead buddies from the class of '68 actually did try this. We were such idiots—and so cheap—that we pooled together our money to catch a movie at the Mann France Avenue Drive-In but could only afford ONE ticket! Three of us piled into the trunk, and our friend Tom Sanner paid for his ticket and drove in all by himself. First, the car had about 500 pounds of dead weight in the trunk -- so it visibly sagged (way too much junk in the trunk). Not too obvious or anything! Second, who goes to the drive in by himself!? How stupid! Shortly after buying his one ticket and moving past the ticket booth, Tom pulled into the drive in and- a short time later- realized that he was being followed. Tom proceeded to "punch it" -- and a drag race through the gravel roads winding throughout the drive-in ensued. My two idiot trunk buddies and I were thrust violently (and painfully) from side to side in the trunk as Tom tried to elude his pursuer – to no avail. After a few minutes of this nonsense, Tom realized the gig was up and he pulled out of the drive in. After driving a couple blocks, Tom pulled over and let us climb out of the trunk. We lost our two dollars, and we didn't get to see the movie. But at least we ended up with a story!

# SWIMMING LESSONS

**BARBARA MATTSON RENNEKE**

*72ND AND OAKLAND AVE. SO..*

I grew up in Richfield from 1950-1969. My parents were very big on swimming lessons. I started them in third grade at the Navy Pool, by the airport. I walked to Elliot school early in the morning to get on the bus. We'd sing, "The Ants Go Marching", 99 Bottles of Beer", etc. All the way to the pool and back. The pool was huge, freezing, and intimidating, especially the diving boards- 3 ft., 10ft., and 25 ft.). But I learned to swim there. The Richfield Pool opened in 1962. Everyone in my 6th grade class at Elliot was excited. My best friend, Cindy, lived on 66th and Portland and asked me to sleep over so we could be first in line when the pool opened. We set our alarm for 6:00 am and jumped out of bed when it rang. We put on our swimsuits and ran down to the pool. Alas, we were third in line. But that was good enough for us. This began three summers of fun and drama. My swimming lessons during those years (12-14) were Junior Life saving. The same cold mornings and water but now I was learning to save people! Fast forward to 1971. I became a Richfield Pool lifeguard. It was great being back as nothing much had changed in nine years. Many of my fellow guards were RHS grads. I remember Barb, Jeff, Dennis, and Ron. We took our job seriously, "No Running!", Only one person on the board!", etc. This time my swimming lessons consisted of me teaching little Richfieldites to float, swim, and dive off the board in chilly, early morning water. Now I realized why the teachers never got in the pool!

# OUR AUNT AND UNCLE AND THE MAGNUSON SOD COMPANY

ROBIN WAGGONER-JOHNSON
AND MIKE WAGGONER

Among the Richfield entrepreneurs who emerged after the 2nd world war were our uncle and aunt Manley 'Bud' Magnuson and his wife Nita (Waggoner) Magnuson. After serving in the Air Force, Bud came back home, and he and Nita settled in Richfield in a little 3 room house (formerly a garage) at 6320 Standish Avenue. Nita worked at the then airport restaurant, and Bud worked for a shirttail relative, (Ray Jordan) who had a small landscaping company. About 1946 he and a fellow named Don Grey created a small company which was then involved in doing 'highway work' which meant sodding along the many new Minnesota highways that were being built to satisfy the ever-growing travel needs of the growing population after the 2nd world war. In about 1948 Bud split off on his own and created Magnuson Sod Company and worked out of Richfield. He had a friendship with Ben Jorgenson who owned the Philipps 66 station at 66th and Cedar and that's where he kept his ever-growing fleet of trucks and equipment. A note here to establish that, at this time (1953) Bud re-directed his sod and landscape business to become solely a wholesale sod provider to landscapers and nurseries and no longer did sod laying and installing and was clearly an early pioneer in this direction. Soon after, he outgrew the 66th and Cedar location and bought the Phillips Station at 6401 Cedar and relocated his equipment and office to this location. Up to this point the only sod available was called 'pasture' sod, which meant it was harvested from farm pastures, typically cut in the Glencoe, Norwood-Young America, Gibbon, Green Isle, Waconia areas. By the late fifties his need for sod was quickly exhausting the supply he could find. In about 1962 Bud and Nita decided to grow their own; something that was very new across the nation. They bought several acres of 'peat' ground in the Andover and Ham Lake areas and were early pioneers in growing what is known as 'Cultured Sod' on a sod farm. Many of these new sod farms were formerly vegetable farms. All told about 70 acres was purchased and repurposed and exists to this day. At this time Bud moved all trucks, semi's and harvesting equipment to the farm and new garages and buildings. The Richfield office and retail was then moved to 65th and Cedar and he maintained this arrangement until his retirement in about 1988. In 1964, Bud and Nita built a beautiful home at 6316 Standish Avenue where they lived for many, many years. They were charitable with their families and friends and helped many families financially through hard times and unexpected needs. A true pioneer couple, and entrepreneurs who called Richfield their home.

# YOUNG OR OLD, LIFE WAS FUN HERE

**PAUL LARSON AND WENDY HOVERSTEN LARSON**

*76TH AND 11TH AVE. SO.*
*72ND AND GARFIELD AVE. SO.*

This is Paul and Wendy Hoversten Larson. We both graduated with the class of 1972. Wendy is from a family of 8 kids and the story goes there were 100 kids living on the block at 72nd and Garfield Ave in Richfield. Or we would like to think so! We kids enjoyed living on the block that was the same name as our dad's name Garfield! Many of the kids would gather at Carlson's garage in the middle of the block and make plays inside all with curtains, staging and plenty of audience and actors. It was great fun! Our dad was a science teacher at East Junior High. We loved going after school when it got out for summer to clean the hallways of pencils, erasers, notebooks and paper and keep it for next year's stash. Many of the Richfield kids would possibly have graduated with the Hoversten Family since they spanned from 1968 to 1980.They were with graduation year: Ralph 68, Linda 70, Elise 71, Wendy 72, Peter 73, Jon 74, Laurie 75, Nina 79...Paul lived on the East Side while Wendy lived on the West side. Dad couldn't teach in the same school we were at, so he got to teach at East Junior High for that reason. Wendy's dad was also a summer Driver's Ed teacher and Paul recalls a funny incident with her dad since he got to have him as an instructor for Driver's Ed. Garfield was behind the wheel showing all the incidentals while Paul was on the passenger front. In that day they had installed an additional brake on the passenger front side for the instructor to stop the car if need be. Paul noticed that the brake by him would go down when Garfield was using the brake pedal, so Paul compressed it down when Gar was trying to go in reverse and found it bewildering that he couldn't move anywhere so he pushed the accelerator a little more and then Paul took his foot off the brake and the car sped backwards pretty fast. Luckily they were in an empty parking lot! Paul wasn't allowed to ride in the front seat again except to drive. LOL!

# RICHFIELD MEMORIES

**HAL HINCHLIFFE**

*73RD AND GARFIELD AVE. SO.*

We moved to Richfield in the late 1950's. My parents bought a lot and had a home built on the 7300 block of Garfield Ave. Our house at that time was the last home on the east side of Garfield and the duplexes that are currently on 74th Street were not built yet, the upside to that was a vacant lot for the neighborhood kids to play in, and alas as the late summers would go it was a breeding ground for sand burrs. Early Richfield, school year 1958/1959 as the Class of 1965 was finishing elementary school and ready to move to Junior High School, alas, East Junior High didn't have enough room for the whole class, and plans were developed to build another Jr. High on the West side of town. Meanwhile where do we put some students for 7th grade while we build West Jr. High. The decision was made by the School Board to put a portion of class in a wing of the High School. Here we are, a group of 11 and 12 yr. olds in a school building of BIG kids. Things went along for the better part of the school year, that was until March 1960. The Lake Conference Basketball Champions, and soon to be in Minnesota State High School Tournament. For whatever reason, I don't recall right now, the decision was made there would be no pep fest……. The High School students took it upon themselves to have a pep fest. They stormed the gym, pulled the bleachers and had the pep fest. This little 7th grader was in awe of what the big guys were doing.

# RICHFIELD CAMPING?

**ROBERT "BOBO" PATRICK**

*68TH AND 18TH AVE. SO.*

Growing up in a small suburban community was difficult with a family of 6. We only had 3 bedrooms and no basement. Everyone else had a basement. Us 2 boys shared an 8X10 foot bedroom with a bunk bed and two dressers. During the summer we often put the family tent up in the backyard. It was a gigantic 10 X 10 tent with 3 windows and a zipper door. It only had one center pole but was very spacious. One summer day my brother Mike invited his classmate Bill to a sleepover. I was asked to join the older boys in the tent. I was surprised and thrilled. All went well until later in the night when the older boys told me we were going to sneak out after the folks went to sleep. We were going to walk to West Richfield where Mike's girlfriend lived. This was 1963 and the city of Richfield had a curfew for minors. As we walked the city streets, we would occasionally see approaching headlights, all three of us would jump behind a bush or tree so we wouldn't get spotted by the police. We made it to West Richfield and Mike got to talk with his girl at her bedroom window. Bill and I waited out front and we were quickly tired and bored. Bill and I decided to head back to the tent. So we struck out for East Richfield and left Mike there. As we walked, we realized we had been ducking behind bushes and trees and never saw a cop car go by. The very next car came our way and we just kept walking. Yep, it was the police. He had us get in and took us to the Richfield Police Department. He phoned my house and woke up Mother. He said he had her son at the police station. Mom said, "Not my boy, He is out back in the tent." The cop said, "You better go check". I think Mom sent Dad to check and no one was there. Dad had to drive to the Police station and pick us up and then started looking for Mike. He brought us all home with a stern warning. Dad said, "Mike, that girl's father might have shot you thinking you were a prowler".

# THE 11TH AVENUE GANG

**BRENDA GRANQUIST OLSON**

*68TH AND 11TH AVE. SO.*

I drove by my 11th Ave house in Richfield the other day and it brought back so many great memories of the fun we had as kids. We lived just two blocks from Elliott Elementary and East Junior High Schools, and we would walk to school every day. Richfield was a growing community and we had 44 kids on our block at one time — 44 Wow! Many of us grew up together over the years because our families were so young when they moved to Richfield. My best friend lived across the street, and we did everything together. And to this day we are still friends even though my best friend lives in another state. For many of us, we would ride bikes outside after school or would just hang out at each other's houses. I will never forget all the games we used to play such as "60" where someone would have to count to 60 and run all over just to find and tag you. There were so many kids that you can imagine how long it took sometimes to find them. Other games we played were "Kick the Can" and "Red Rover." My friend's dad worked at the Air Force base and one day brought home a huge airline inner tube tire that we jumped on for days and days. This became our hangout for a long time. After school or after dinner we would jump and jump on this tube until of course it popped one day. I also remember that 11th Ave became known as the 11th Ave Gang because we would hang out on a Friday or Saturday night right in front of our houses on the street. Friends would drive over, or the neighborhood kids would just hang out in the street until late at night. At least our parents knew where we were. I think about the kids these days. You don't see them playing outside as much anymore. We are fortunate to have lived in our Richfield neighborhood during the 60's and 70's!

# RICHFIELD CONNECTION

**GARY NIELSEN**

*75TH AND EMERSON AVE. SO.*

Anyone who has travelled to a far country can attest to the fact that the further you get from home, the less English you hear spoken. The year 2000 found my wife, two daughters and myself in Europe. We had started in England going to France, and then Germany. English wasn't a problem in any of these places but now we had a choice to make. We were in Europe for a family gathering in France and had a few extra days to spend, but where to go? Finally, the choices were narrowed to Madrid and Prague both being equidistant to where we were. Madrid was tempting. After all, I had enjoyed two years of Spanish at dear old RHS! But Prague was further east and seemed so mysterious. Finally, a decision was made. and we turned our little rental car to Furth im Wald, Germany. Upon arrival we found that our rental car wouldn't be allowed in the Czech Republic because of fear of theft of the car or any of its parts! We would have to leave our car in an open public parking lot. Then we needed to take a train into Prague. On arrival in Prague daylight was already slipping away and we needed to take two trams to get to our hotel. We grabbed the first one without a problem leaving us at kind of a central station where several trams stopped. Now it was more dark than light and as trams came and went but none of them was our coveted tram #11. The drivers of the others were either unable or unwilling to give us an answer. Finally, in the pitch dark, one driver told us that tram #11 didn't run that day! We had been warned that the cabs there were not safe and not to be trusted. Now what!? Unsure, we re-entered the station to make some decisions. It was then that we heard the most wonderful sound. English!! English!! The sound lifted our spirits. Right away we all started talking. There was a middle-aged woman, her daughter, and her niece. They told us they had come to Prague six months earlier and assured us that in spite of the inky blackness of the 10:30pm sky it would be safe to walk to our hotel. Yikes! The chaos of several conversations found me talking to the niece who told me she was from Minnesota. When I asked where, she replied, "the Minneapolis area". I asked her what high school she went to, and she said she had moved when she was 12 but had gone to Richfield Middle School!! I was shocked and then she was shocked when I told her I had graduated from Richfield High School. Well, we took their advice and walked. Was it scary? Yes, very but we made it thanks to our new Minnesota friends and my new classmate, one I can't name and can't even name what class she would have been in, but I'll never forget that Spartan bond, strong even so far away from home.

# THE NIGHT I MET THE TEEN KING

**TERRY AHLSTROM**
*75TH AND 5TH AVE. SO.*

It was towards the end of February 1972 in that transition period where the ice had melted at the rink and you felt let down because you had spent the whole winter there playing hockey, skating, and hanging out. You now had to find something to do. One of the warming house attendants that season at Roosevelt Park was Ron. Ron was a hip guy and I remember that he always had a somewhat new radio station called KQRS going. For those who would not know or remember, at the time it was not unusual for KQ to play a whole side of an album including the silence between album tracks. It also was on something called FM? This was out of the box thinking for many of us Richfield kids who lived in the AM world of WDGY and KDWB. One day up at the warming house just doing a bit of hanging out before some hockey Ron had the radio on tuned to KQ and they were playing a live album from a band that had been at Woodstock that dressed up like hoods, had greased back hair and were singing Elvis, Jerry Lee Lewis and some great fifties tunes. The audience on this live record was going nuts, especially when they swore and were belching into the microphones. Very sophomoric I know, but right up my alley. I loved it and it made a huge impression on me. Back in those days our main entertainment was the same as our mode of transportation, just walking around. You'd put on countless miles walking from one side of East Richfield to the other, stopping at a friends' house and picking up more friends along the way and having lots of fun doing basically nothing accept walking and hanging out. But occasionally there would be a Dance with live music. ACT dances at Assumption, House of Prayer Dances in the lower level and even Teen Club (especially when they had a live band) and there were certainly others...Back to February of 1972. It was early Saturday evening I went up to the park, no more ice to skate on, no more open warming house. I met my friend Tom who was with a girl he was dating. What did we do? Of course, we just started walking. We had walked about 4 blocks up to where Hope Church on Portland Ave. is and It looked like they were going to have some sort of dance because I saw some guys taking amplifiers and drums out of their cars. The area of the Church where they needed to get in was not opened yet, so I struck up a conversation with these band guys. What kind of music do you play? They said Oldies. Not really knowing what that meant I asked if they were like the band that was at Woodstock with the greased back hair that dressed like hoods and screwed around? They said they play old Rock n Roll music from the 50's, but they don't do all the other stuff they just play the music… Tom and his friend decided to go on their way, but I stayed, and as per usual not having any money, but being a somewhat resourceful kid I volunteered to help them carry their gear downstairs if they'd get me in to the dance for free and they agreed. We got all the stuff downstairs and set up. They said their singer was not there yet. I got the idea from the band guys that this wasn't unusual. The Singer finally shows up along with his pretty girlfriend, eventually sees me, and asks who I am. The band guys told him I am some kid who helped bring amps and equipment down and he proceeds to hand me his gold spray painted cowboy boots and said here you can carry these in for me. About 15 minutes before the dance was about to start the band disappeared. It looked like they had gone into a kitchen area to tune their guitars or something. I just huddled by the small stage hoping not to get kicked out. The place starts filling up with kids and it was packed. Someone got up on the stage did a few announcements and then said, "Please welcome to The Coffee House Teen King and the Princes!" and here comes the band walking out of the kitchen all dressed up looking like Hoods with their hair all greased back, the singer had on his gold cowboy boots and a gold lame' suit , they were belching and being smart mouths doing all the things they told me they didn't do! They told the crowd they don't do any requests and that they only play what they want and they don't do any of that modern crap. They plugged in and started playing. I was hooked. To this day I remember that it was so bad that it was GREAT! and is one of the coolest things that I had ever seen in my life. It was just like the band I had heard KQ play on Rons radio at the warming house. I grew up in a time where all my friends that played music or aspired to be musicians wanted to be in The Beatles or in The Rolling Stones. I knew my limitations and I became the kid who wanted to be in Sha Na Na ... I am happy to say that about 3 ½ years after this very true story I became a part of Teen King and the Princes and was a Prince for about the next 7 ½ years. Besides meeting some wonderful lifelong friends and lots of characters along the way, I had more Rock 'n' Roll fun than I should have ever been allowed to have…I owe it all to that night in February 1972 in the basement of Hope Church when I met The Teen King!

# CLINTON AVENUE

**DONNA JOHNSON NEU**
*75TH AND CLINTON AVE. SO.*

Clinton Avenue was an adventurous street to grow up on in the 1950s and 60s. My two older brothers and I were among 50+ kids of various ages who lived there. The most amazing thing was that all of the neighbor kids got along well, no matter how old we were. Knock on a door, ask any available kid to play, and out someone would come. That was the norm. Summertime was endless days of fun, at least before we got to the age where we had to get regular jobs. The school year would end, and suddenly the next three months of vacation stretched out in our minds, as if forever. The first two weeks were swimming lessons at the new Richfield Pool. **Brrrrrr**. The water was not heated – it was ice cold. I remember that it was usually cloudy, rainy and cold for the early morning lessons. But after they were done, we could enjoy just using the pool on hot afternoons or balmy evenings. Mornings on our street were usually kickball or softball games. After lunch, we would head to the afternoon Parks & Recreation activities at Roosevelt Park which was nearby. The park staff had us do everything from making ash trays with soda bottle caps (my brothers did that), to rehearsing one whole week for a performance of songs from the musical, "South Pacific." They even had a Doll Contest, and everyone could bring their dolls to be "judged." Of course, every doll got some type of award. I still have the doll and the award certificate! And then we'd mosey on home for a game of softball, always on the street. We originally played ball in a vacant lot near our homes, but the lot's older owner was angry about the noisy kids on his property. So one of our neighborhood Dads developed a strategy for our street games to keep all of us safe. The minute a car appeared at either 75th or 76th streets and started to turn onto our street, one, or all of us, would yell "CAR UP." Then we'd all run to the curbs on either side of the street. When the car had safely passed (probably creeping at no more than five miles per hour!!!), we would yell "CAR DOWN" and resume playing. We had tots to teens playing or watching our games, so it became a habit to do and it was a normal part of our play routine. Summers were long days of riding bikes to Lake Nokomis, visiting the library at Augsburg Park, riding the bus to shop at the Hub or Southdale, walking to the Milk House on Nicollet Avenue for popsicles and fudgesicles, perusing the aisles of Atlantic Mills, watching matinees at the old Richfield Theater, attending Twins games at Metropolitan Stadium and playing games. As the long days ended and darkness set in, my childhood friend's father would step out onto the porch and give a loud whistle that resonated throughout the neighborhood. It was like a whistle at the end of a workday, or for us, a play day. Then we'd all head home. By the end of the summer, we were ready to go back to school after attending the State Fair. And my birthday was at the end of August, on the same day as my childhood friend, Clare. So we had two separate birthday parties on the same day. Wow, two parties, two cakes, lots of presents. It was quite the way to end the summer for us and our neighborhood pals. The Richfield Parks Department did a fantastic job arranging summer youth activities. And of course, the skating rinks with warming houses were wonderful during the winter. I remember lots of burned mitten smells from the old stove inside the warming house at the ice rink. My two close childhood friends and I often reminisce with fun stories about our old neighborhood, and it seems like yesterday. Most of the neighbors kept in contact through the years and supported each other's families. We three feel that we were very lucky to have had such wonderful times together. I will always be grateful for my childhood on Clinton Avenue.

# GROWING UP ON 68TH AND 18TH

**MARY HERZOG RYAN**

*68TH AND 18TH AVE. SO.*

Our neighborhood had about 60 kids in a 4-block radius. We played all the time… Kick the can, Ghosties, Mr. Tangleweave( I think that is what it was called) where we all held hands and then twisted up and someone had to come and untangle us without breaking the chain. Annie Annie over…. Christian Park was a blast!! Big sliding hill and huge Ice-skating rink. The hockey rink as well where the Christoff brothers played. As you know Steve Christoff went on to win a gold medal in the 1980 Olympics… Summer at the park was the hump a jump. My sister Judy and her friend Nancy Mason were the champs of the park. Kick ball. Riding bikes to other parks to partake in games. I could go on and on…What can I say about the Richfield pool???? Every kid in Richfield practically lived there all summer long… Richfield little league looking to see if the white flag was flying after the rain to see if we could play. Racks of bikes at the field. Getting snacks at the snack shack… Plane crash on 67th and 18 in the 70's. My dad watched it crash as he was coming home from Richfield liquor store. My little brother was riding his sting ray bike as fast as he could to let us know what happened. Very vivid memory. So sad… The day we got city water, and they filled up our well. When we got cement curbs put in, we all watched the trucks come poor the cement… Sitting on our garage listening to the Twins games…. The Barnum and Bailey

Circus. They would come by train to Minnehaha and then walk the animals to the Met center. My mom would take us across Cedar Avenue to watch. Clowns, animals, and I think they even gave us popcorn… There were Fireworks shows across cedar Ave where one year something happened, and they all blew up at once. We kids thought it was cool, but it was a big mess.

# WORKING FOR MR. EMBERSON

**WAYNE JOHNSON**

*75TH AND CLINTON AVE. SO.*

I have many fond memories of growing up in Richfield. One of them pertains to a job I had while attending East Junior High in the late 1950s. I worked for Mr. Curtis Emberson, who was a teacher at East. He had a small part-time business of delivering hand bills for grocery and hardware stores. He hired several boys from the school to work two to three hours after school to help him. We would typically work one afternoon a week, and maybe an occasional Saturday. A typical afternoon job after school would be to ride in his panel truck to one of his customers. The truck held about six boys. Once he picked up the hand bills, Mr. Emberson would tell each of us how many bills to count out, depending on the route. He would give us an apron which held the bills and to grab a handful of rubber bands, that were used to attach the bills to house doorknobs. When we delivered in Richfield, he would drop each of us off on a different avenue on 76th street. We would then deliver handbills on one side of the street, going all the way to 66th street. Once there, we would cross over the street and return to our starting point, doing the same thing. We were paid about a penny per handbill. In East Richfield, there are about eight houses on each side of the block, so ten blocks up and ten blocks back totaled roughly 160 bills delivered. This came to a grand total of $1.60. If we worked on a Saturday in Minneapolis, we could easily deliver 800 to 1,000 bills that day, especially if we had several larger apartments on the route. Not much money, but better than returning empty Coke bottles to a grocery store for three cents each! One late afternoon in November, we were delivering in East Richfield. One of my best friends was with me that day. At the end of our routes, we were getting picked up and ready to go home. I was already in the truck when my good friend got picked up. It was dark at that time and my friend was very quiet. I asked him how it went but he didn't say much. He then took his hand away from his face and I was shocked to see him bleeding from his face and lip. He told us that while on his route, he met a fellow student who punched him in the face for no reason. I knew the kid who punched him. He was a wanna be 'tough guy' in eighth grade at our school. Shortly thereafter, I'm sure Mr. Emberson handled the issue with my friend's parents and the school. I lost track of the wanna be 'tough guy' and knew he didn't graduate from high school with me. I think some of the good old days aren't always as pleasant as we remember, but I continued working at that job until the end of 9th grade, and felt safe working for Mr. Emberson.

# THE GRANARY ANTIQUES AND FLOWERS

**MOLLY MCGINNIS**
*69TH AND 5TH AVE. SO.*

Many of you may remember the Granary Antiques and Flowers, a true hidden gem located on 68th and Emerson Lane in Richfield. Most referred to as The Granary. This popular shop was owned by my second Cousin Carolyn Bachman Haglof and her husband Milo Haglof. A little snippet of our family history – Carolyn was the daughter of Henry Carl August Bachman and Betsy Deborah Smith Bachman. Betsy was the sister of my maternal grandmother. Upon retiring, Carolyn and Milo opened The Granary Antiques and Flowers. Carolyn had quite a creative talent for floral arrangements and antiques. There was always something new to see while you were there, from dried florals to antique collectibles. Everything was displayed just perfectly. Carolyn had a glass display case showcasing her middle daughter's toys from the 1950's era when she was a young child. On display were metal spin tops to antique dolls. One of my favorite displays to look at when I was there. I always enjoyed Carolyn telling me about each toy. A wonderful keepsake and memory. During the holiday season Carolyn always had a special event at The Granary which would bring many shoppers and antique collectors. A shoppers haven! One of my favorite purchases was an old round wooden cheese box, although I always referred to it as a hat box. It was the ideal round cheese box to hold many special

Christmas ornaments in. Where they are kept today, years later. As time passes by, and many years later Richfield shops that were once are gone. The memories and history shared will always be there.

# HENDRICKSON HOCKEY IN RICHFIELD!

**JULIE HENDRICKSON-OSS**

*FOREST DRIVE*

As soon as I can remember, hockey has been a huge part of our life in Richfield as the youngest member of the Hendrickson Family. While other friends' parents parked in their garages, our Hendrickson garage was a full fitness gym equipment with strong men lifting all the time. I didn't know at the time, but the weightlifters were players from the 1980 Olympic team and players for the MN Northstars. My dad Larry was a young teacher & coach in Richfield in the 70-80s and he had a player named Steve Christoff that was scouted by Coach Herbie Brooks for the 1980 Olympic team. Larry & Herbie instantly became fast friends & Herbie would bring the players over for weight training & the first notion of "off ice" training. The joke is that Larry was the "unofficial" official strength coach for the Olympic team so never got that gold medal! I am told my father was a big part of bringing to light the importance of strength training outside of the ice rink. Larry was pivotal in getting the ice rink made in Richfield & working for the Spartans to have a powerful hockey program. As we resided in Richfield, the weightroom was then used by my brothers Danny & Darby (1991 State Tournament contenders) & as well as my sister Christine's friends & boyfriends, who was a hockey cheerleader & skater. Our garage was a free gym that kids could use, as long as you had a spotter! It was a special place to grow up as you just never knew who would be coming in the door & how famous some of these players were! Hockey has really brought our family together with so many people in Richfield today, who have become lifelong friends. We are proud of the legacy of Richfield hockey & the impact my father & family had on the program. Today we continue our late father's legacy with Hendrickson Foundation, whom seeks to enrich the lives of individuals with disabilities, and their families, through the game of hockey. Our focus is to make hockey accessible for ALL who want to play the game. By supporting adaptive and Warrior hockey programs' growth and participation nationwide, we aim to break barriers and promote inclusivity in the game. I now have 3 boys that play hockey in Bloomington, and we have now merged with Richfield so I get to relive my wonderful childhood with my boys with the next generation of Richfield Spartans! It all started in Richfield for our family and amazing the impact that has grown through the decades to connect families from all over the country and continue our Spartan PRIDE!

# HELLO?

**LINDA MAHER**

*68TH AND PENN AVE. SO.*

Looking back, one of the everyday essentials that changed most dramatically for me was the telephone. In the 50's, most homes had a phone. It was a heavy black metal phone that would sit in a prominent corner of your house. I remember my grandparents' phone being in the "front porch" sitting on a desk. This thing could be used as a weapon as it weighed more than a baseball bat! To make a call, you had to put your finger in the correct hole and drag the dial around until it stopped. You had to dial the prefix, a single number, and then a 4-digit number. The prefix was the first two letters of a word, and if you made a mistake, you started over. Most phones in the Richfield area had exchanges such as: Tuxedo (TU), Union (UN), Rockwell (RO), etc. It could take a while to dial someone. That is, if you had a "line" open. Most homes had a party line (a phone line shared by a neighbor close by). So, you "could" pick up the phone and listen to what was going on in the neighborhood. Not that anyone would do that. In addition, since the lines were often shared, you had to identify your calls before answering by a ring sequence. Maybe it was one long and two short or one short and one long ring. But you had to pay attention and not jump on the line too quickly because it may not be for you. A fun feature that got me in trouble was a two-digit number you could dial, and the phone would ring back to you. Testing, as it was. It was also very annoying for the adults in the house. Another feature allowed me to call a phone number to get the time. It was novel. Not that I couldn't look at the clock in the room. But, if there was any doubt as to what time it was, that's how you could verify it. No re-dial, no calling history, no pre-programmed numbers, just numbers in a circle that you pulled along with a finger until you created the phone number you were calling. Back then, phone books were heavily relied upon. The Richfield one listed our name, address, phone number, age of kids and place of employment for the head of household. It was more like a mini census report. There was never a "hold" feature. "Hold" consisted of hanging the phone on the closest thing possible and yelling, "you've got a call". "Do Not Disturb", consisted of leaving your phone off the hook. And, hopefully remembering that you need to put it back on at some point. On the plus side, you could never lose your phone. It wasn't very mobile. And, if you wanted to make a dramatic exit from a call, your caller knew when you slammed the receiver down. As I got older, wall phones became popular. My parents got one for the kitchen with a very very long coiled cord on the handset. It often got beyond tangled. It looked awful and sometimes ended up in a big ball of wires. That cord would stretch across the kitchen and down the hall into my room. It became kind of a tripping hazard, but at least mom and dad couldn't listen in. When I was a little older, the Princess phone came on the market. I thought I died and went to heaven. Granted, this was an extension, but it was MY VERY OWN PHONE. It was beautiful. Aqua. I loved that phone. And, had to work to pay for it. The evolution of the everyday phone was quite mind-blowing.

# FIND YOUR PASSION

**MICHELLE HAMMOND**

*67TH AND SHERIDAN AVE. SO.*

My Junior year at RHS my 11th Grade teacher Mr. McMartin took his glasses off and told our class "People, I will NEVER dock your grades if you miss my class to travel. Mark my words, you will learn more about life and people than you ever will in my classroom". My Senior year my parents took us to Hawaii for my Spring break. I fell in love with travel after that trip and swore I would become a Flight Attendant so I could travel. In 1989 my dream came true as one of the last classes of Northwest Airlines Flight Attendants to wear the traditional "stewardess hat". By the time we were flying they had retired the hat. I have traveled the world and been to almost every state in the good old USA. Mr. McMartin was right. To this day I am so thankful for the 15 years I worked as a Northwest Airlines Flight Attendant. I met wonderful people from all over this great world. I am forever thankful for Mr. McMartin and his passion. There were countless teachers at Richfield that not only taught us what they were supposed to, but the ones who shared their passions taught us to follow our own. Leo Poehling is another one of the most beloved... I'm proud to be a Richfield Spartan, always have been and always will!

# RICHFIELD BASEBALL IN THE 60'S AND 70'S

**BARRY AND BOB BISHOP**

*64TH AND NEWTON AVE. SO.*

Under the guidance of coaches Gene Olive and Jim Hare, Richfield baseball established itself as one of the most successful baseball programs in the State of Minnesota. The contributions of these two men along with the many volunteer coaches, parents, community members and businesses, were vital to that success. The 1000's of kids that were involved in the Little League (ages 7-12) and Babe Ruth (ages 13-15) programs served as the foundation that made Richfield baseball one of the premier programs in the state. RHS won 4 of the 5 State Tournaments they qualified for. The overall Tournament winning percentage of 93% is still the all-time best State Tournament winning percentage. Many of the players went on to have success playing collegiate baseball, with a number of players signing contracts with major league teams.In the 60's and 70's, the community of Richfield distinguished itself as the Gold Standard for outstanding youth baseball programs.

# THE NEIGHBORHOOD

GAYLE M. SKLUZACEK

*64TH AND 19TH AVE. SO.*

My parents moved to New Ford Town in 1955. My father bought our house at 6444 19th Avenue with a loan from my maternal grandfather and the GI Bill. They paid $11,000 for a two-bedroom, one bathroom rambler on a large corner lot. The house was ideal for a young family with two small girls aged 2 and 3. Within weeks, my sister, Cheryl, and I met our first best friends - the three-year-old Ayres twins, Darcy and Diane. The four of us were inseparable in our Pre K years. We did sleepovers, shared meals, Popsicles, Kool Aid, our meager toys, and our parents. Their father taught me to ice skate and eventually was my softball coach. My father taught us to play "horse" as we shot basketballs into the hoop on the side of our garage. Seasons went by, and more and more kids entered the neighborhood. Gradually our inner circle was joined by the Montori girls, Carla and Patty. Carla was my age and Patty was a year older than Cheryl and the twins. As school and younger siblings took a toll on our friendship, Christmas breaks, weekends, snow days and those wonderful summer nights rekindled our bond.

Our house faced 65th Street (south) and was one house away from the one-way Longfellow Avenue (to the west) which was a dead end due to the construction of the Cedar Avenue Highway (called Highway 77 today). There was very little through traffic, making the street in front of our house perfect for softball, kickball, foursquare, hopscotch and any imaginative chalk-defined game. Since Cheryl, Darcy, Diane, Patti, Carla, and I were an easy two teams, we often met in the street and other kids joined in. We welcomed any child whose parents let them play with us. We would play until we were called for dinner. Once school was out in June and the days became longer, we met every day (always after chores) until dinner (usually around 5:00). Then returned after dinner to our corner for some night action. We played in the street until it was too dark to see when we played Starlight/moonlight - a scary version of hide and seek in the dark. Our mothers usually called us in around 9 or 10 o'clock. The next day we got up and did it again!

# THE MORRIS NILSEN BOYS CHOIR

**DAVID WALLER**

*72ND AND GARFIELD AVE. SO.*

Founded by Morris Nilsen Sr., this group of 60-65 boys with unchanged voices was a dream to bring something similar to the Vienna Boys Choir to the Twin Cities of Minneapolis and St. Paul. When people heard about the choir, we were often asked if we just sang for funerals, as our sponsor was the Morris Nilsen Funeral Chapel in Richfield. I was a member of the choir from 1968-1972. During those four years, we only sang at one funeral, and that was the funeral of one of our fellow choir members, who tragically died while he was still singing with the choir. We sang for churches, schools and organizations throughout the Twin Cities and greater Minnesota. As Morris Nilsen Sr. grew older, his son, Morris Nilsen Jr. continued the tradition of offering young boys in the greater Twin Cities area the opportunity to sing a wide variety of song styles, including sacred, secular, show tunes and even songs in German and Latin. Under the direction of David Van Fleet and later Bea Speed, this choir gave us a platform to develop our voices and musical skills, but also built a foundation of confidence and created a brotherhood within our membership. Young boys became young men while singing locally, which prepared us for our annual tours. These tours included the World's Fair in San Antonio, TX, the Portland Rose Festival in Oregon and Washington DC during my tenure with the choir. Many special memories and a great learning opportunity in addition to wonderful chances to sing some special music were all part of participation in the Morris Nilsen Boys Choir, right here in Richfield, Minnesota

# DREAM HOUSE

**SARA BARNABY AND DAVE BURGWALD**

*73RD AND LYNDALE AVE. SO.*

I got my dream house early in our marriage. We lived in an old farmhouse at 7329 Lyndale Ave. South in Richfield, MN for 23 years. We still live in Richfield. But before Richfield, we lived in Minneapolis. We were a family of four, 2 adults, a 4 ½ year old daughter and a18 month old son, living in a two-bedroom house in South Minneapolis. We were looking for a new home for our growing family. We had been considering a dream house on acreage in the suburbs. My grade school friend was urging us to come to Richfield. Richfield had a K-6 school at the time. One Sunday, I scanned the "For Sale" section of the paper for houses. I spotted an ad for a large four-bedroom home on Lyndale Ave. I thought our future home was on the west side of Lyndale. So, I told my daughter, the oldest, "I bet we can't afford this house but let's go look at the house anyway". I drove by the homes on Lyndale and realized that I was wrong. Hidden behind a hedge was this large white farmhouse, on the east side of Lyndale. My daughter and I started exploring the house. We both became more and more excited as we checked out all the nook and crannies of the 78-year-old house. One unique feature was a stump of a tree, in the middle of the backyard fence. It also had an old apple tree and a tree in the front yard with oddly twisting limbs. Could this become my dream home? A farmhouse in Richfield of all places? I looked at the listing. We would be the fourth owners of this house. The first owner was a prominent Holstein breeder, John B. Irwin, and the home was part of the Irwin farm. The farm had an award-winning cow, Duchess Skylark Ormsby also known as "World's Greatest Cow" until she was de-throned in 1921. The second owner was E.C. Kelly who had a poultry farm (Bonnyview Farm). Kelly sold it to Richard Rendahl in 1963. He owned the home until 1993 when it was put up for sale. We could afford this house! My daughter and I headed home. We rounded up my husband and toddler son and toured the home again. The home had a wonderful built-in China cabinet that opened to the pantry and the dining room. (We had a dining room set finished to match the cabinet). There were wood floors throughout. The closets were all deep. There was a porch off one of the upstairs bedrooms. These quality touches to the farmhouse reflected the first owner of this house, John B. Irwin, he also served as Richfield Mayor. The excitement spread to my whole family as my children checked out the four floors. This would be the best house for hide and seek. We knew this home would not last long on the market. I had been seeing a realtor's sign in my neighborhood. We called her that Sunday. She was over by 4:00 pm. We were truly blessed with the ability to afford two house payments. We put in a non-contingent offer that night. Within hours, the house of our dreams was ours. The magic of this dream home continued, as we sold our old home. It sold the first weekend we showed it. A young couple bought their first home and our realtor got the whole commission on our old home. Fast forward 23 years, we had aged out of the house. We planned a 100-year birthday party for the house. It was a great day. A highlight was the older couple who told about the strawberry fields that they grew up with, behind our farmhouse, our dream house.

# MY TRIP FROM EDINA TO RICHFIELD

**MIKE MCLEAN**

*71ST AND STEVENS AVE. SO.*

My journey from 3rd grade in Edina in 1956 to my Richfield residency which began in 1970 was by no means a straight trip. My parents built a house in rural Edina in 1956 on West 68th street. It was located about 2 blocks East of where the current Edina High School is located. The current high school location was all horse pasture. Across the street from our house was a corn field and a horse barn and riding stable. Between 68th south to 70th, Antrim east to Tracy Ave there were less than 15 homes. I started third grade at Cahill Elementary which was at the time a six-room school. First through sixth. They started an addition on Cahill as I started fourth grade at Concord. Fifth grade at Highland. Sixth grade at Wooddale for the first half year and the second half back at the completed Cahill. Seventh grade at Edina Junior High school. After seventh grade we moved to Tucson for eighth grade, freshman, and sophomore years. In 1963 we moved back to Edina and bought the house right next door to the house that my parents built. I graduated in 1965 from Edina High School. Attended the U of M for one year and then joined the Navy. Spent two years in California at boot camp in San Diego and the Schools Command in Vallejo north of San Francisco. Back to Edina to start at Brown Institute days and work at Control Data second shift. I married a 1964 Richfield graduate in 1970 and moved to Century Court apartments on Penn and 494. We were paying $145 a month rent. Moved in with her mother on Clinton Avenue, divorced and moved into New Orleans Court apartments 1975.In 1977 I bought a 22x22 little Richfield house on the back of the lot. Moved in on Sept 1st. I bought a house plan with materials from a company called Capp Homes. Once you have the basement foundation in, they would deliver the first stage of materials. They then would build your house to any degree of completion that you wanted. I had them stop when they had installed all of the exterior walls and roof along with the windows and doors. Then with the help of family and good friends, we wired, plumbed, and installed the HVAC. We also roofed the house and installed all of the siding. We also sheet rocked and painted the walls. Had the carpet installed and moved into the new house in May of 1978. We converted the little house into a two-stall garage. I lived in the little house the winter of 77. The biggest surprise was the first time the snowplow came down the alley about 5 feet from my bed…I've lived in Richfield 53 enjoyable years!

# MEETING TONY O.

**REBECCA BENSON SEVERSON**
*76TH AND GARFIELD AVE. SO.*

One of my earliest Richfield memories was meeting Minnesota Twin Tony Oliva! He was sitting in the back of the National Tea grocery store on 76th and Lyndale signing his autograph to his TWINS picture. I'm guessing this was about 1965. I was as shy as he was! Not sure if I was alone or with one of my sisters. I feel like I went up there alone. The only players I remember at the time were him and Harmon Killebrew. I mean I was all of 6 or 7. I don't remember a line of people to meet him. Just a ballplayer sitting at a table. After I received my signed picture, he handed me a popsicle. Pretty sure NO words were uttered between us. But it was a memory that has always stayed with me. I met him years later in 2013 at a TWIN'S Fest. It would have been fun to share this story with him.

# THE STORY OF ROYAL AND ESTHER BAUSER

**ROGER BAUSER**

*67TH AND HUMBOLDT AVE. SO.*

My parents Royal and Esther Bauser (née Lloyd) moved to Richfield from the state of New York. Their respective upbringing was entirely different. Roy grew up in the middle of New York City and Esther grew up on a poor farm in the small town of Lima located in upstate New York. Esther's family had no running water, no indoor toilets, and the only source of heat was derived from fireplaces. The house was built in the 1770's and was very crude. Knowing a secondary degree could provide a better life Esther enrolled in Gene State and received her degree in Elementary Education and Library Science. Roy was attending divinity school when they were introduced. They met one another through a mutual friend, and they had a short courtship. Upon graduation Roy took a job in Richfield, MN at the Richfield Baptist church. A minister friend from NY, Homer Armstrong having relocated from NY, recommended Roy for the position at Richfield Baptist. Roy took the position sight unseen. Roy and Esther were married in 1943, and immediately traveled to Richfield. Traveling was difficult on single lane roads at that time because during the WWII wartime gas and tires were rationed. Neither of their family members had ever left New York so it was an entirely new experience for both of them and their families. Out of blatant ignorance their older relatives told them that beyond New Jersey the earth stopped and if they got to Richfield they would live in an igloo amongst the Indians. Upon arrival Esther and Roy were greeted by an old run-down church and parsonage. Esther wondered what she had gotten herself into. After putting herself through college she never expected that she would end up living a life worse than where she began. The church was located on 61st and Lyndale and at that time the boundaries of Richfield went further north than they do today. Lyndale was a dirt road with farms surrounding the church. As disappointed as Esther was Roy, the eternal optimist, lived by the mantra of "my glass is half full not half empty". Roy was determined to make the best of things. And making the best of it he did. Roy built a new church in 1949 on the opposite side of Richfield on 77th and Emerson. He was able to do so because a church member donated the property to the church. The corner where the church stood on 77th and Emerson is now the northeast corner of 494 and 35W. During this time Roy became disillusioned with the Baptist approach to religion. After much deliberation he decided to break away from the Baptist religion and build a church in the Congregational faith. Prior to building the church his congregants held services at Woodlake School. During this transition period the US Baptist denomination sued Roy claiming he stole furniture and parishioners from them. The US Baptist denomination lost their lawsuit in court because the charges were falsely accused. The old Baptist church stood empty for many years and vandals eventually ruined it. Even though it was in terrible condition in the late 1950's a beautiful pipe organ remained. Roy was unable to appreciate many of the fruits of his labor. The Congregational church grew generously and became very successful. The pews were always full. An education wing was created and brought to fruition in August of 1959. However, in 1955 Roy was diagnosed with colon cancer and he died in October 1959 at the young age of 45. His successes were many but his time at the Congregational Church was brief at only seven short years. Esther was able to put her degree to use when she became the first degreed librarian in Bloomington. Fortunately for Esther not many women had a college degree in the 50's and because Esther did, she was able to provide an income (which paid the same salary as a teacher) to support her family after Roy passed. Unfortunately, most ministers in the 1950's typically lived in a church parsonage as part of their compensation. Because Roy and Esther never purchased property and their home was church property Esther and her children were technically homeless when Roy died. However, out of the charity of the church they were given housing until they found another home. Fortunately, times have changed, and most ministers realize that they should own their own home today rather than receive housing from the church. The Congregational Church persevered over the years. However as most of Richfield's population aged out the population of Richfield diminished. It appears as though Roy kept watch over his church from above because an anonymous church member paid off the mortgage in the 1980's for approximately $80,000. Shortly thereafter, Best Buy bought the church for $1,000,000 that allowed the congregation to construct a brand-new church at no cost to the congregation. The church was built a block north on 76th and Grand and still stands proudly today.

# RICHFIELD HISTORY - IN THE "CENTER" OF THINGS

**JOHN BJOSTAD**

*70TH AND HARRIET AVE. SO.*

Do you think we could make a history Center out of this? That question was asked time and again in the early 1990's when the school system decided the Richfield Historical Society could utilize the shed previously used as a wood shop. Under the excited direction of Ruthann Clay, the building was creatively made to stand straight again by workers like Dick & Cherill Lindquist, Jon & Don Clay, Herman & Nel Swanson and Greg Olson. Book sales, ice cream socials, and art sales took place to pay for the sparse materials,– and the work progressed very slowly for several years. A new leadership regime came on board in the early 2000's, and the realization that we could really do this was spearheaded by David Butler, our fundraiser guru at the time. So, in 2003, plans were drawn up by an architect and many of us caught the fever! By May of 2004, we selected a contractor who said they could give us the building of our dreams for about $120,000. They swooped in and started demo of a few of the things we had already done, like stairs to the upper level. We were aghast at their actions and called for them to slow down. A few days later the bosses came in and said their estimate was too low. They would need about $250,000. to do the work. Our jaws hit the floor, but we could not afford the higher cost.

Thank goodness we had a lawyer on the Board, and they were fired immediately. Now what to do? Why don't we do it ourselves? And a work crew was established right then and there. Joe Cleaveland, Norm Hines, John Bjostad said they were willing to work every day. Other members helped on weekends and the transformation took place. We hired a part time experienced carpenter, Paul Anderson, to keep us on track Our main crew put in over 1,500+ hours each over the last half of 2004 and into the winter of 2005. A gallery area, office, library, and two climate controlled areas were the result. Early in 2005 we hired our first Director with museum experience to establish our programs. On May 5, 2005, we held a grand opening of a History Center to go along with the 1852 Bartholomew House Museum that Richfield residents and visitors have been using and donating artifacts to, ever since.

# HOW I ARCHIE WARD'ED THE SYSTEM

**TOM TANK CHRISTENSEN**

*FERN DRIVE AND DIAGONAL BLVD.*

At Richfield High there was a protocol football players had to follow in the locker room ONLY Backs and Receivers could wear the classy lowcut shoes while ALL Linemen must wear the ugly high-top shoes on game day. It was a rigid protocol followed by the coaches taping the ankles of all backs and receivers on Friday afternoons in the Locker room before the Friday night game. NO Lineman allowed. The taping was considered by the backs and receivers as a ceremony for the 'elite,' while the poor linemen had no ankle taping and flopped around during the game in their high-top foot boots. Yet, though I was a lineman, I was determined to not be excluded by this tradition. Let me explain. I had been a full back all my football career since the age of 8 until my junior year. My 8th grade coach named me "TANK" because I just ran over opposing players so effectively. The name and my specialty stuck. However, in 1966 Coach Collison (Head Coach) and Archie Ward (Line Coach) came up with a new offensive scheme. Previously, the one distinction of my role was that as a fullback I had run around mowing down defensive players to set loose our running backs. Now, with the new offensive scheme, my position was changed. My job was still to pull out on most plays and run around knocking down defensive players, but this time as a lineman. I really couldn't protest as being a team player on the Spartan team was expected of any participant. Wherever the coaches thought you were needed, that is what you did. But here's the thing, as a lineman, I must wear high top shoes for the games, have no low cuts provided to me, and certainly no taping of my ankles on Friday afternoon by the coaches! Hurrupph. I thought this was going to call for a bit of a quiet yet forceful revolution in the football locker room. So, the week before the first Friday night game, I purchased my own set of snazzy low-cut shoes, and new white socks to wear for our first game. The test was now to storm the Bastille of the Friday afternoon ankle taping tradition in the locker room. So that Friday afternoon I screwed on my courage, I walked into the locker room, sat up on the taping table amidst some confused and hostile stares of the backs and receivers, and stuck my ankle out. I could smell the thoughts coming from the other players. A LINEMAN in the taping room? What has the world come to? The coach at the table began to say, "Christensen what are you doing in here," but Archie Ward sensing the tension, came over to the table and said to the coach, "I'll take care of this one." As Archie stood there, I thought, "Oh, oh, I'm going to get it now." But then something amazing happened. He said not a word, gave me that cat caught the mouse smile and quietly began taping my ankles. That night and all the other game nights for two years I got my ankles taped and wore my snazzy low-cut shoes. What an amazing example of character from Coach Archie Ward. I have never forgotten it.

# THE RICHFIELD NEWS

**JON WICKETT**

*72ND AND 3RD AVE. SO.*

On Thursday, January 23, 1941, hot off the presses came the first issue of The Richfield News. This predecessor of the Richfield Sun Current was the creation of owner, Aubrey Smith and Managing Editor, Oscar B. Strand. They had the idea that Richfield, with a population similar to that of Stillwater and Eveleth, did not have a "majority voice" when it came to sources of news. The area was dominated by the big city newspapers of Minneapolis and St. Paul.

From the first edition:

Sincerely Yours...With this first issue the NEWS makes its bow to the Village of Richfield. We come to you with a definite purpose and promise: to bring into your home every Thursday a complete report of what's new and news in Richfield. The kind of news you'll want to read because it is closest to home…

The Richfield News came to be one of the largest circulated locals in the metro area. Covering major national stories, such as World War II and the Kennedy Assassination. Major local stories including the death of the only Richfield Police Officer killed in the line of duty, Fred

Babcock. But the Richfield News primarily focused on the issues that really mattered in a growing community like Richfield in the post-war era. The paper informed the public about the need for a sewer and water system, the need for a high school, and other city needs while still balancing coverage for the farming community. In the 1950's the paper was bought by Robert Broad, Ted Farrington, and Larry Farrington who continued the paper's proud traditions as a major voice for the southern suburbs. The paper ceased publication in the mid-1960s, but its legacy continues in the Richfield community. After Larry Farrington's untimely death in 1968, the Richfield Chamber of Commerce established the Larry Farrington Award in 1969 to recognize his long service to the Richfield community and the Chamber. This award is still awarded this day to the person who best exemplifies the spirit that the "world is not just a profit-and-loss statement, but a combination of community spirit and being supportive of Richfield businesses"

The Richfield News may be no more, but the imprint it left on the now City of Richfield can be seen every day, from our fantastic municipal water to becoming a major shopping destination with the Hub.

# MY RICHFIELD STORY

**DAWN NILSEN WENNER**

*64TH AND 11TH AVE. SO.*

Our family moved to a new house in Richfield in 1955, on my sister's first birthday. 6435 11th Avenue was across the street from "the swamp," a fabulous playground for kids. My first wedding was at the age of 5 and was held in the back yard of Clarence and Dagmar Christian. Neighbor,

Lisa Hanto (age 7) officiated the ceremony and my groom, also age 5, was another neighbor, Steve Bingea. With so many kids on the block, we played kick the can nearly every night. We explored the swamp, climbed trees, played in the street until someone yelled "CAR" and we ran to the curb. The swimming pool was our babysitter most of the summer. How many of us kids were upset when it was ADULT NIGHT at the pool, and we couldn't go swimming after supper! I could ride my bike to the pool right after lunch and pedal back home for supper. No wonder most of the kids in school were blond, all that chlorine did a number on our scalps. East Elementary was my grade school. The year the school was closing, our family moved to WEST Richfield. I graduated in 1980 with many of my east and west side friends. The HUB, BRIDGEMAN'S, FIRESIDE PIZZA, and SANDY'S were my favorite hangouts. Does anyone remember Rich Acres Golf Course? I worked there for a couple years right after it opened in 1980. With my parents, I got to play the first round on the Par 3 course. It was a sad day when it closed and was taken back over by the airport. In my mid 20's I was hired by the Richfield Fire Department and worked for 23 years as a firefighter. It was a tremendous opportunity serving the citizens of Richfield! I saw many changes over the years. The building of more senior high rises, the demolition of Ford Town and the Rich Acres neighborhoods, changing over the road from 76th Street to 77th Street as the main thoroughfare across the south end of town, roundabouts built at many intersections, an increase in the number and severity of the calls to which the FD would respond. I'll always be thankful for the way the FD put the citizens first. My family has owned a funeral chapel in Richfield since before I was born. Knowing that my grandfather, dad and brother were also serving the Richfield community gave me a great deal of pride. The phones would ring at our home some evenings. We all knew it was time to be quiet when Dad had to answer, "the business phone." The family business is still being run by my brother and his tremendous staff...Richfield will always be my hometown!

# HOW MUCH OF AMERICA CAN YOU GET TO FROM RICHFIELD IN A MONTH?

**PETER MCKENNA**

*LYNDALE AND OAK GROVE BLVD.*

As I journey by bus this afternoon between Washington, DC and New York City, I am reminded of the "ultimate" bus trip I set off on 50 years ago this week. In 1973 I was 15 and my neighbor Bobby Peterson was 14. I had heard about a new program the Greyhound bus company launched that year called "Ameripass" which offered UNLIMITED bus travel throughout the USA for an entire month for $149. So, Bobby and I made a plan. We set up a business engraving people's names on matchbooks, which we pedaled around the neighborhood for $2.50 for a box of fifty matchbooks. (Back then everyone smoked, and it was a status symbol to have personalized matchbooks laying around.) We raised almost $800, and after buying our two passes, had $500 to spend on other travel-related expenses for the month, which we figured we could do if we spent as many nights as possible sleeping on buses or visiting relatives rather than springing for a hotel...And travel we did! We boarded our first bus in Minneapolis, Minnesota and made our way through North Dakota, Montana, Idaho and Washington, stopping for a day of sightseeing in Seattle. Then down through Oregon into California, where we visited San Francisco, Los Angeles and San Diego. Next we hit Arizona, New Mexico and Texas, overnighting in Dallas and Houston. Then Louisiana, for two nights in New Orleans, before heading off to Mississippi, Alabama, Georgia and Florida. Got as far south as Fort Lauderdale and Miami, then headed back north, again through Georgia, then South and North Carolina, Virginia, and Washington, DC. Next came Maryland, Delaware, New Jersey, and New York. After two days in NYC, we continued north even further to Connecticut and Massachusetts (Boston) before turning west again to visit Pennsylvania, Ohio, Indiana, Michigan, Illinois (Chicago) and Wisconsin, arriving back in Minnesota on the very day our month-long passes expired. We calculated we visited 30 U.S. states, saw 10 state capitals, swam in two oceans, traveled a total of just over 10,500 miles — and had the time of our lives doing it! Decades later I joked with my mom she would be arrested and charged with "reckless abandonment of a minor" if she ever let me do something "unchaperoned" like this nowadays. But I'm sure glad she did. What a fun adventure!

# FROM DUELL'S CAFÉ TO THE BROADWAY LEMONS

PATTI STERBUCK AND STEVEN O. LINDGREN

In 1949, a group of business folks at 76th and Lyndale (Highway 65) started meeting for coffee at 10:15 a.m. every day at Duell's Cafe in the 7600 block of Lyndale Avenue South in Richfield. Our best recollections indicate the group included Don Anderson (Woodlake Barber Shop), Dr. Mitby, Bob and Merilyn Jensen (Tandem Printing), but no doubt included many others. While we don't go back to 1949 as coffee drinkers, we do go back to 1949 and 1950 in Richfield. After Duell's Cafe closed, the group moved closer to Tandem Printing to the Plaza Cafe on I-494, as the Richfield SUN-CURRENT chronicled in a story written by Don Heinzman in December 1980. By this time, it had been named the Lemon Tree group and according to the article: "Present when the roll was called (there were no minutes) were Bob Jensen, always the president, Rinky Sanders, Don Anderson, Larry Loeffler, Denny Nuenfeldt, Gordy Herboldt, John Hamilton, Clayt Eggsaard, Bob Elliott and George Karnas." According to the article, the group had been meeting for coffee since 1957. However, this reference might be only to the years at this location. In 1984, when the Lemon Tree Restaurant was destroyed by fire, Merilyn Jensen headed to Broadway Pizza at 7514 Lyndale to meet with Patti Sterbuck the owner about the possibility of having the group meet there every day at 10:15 a.m. Monday-Friday. When Patti informed Merilyn the restaurant didn't open until 11:00 a.m., Merilyn, quickly responded with "that's ok, we will make our own coffee." Thus, was born the renamed Broadway Lemon Coffee Group. Now approaching nearly forty years at this location, the group has lost most of the members from the days of Duell's Cafe, the Plaza Cafe, to the Lemon Tree Restaurant, but Patti and Steve have attempted to keep the tradition going to this day. While the Monday-Friday tradition has been abandoned, there are many who still gather around the round table being greeted every Wednesday by Donna Gage who has served the group since 1984. Nina and John Sterbuck, the owners of the business now welcome the group, as well. As Bob Jensen regularly would say to newcomers to the group, "you come once, and you are a visitor and the second time you are a member." We hesitate to mention some of the names who have frequented the round table over the years, but it would be fair to say there have been several hundred. A final word about the stories which have been told at the round table. Some have speculated about the value of this coffee group and the contributions made to the City of Richfield as a result of the people who have participated in the conversations. Perhaps VOLUME II of this book of recollections might include a few of these historical references but suffice it to say the idea of this VOLUME was initiated at the round table. We hope to see you for coffee.

# MILES LUNDAHL'S MAGIC AT RICHFIELD HIGH SCHOOL'S 50TH ANNIVERSARY PROGRAM

**NORM PLASCH**

As coordinator for Richfield High School's 50th Celebration in October 2004, I witnessed many memorable moments. The occasion that stands out most vividly is former band director, Miles Lundahl, speaking to a packed house at the RHS auditorium on Saturday, October 16, 2004.The program was one of several events that seven RHS alumni committees planned for a full week of anniversary activities prior to the big Saturday open house event. Some 5000 people arrived at the school that day and experienced a memorable time of celebration. In addition to directing activities involving representatives from each of the prior 48 graduating classes, I had the opportunity to plan and host the Saturday program in the school's auditorium. About two months before the program, I spoke with former RHS Band Director Miles Lundahl by phone. I mentioned that I was looking for a secret guest speaker for the RHS 50th Anniversary Program and asked if he would be interested. Mr. Lundahl humbly hesitated at the offer but soon agreed to be our speaker. The printed program did not list Miles Lundahl's name on purpose as I wanted to keep his part in the event a surprise. He had initially agreed to keep his comments limited to 4 to 5 minutes and the message was to focus on his memories while serving as the RHS Band Director for 35 years. On stage at the podium, I noticed an electric atmosphere during the first part of the event in the RHS auditorium on that Saturday. Perhaps it was due to former students seeing old friends for the first time in years or it may have been due to the Teddy Bear Band that was playing in the hallway outside the auditorium before the program. A dynamic energy was building up to the program. When I announced that a secret guest speaker had arrived to address the group a silence took over the auditorium. I then invited Miles Lundahl to the stage and the entire auditorium went wild. The local paper compared it to a scene from the 1995 movie, Mr. Holland's Opus, where actor Richard Dreyfuss, playing retiring school band director Glenn Holland, arrives to the school auditorium to see a full house of former students who shared their admiration and love for a former teacher. Miles Lundahl took the RHS auditorium stage on that Saturday and expressed his sincere appreciation to all who were there. He also shared some memories from his teaching career and then explained the story behind the cherished school song, Hail Richfield! He explained that the song was written by himself and another RHS teacher, Mr. Frank Curry, and that no other school had rights to this song. As the program progressed, we were going overtime but I soon realized that, as host, if I had attempted to shorten this speaker's message, I may not have been able to exit the auditorium alive. The program script called for me, as host, to introduce the school song to the audience but Miles Lundahl put on his Band Director's role and invited the Spartan band to play the school song where an energized audience fully participated. A moment forever etched in the minds of all who were there on that day. In October 2017, I had the opportunity to briefly speak at a funeral for a beloved band director where, in a heartfelt message to his family, I expressed an ongoing love and appreciation from students over 35 years for a teacher who taught many about more than music, but helped to equip us for life, Mr. Miles Lundahl.

# THE STORIES OF – "THE GREATEST PRANK IN THE HISTORY OF RICHFIELD HIGH SCHOOL"

In 1969, just a few days prior to graduation, a handful of graduates decided to pull off "The Greatest Prank in the history of Richfield High School." This prank was pulled off during the evening hours. The following morning this "prank" was the talk of the school. Two tires were on the very top of the flagpole, with several others "around" the pole at the base. When I arrived at school that morning, several custodial staff were standing around the flagpole scratching their heads trying to figure out how the pranksters could have pulled this off. The following is their story, in their own words of that legendary night.

Respectfully submitted,

Al Malmberg

* * * * * * * * *

I am writing this at the request of my friend Al Malmberg who wanted a first-hand account of what he considers the "Best Prank of All Time at RHS".So, as the story goes, on a late evening in June 1969, a group of mischievous Richfield High School seniors, coming to the end of their thirteen years of public-school education, felt compelled to do something, a prank, that would someday be considered remarkable. Not that this type of thing had become a tradition, but the year before, the class of '68 pranksters added some trees to the school's courtyard that turned out not to be planted at all. These trees had been cut off at their base and just stuck in the ground to look like they had been planted. Maintenance was not happy when they figured out the trees didn't have any roots. The '69 pranksters gathered around the school's 70-foot flagpole (approx.) that night to discuss some options and possibilities for a good rouse. The idea of dropping tires over the top of the flagpole was suggested and seemed to be the best idea at the time. Knowing there was a supply of old tires located near the athletic field, the gig was on. Now the problem was how to get the tires over the top of the pole so they could be dropped down around the base. It all came down to this, someone needed to shimmy up the pole. Doug Quick, one of the bravest of us all, volunteered. To get the traction he needed, we found some foam pads to tape to his thighs before he began his ascent. The rest of us knuckleheads gathered around the base of the pole, to catch him if he should slip down or fall. Slowly, Doug worked his way to the top and reported he was ready to receive the tires. The first tire was then attached to the flag halyard and hoisted up. When it got to the top, Doug slipped it over the top of the pole and then passed his grip so it could slide down to the bottom. This went on for six or seven times until finally, it was decided to leave the last tire hooked over the top of the pole. Doug then worked his way to the bottom and the prank was complete. We then celebrated this great achievement and took pictures of ourselves to document our participation and went home feeling quite proud. The next morning when students and staff arrived at the school, it was the buzz that everyone was talking about. They wanted to know "How did they do it?" and "Who could have done such a thing?" It was a mystery! Shortly after the school bell rang that started first period, the Principal got on the intercom and spoke to the student body. He said something like "What you see is a clever prank, but what you do not see is that the Teacher's Lounge was broken into and vandalized. It is suspected that it was the same individuals that put the tires on the flagpole." Well, of course we could not wait to turn ourselves in and confess. They then marched our shameful butts out to the flagpole to resolve this dilemma. Doug then shimmied back up the pole and released the sole tire hooked over the top. Again, Doug's performance was heroic. Once down, the rest of us were given a hack saw and instructed to cut away the remaining tires. Needless to say, we were identified as the pranksters and given the notoriety for pulling off one of the "Greatest Pranks of All Time at RHS"! The only person named in this story is Doug Quick who is the one who volunteered to climb the flagpole and make this happen. Doug is one of the bravest people I know! He has been and is now successfully fighting a battle with the life-threatening Lou Gehrig Disease. His courage, determination, and toughness in this fight are a tremendous example for others like him, who are facing similar life challenging diseases!

Respectfully submitted,

One of the '69 Pranksters

* * * * * * * * * *

How Doug Quick remembers that night:

We went to the football practice field to pick up tires, and the police got a phone call. We drove to the high school and dropped off the tires in the bushes on the southwest corner of the building. The police received another call. We then parked the vehicles down the block from the school and ran back to the school. The police received yet another call. Guess who showed up? A police car! We spoke to the officer and told him our plans. His response was, "Ok, I'll cover for you."

* * * * * * * * *

I was in awe watching Doug climb that pole and then getting the tires over it. I don't know that anyone else could have done that. I think there were 8 of us. I take great pride in being with this group of men. I borrowed my dad's old truck to pick up some of the tires from the track at West Junior High. Unfortunately, it had our family name on the side. Someone called my dad about this the next day. Not very smart on my part. The principal told us we would not graduate with the rest of our class, but he relented later. Several of us sat in the main entrance to watch people's reactions as they came to class. None of us had ever been early for class before so that gave us away.

Anonymous '69'er

* * * * * * * * * * *

Doug Quick gets the credit, and the rest of the knuckleheads are accomplices. This caper will go down in history as the greatest achievement known to mankind. I am very proud to know our leader, and the educated idiots who were involved. There was much conversation about this caper, and it was Doug's idea. I couldn't imagine him sitting at the top of the flagpole with only the horse harness, holding him to the ball at the top. The horse bridal looked like something Jesse James had on his horse. He said don't worry about that.... PREPARATION : Where do we find the tires and are they going to be big enough to work? We learned in RHS Geometry class to measure the circumference of the bottom of the flagpole, to find out what size tire would fall all the way to the bottom of the tapered flagpole. A 15" tire will work the 14" tire will not. So, the plan was to have the bigger tire over the flag pole, the smaller tires in the court yard. I really felt the need to have the biggest thing ever at RHS documented. So, I brought a camera, new batteries, film and flash bulb. We located the tires in advance at West Junior High on the football practice field. There were many and both 14" and 15". We needed a truck, unknown to Maurice Hagen, he provided that. We were ready.

* * * * * * * * * * *

Points I remember:

I was sitting on Ruth Bonstrom's couch when Doug called me. Where are you, Hagen. I sprung into action immediately. The next thing I remember I was driving my dad's truck at night with no lights around the water tower at West Junior High. I don't remember who was with me. I thought this is crazy, but how much trouble can I get into with such upstanding accomplices. We took the tires to the flagpole, here the rest of the idiots awaited. Doug climbed to the top of the pole. He said the funniest thing ever looking over the top of the school. "I can see the Sears Roebuck tower from here" The accomplices hoisted the tires to Doug, being sure he only got the big 15" tires, using what we learned in geometry class. Doug left one tire on the ball. After the caper, I snapped a picture of the morons next to the flagpole and the tires dropped over, as documentation. The next morning several of us were there very early. We were never early. I had the camera and wanted to document the flagpole and who might be standing there next to it. We were in the hallway by the gym, and health room. What I saw and heard next will never be forgotten. The doorway was opened in the hallway, and I saw several janitors scratching their heads looking at the flagpole. As I snapped the picture the principal walked by and said under his breath out loud, "When I find those guys, I am going to kick them out of school." At that moment I knew it wasn't good for us. How did the administrators get us to confess? Over the loudspeaker for morning announcements, we heard that glass was broken in the science wing and if anybody was around the building to let us know. There were two typing classes. I was in one and one of the other pranksters was in the other, we both bolted out into the hallway at the same time. He said let's get down to the principal's office and confess. We did. I was very proud to be part of the greatest bunch of guys ever. Some may call us morons, but I consider us Brilliant. Doug the most brilliant mind of all. Sincerely, an accomplice.

* * * * * * * * * * *

Didn't we kind of plan that or at least discuss it when we went to, I think, the Mann drive in movie one Friday night? Not sure who was all there as we made our devious plans.

I remember that the next day the school would not let Doug climb the pole again, for obvious safety reasons. We tried numerous tools to cut the tires off the base of the pole but could not get through the wire that formed the cord of the tire. You even went home and got a hunting knife and we were able to cut the rubber but not the cord. If I remember it right, somehow, we got a large bolt cutter and used that to cut the cord of the tires and remove them. One thing that stands out to me was when we were out by the flagpole trying to figure out how to get the tires off many other students, who were supposed to be in classes, were watching through the windows to see what would happen next.

Don't forget we also strung a rope across the inner courtyard with tires on it.

That was quite an adventure. Long time since I thought about that night. You with your red truck. Taking the tires from the West Junior High School track area. Wow! We were crazy!

Anonyomous

We have run it up the Flagpole and have determined that the best place to end this book is on a high note!

I hope you enjoyed these stories.

Do you have a Richfield Story to share? Feel free to send it to

Ourrichfieldstories@gmail.com It may very well be used in a future volume of Richfield stories.

# PHOTO AND IMAGE CREDITS

1. Fred Babcock killing article image licensed by the Star Tribune copyright 1949 Star Tribune
2. Cloverleaf Motel postcard courtesy of the Richfield Historical Society
3. Barry and Bob Bishop Co-Captains photo courtesy of Bob Bishop
4. Millers Fireside Pizza photo courtesy of the Richfield Historical Society
5. Leroy Howe won a door prize photo courtesy of the Richfield Sun Newspapers.
6. Finian's Rainbow advertisement courtesy of the Richfield Historical Society
7. Float plane on Wood Lake photo 1 courtesy of Laurie Kollar Smyrl
8. Float plane on Wood Lake photo 2 courtesy of Laurie Kollar Smyrl
9. Float plane on Wood Lake photo 3 courtesy of Laurie Kollar Smyrl
10. Softball Marathon photo 1 courtesy of the Richfield Sun Newspapers
11. Softball Marathon photo 2 courtesy of the Richfield Sun Newspapers
12. Augsburg Park warming House photo courtesy of Dave Jackelen
13. Otto Hardt's Automatic tees photo courtesy of Paul Hardt
14. First set of golf clubs photo courtesy of Paul Hardt
15. 1963 Lake Champs courtesy of the Richfield Historical Society
16. Country Club Market hold-up article image licensed by the Star Tribune copyright 1974 Star Tribune
17. Al Payne Hurls No-Hitter courtesy of the Richfield Historical Society
18. The Peterson Family 1964 photo courtesy of Patty Peterson
19. Willie Peterson in the Twins organ suite photo courtesy of Patty Peterson
20. Billy Peterson in Twins organ suite photo courtesy of Patty Peterson

21. The Peterson Family 2007 photo courtesy of Patty Peterson
22. Mark Jimmy and Skip visiting Santa photo courtesy of Mark Foster
23. Shawn Phillips ticket photo courtesy of Jan Hatfield
24. Mr. Duane Wold article photo courtesy of the Richfield Historical Society
25. Pam Syverson Girls in Boys classes courtesy of the Richfield Sun Newspapers
26. The Rave-Ons article photo courtesy of the Richfield Sun Newspapers
27. Bill Davis 1960 photo courtesy of the Richfield Historical Society
28. Bill Davis photo courtesy of Bob Strandquist
29. Reiter Realty photo courtesy of Rick Reiter Sr.
30. Tait's boat giveaway photo courtesy of Mike Tait
31. Sherm Booen photo courtesy of the Richfield Historical Society
32. Edgerton.vs. Richfield photo courtesy of the Richfield Historical Society
33. Mike Waggoner and Bops ad photo courtesy of Mike Waggoner
34. Looking across 76th Street to Hank Ranft's Farm photo courtesy of David Turk
35. Nelson's pie tin photo courtesy of the Richfield Historical Society
36. Nelson's Restaurant photo courtesy of the Richfield Historical Society
37. Mike Fossen and his 6 tickets photo courtesy of Mike Fossen
38. Leffler's Dairy Store photo courtesy of the Richfield Historical Society
39. Deb Browning My Sunflower photo 1 courtesy of the Richfield Sun Newspapers
40. Food fight photo courtesy of the Richfield Historical Society
41. Scholz Store ad courtesy of the Richfield Historical Society
42. 66th Street July 4th, 1955, parade photo courtesy of Chuck Strauch
43. 1964 Bike trip to Worlds Fair photo courtesy of the Richfield Sun Newspapers
44. Richfield Pool photo courtesy of the Richfield Historical Society
45. Dennis Dietzler and Mike Fossen photo from annual Augsburg Park Hockey game courtesy of Mike Fossen
46. Becky Bingea with sister and patrol courtesy of Becky Bingea
47. The Bingea Family photo courtesy of Becky Bingea

48. American Legion Post 435 photo courtesy of the Richfield Historical Society
49. Circus came to town photo 1 courtesy of Geoffrey Grudzinski
50. Circus came to town photo 2 courtesy of Geoffrey Grudzinski
51. Circus came to town photo 3 courtesy of Geoffrey Grudzinski
52. David Nye Iron Cross photo courtesy of David Nye
53. Tom -Tom Drive In photo courtesy of Debbie Nielsen Palm
54. Tony O. Advertisement courtesy of the Richfield Historical Society
55. The Christian Family Farmhouse courtesy of Edward Christian
56. Magnuson Sod photo courtesy of the Richfield Historical Society
57. The Granary House photo courtesy of the Richfield Historical Society
58. Duell's Café photo courtesy of the Richfield Historical Society
59. Richfield Spartan baseball field photo courtesy of the Richfield Historical Society
60. The Morris Nielsen Boys Choir bus photo courtesy of Dave Waller
61. Sara and Daves Dream House/Farmhouse photo courtesy of the Richfield Historical Society
62. Tank Christensen in his low cuts photo courtesy of Tom Christensen
63. The Richfield News banner courtesy of the Richfield Sun Newspapers
64. Miles Lundahl photo courtesy of the Richfield Historical Society

* Road Ramblers story photos courtesy of the Richfield Sun Newspapers. Photos in the 71st and Nicollet Champs story provided by Jim Ondich.

* Photos of The Greatest Prank in the History of Richfield High School courtesy of Al Malmberg and anonymous '69 Pranksters